LINVOY PRIMUS
TRANSFORMED

LINVOY PRIMUS
With Peter Jeffs

*'I alone know the plans I have for you, plans to
bring you prosperity and not disaster, plans to bring
about the future you hope for.'*
Jeremiah 29.11

Legendary Publishing

First published in 2007 by
LEGENDARY PUBLISHING
11 Rosedale Close, Fareham, Hants PO14 4EL

Reprinted in 2009

British Library Cataloguing in Publication Data

A catalogue record for this book is available from the
British Library

ISBN: 978-0-9526760-3-4

Print Management by
Verité CM Ltd, 8 St Johns Parade, Alinora Crescent,
Goring-by-Sea, West Sussex BN12 4HJ
www.verite.co.uk

Printed in England

*I dedicate this book to my Lord and Saviour
Jesus Christ that all may come to know Him.
And to my best friend and soulmate,
my wife Trishia and my dear children
Nathan, Atlanta and Cameron.*

Acknowledgments

To my Lord and Saviour Jesus Christ without whom I would not be where I am today. Thank you for loving me and guiding me always Lord.

To Trish my wife, thanks for all your love and support through the good times and the bad times. You know me better than I know myself.

To Nathan, Atlanta and Cameron. You truly are blessings, I love you.

To Mum and Dad for your love, guidance, all the family values you instilled in me, and for introducing me to church in my early years.

Love to all the family, especially Leon, Fran and Luke.

To our good friends Darren and Angie Moore. Darren for his part in leading me to God, as someone I looked up to as a footballer and a person who is sensitive and thoughtful to everyone's needs, not to mention his valuable work in Faith and Football in the Midlands.

To John Mac, my agent, who's grown to be my surrogate father and values me as part of his family, for negotiating and making decisions as if they were for himself ('he was the helicopter').

To Mick O'Brien and Mick Mellows for setting me on my spiritual journey, guiding me, persevering with me and my family, and using their special individual gifts to lead me to God.

To Keith and Sam Richards for their prayers, for being obedient to God and bringing us to the church.

To all the 'Faith and Football' stalwarts and volunteers who do so much to serve our community in Portsmouth and Birmingham in so many ways.

To good friends from my youth and schooldays – in particular Chris Collins who took me to sign for Pretoria and recommended me to his father, Ricky Anton, Edwin Laviner and Gary Lawrence.

To all those coaches and mentors who have helped me along the road to the Premiership – in particular the Pretoria management and team-mates, Keith Peacock at Charlton, both Terry Bullivant and Ray Clemence at Barnet, and Alan Pardew at Reading, not to mention Milan Mandaric who persuaded Tony Pulis to sign me for Portsmouth.

To all the special friends I have been lucky enough to find during my career in football – in particular Paul Wilson and Lee Hodges at Barnet, John Polston, Carl Leaburn, Alex Dyer, Martin Williams and Alan Pardew at Reading, but too many at Portsmouth to mention

To the Pompey fans and the people of Portsmouth who have given me amazing support over the past seven years in everything I've done.

To Peter Jeffs my co-writer and publisher for all his hard work and support, and to Amanda Hughes, Colin Farmery, Lisa Samways, Di Lloyd and Jake Payne for their valuable help in producing the book. To Jo Scrivener and Scott Suttey at Starfish Creative Design for your great contribution.

To everybody at Antony Rowe printers, particularly Geoff Fisher and Libby Rodger, who made this book possible.

Linvoy Primus, August 2007

Contents

Foreword by Gavin Peacock

Gavin played for QPR, Gillingham, Bournemouth, Newcastle and Chelsea before retiring. After appearing regularly on BBC TV's Match of the Day and Football Focus he has now moved to Canada to study to become a priest.

Football is a humbling game. One minute you are up, the next you are down. You are a hero one week and a villain another. The crowd can idolize you on a Saturday and make you the scapegoat by the following Wednesday. Add to this a constant battle to maintain or regain good form and the agony of training for fitness or fighting back from a mind numbing injury. It is almost satirical of life, with huge highs and lows, and yet they are condensed into maybe a ten year career and played out on very public stage.

Linvoy Primus is a person who knows all about the above; his career as a professional footballer has put him through the whole gamut of emotions. He has felt rejection more times than most and yet has emerged as a fine, top level central defender who has formed a partnership with Sol Campbell to match any in the past season. Even when I watched him and did a little summer training with him back in his early days at Charlton Athletic there were doubts about his ability to make the grade. He had potential, great athleticism and solid character but was it going to be enough? Overlooked for Richard Rufus and then released from Charlton, he knew he was going to have to do things the hard

1

way, moving to Barnet and then Reading, before finally coming to Portsmouth. Even then the doubters persisted, along with injuries and yet he kept coming back and proving people wrong. He now sits as one of the best defenders around and I've seen him play some outstanding games in the Premiership. He holds the respect of team-mates, coaches and fans alike.

Some may say he has it all now and Linvoy would not disagree. It's just that his all is Jesus Christ and his faith burns through him. He stands firm for God and gives Him the glory for everything in his life both on and off the field. To be a Christian footballer is not easy at times and I know, as one who has trodden the path before Linvoy, that it takes strength to say what you believe and to maintain your standards, in what can be such a hard arena. In a world where so many people, young and old, may hold footballers up as role models to aspire to because of the money, fame and celebrity status today's game affords, Linvoy stands apart.

Linvoy lives his life as someone who loves football with a passion but it is not his god. Everything emanates from his faith in Christ and he uses his platform as a Premiership footballer to spread the gospel. He stands as an example for youngsters of how to live your life right and his influence on his team-mates at Portsmouth has been quite remarkable. Footballers are not immune to the ups and downs of life that everyone experiences and Linvoy's tale is one of someone who has come to realize that God is unchanging and will see us through anything. His is an inspiring story of both a footballer and of a man transformed, set against the backdrop of our national game. In all this Linvoy is a worthy ambassador for God. He is a defender of the faith.

Introduction

I remember quite clearly spending hours on a Saturday morning in the back of a coach playing cards on the way to a game in the north of England, running out in front of a crowd of just over a thousand, and struggling to clear the ball from a goalmouth ankle-deep in mud. I would share a shower with my Barnet team-mates afterwards, get back in the coach for the return journey and then drive home in the small hours of the morning in a beaten-up second-hand motor, washing my own kit in the kitchen sink the next day.

Now I fly with the squad to away games that all involve an overnight stay in the very best hotels and amuse myself en route playing video games on a handheld portable console. I run out in front of crowds of up to 70,000 in huge modern stadia like palaces, gliding over pitches that would pass for manicured lawns. Afterwards I take an individual shower and dry my hair in what would pass for a bathroom in an expensive hotel. I pick up my big modern car, after the return flight, to reach home in time to watch our performance on 'Match of the Day'.

That's a measure of how my career and my club Portsmouth's profile have been transformed.

Our rise to the Premier League, widely regarded as the elite club competition in world football, means I am now playing with and against world class players every week, working in a highly professional environment and reaping the financial rewards that such status in the game brings.

But, after my release by Charlton as a youngster, it was vital to my development, not only as a player but as a person, to start my league career at the bottom rung of football with Barnet. I look back on my years in football, with its highs and lows, its upheavals and uncertainties, and recognise their value as stages to learn and experience life. I've forgiven those who rejected me along the way and realise that, although I didn't recognise it at the time, those situations helped form the person I am now.

Like all young footballers, in my early days at Charlton and Barnet, I harboured dreams of playing at the highest level, but in truth I never expected it to happen. I never believed I was good enough or that I would be able to handle it psychologically. I imagined that, even if I was given that chance, I would have found a way to fail, given my inherent lack of confidence and levels of anxiety.

So I was compelled to write this book at such a relatively young age because I wanted to tell people of the changes that have happened in my life because of God's power. Of how God has lifted me up and taken me to new levels of performance and consistency in my career. Of how I have obtained a peace that has enabled me to meet the challenges that have come into my life as a footballer, husband and father. Of how God has enabled me to overcome rejection, anxiety and that lack of self-belief to find a new confidence and assurance.

I want people to know that what's happened to me can happen to anybody who accepts God into their lives. It has changed my heart from being selfish and having football and money as my God. It has also opened up new horizons and directions that have pointed me towards a true course for my future life outside football.

Very early on as a Christian I believed God had told me that I'd have a long future at Portsmouth – its stretched as far as six years to date – and that he would use me for his purposes in the city. He has kept his promise because that's what is going to happen. God has lifted me up to my current status as a public figure to give Him the glory, not me, and I have been called to serve Him as much as I can. I am thoroughly blessed to be able to do what I love for a living but I have found my complete fulfilment and happiness in life through God. Financially I have been given the opportunity to buy my dream home and to enjoy the luxuries of life, but without allowing them to become the centre of my life. I believe I am being blessed financially to be a blessing to others financially.

My career is nearly over but I want to extend my future as a player for as long as I can. It's not my aim in life to accumulate as much money as possible, but I have to do everything I can to be successful on the pitch so that I can provide for my family's future and help my children through life.

The 'Faith and Football' charity that Mick Mellows and I jointly launched has kept me in touch with real life as we try to serve people in the local communities and through our overseas missions. Nothing opens the door to young people like football. There is some really positive news around about the influence and activities of professional footballers in the UK through their involvement in our charity. Footballers have a lot to offer, and responsibilities, because youngsters look up to them as role models. Their influence in helping to put over a message or in boosting morale can be massive.

The Portsmouth area is home to me now and the Pompey fans have been so important to me in the way they have continued to encourage and push me forward with their huge unparalleled support week after week. It's my hope that they will enjoy reading my inside story of the club's triumphant rise to the Premiership and our astonishing four years in the top flight, including the 'Great Escape' of course.

Another good reason for writing this book was as a way of saying thank you to the people who have helped me to achieve my dream, to develop as a footballer and a person, and, above all else, to find God and place Him at the centre of everything. I thank God for placing those people in my life as spiritual fathers and for their help in mentoring and guiding me on my journey of faith. I am looking forward to seeing what God has planned for me in the future.

1
Wigan's JJB Stadium April 2006

No referee's whistle has ever sounded sweeter and, as it reached its climax before dying away, I immediately sank to my knees in a state of collapse, oblivious to the entire clamour around me, and, looking up, thanked God for the victory. I knew that without Him we couldn't have achieved anything. All our focus, all our efforts, and all our thoughts through every waking hour for the past week had been directed towards beating Wigan Athletic at their JJB Stadium. Now it was all over and, at that stage, I was filled with no more than an overwhelming sense of relief that we had achieved what we had set out to do. In those moments as the players ran to embrace each other, we still didn't know whether we were safe from relegation.

We waited on the pitch for an agonising two minutes or so for Birmingham's home match with Newcastle to finish before an enormous roar went up from our fans in the stand behind the goal at the confirmation from dozens of radios that the final whistle had gone on a goalless draw in the Midlands and our safety in the Premiership was assured. I turned to find our keeper Dean Kiely beside me and it was just the look on his face that was enough to bring the tears to my eyes. It wasn't anything he said; I was overwhelmed with his expression conveying not only relief and joy but every emotion you could imagine. It was all in his face – a look that said: '*We have done the undoable and achieved mission impossible, against all the odds*'.

The realisation that we were staying up was the signal for our supporters to invade the pitch and we were being slapped on the back, jumped on, lifted up and some of us even carried aloft. It came home to me then how much more it meant to our support-ers who had not only been absolutely superb throughout the whole campaign, but had lifted us and carried us through those last ten games to ultimate safety. During the six weeks in which 'The Great Escape' had unfolded thousands of them had filled the away ends week in and week out and, above all, believed in us when almost everybody in the rest of the football world had written us off. Now they wouldn't leave the JJB Stadium until we went out again to parade before our fans in the stand behind one of the goals. You couldn't help but enjoy and milk their acclaim and they were entitled to all those long, loud and continuous cel-ebrations.

The club belongs to the fans; it's their club. I've never experi-enced such passionate support at any other club – it's unparal-leled in the country. From the moment I arrived in Portsmouth six years earlier I had felt at home as if I was back in East London. It's a working class city with a strong pride - '*this is my city and no-one can mess with it*' - and a real community that looks after its own. Once you are accepted as part of them then they will sup-port and defend you to the hilt. That fierce and passionate loyalty is translated in their support of their football club. They've had to work hard for what they've got and they expect the same from their football team. Win, lose or draw that's the least they expect. I like to think the fans recognise that I've always given everything I can, and have warmed to that and responded with their com-plete support.

In the week before the game at Wigan, with just a home game against Liverpool to follow before the season ended, the players, like our supporters, had come to a single conclusion - with Liverpool still needing points to claim a Champions League spot we simply did not want to go into that last game needing a result to reach safety. So we were desperate to try and nail it at Wigan and the equation was simple: if we won and Birmingham failed to win against Newcastle then we would have achieved the 'Great Escape' with that Liverpool game to spare. The overwhelming feeling in the squad was that we didn't want all our hard work and what he had achieved in the last six weeks or so to go to waste. Of even more consequence was the cost to the club in so many ways of losing a Premiership status that had been so coveted and hard-won after so many years in the wilderness of the lower leagues.

After being eight points adrift of safety in early March after our dismal defeat at Aston Villa, we had been on a great run and went into the Wigan match in great form with just one defeat in our last eight matches and an astonishing 17 points out of a possible 24. The doubts do niggle away at the back of your mind however. After all we had managed only four wins on the road all season and you thought – could we conjure up one more? To counter that we knew that Wigan had won at home in the league only once since Boxing Day and, despite their great start to their first season in the Premiership, had found the going hard in recent months so the opportunity was there for us.

The thought of relegation has some players and managers waking up in a cold sweat in the middle of the night. But during the week leading up to the Wigan game the peace I had found in my faith enabled me to sleep well and I couldn't help compare that with the sleeplessness I came up against during the week before some must-win games at Reading, and in fact back in May 2001 before Pompey's relegation-decider against Barnsley.

The build-up and media attention was intense as the trip to Wigan drew closer, but happily our training was very light after the number of games we had played in the previous weeks. Defensively we worked with coaches Joe Jordan and Kevin Bond rehearsing certain defensive situations, on our shape and on how we were going to combat their strengths, very much as normal really. As much as it was a 'must-win' game it was equally a case of 'mustn't lose'. The first priority in any game is not to get beaten and to make it as difficult as possible for the opposition to score. Sometimes that means you only play one forward in a 4-5-1 formation that doesn't appear to be of an attacking nature and not as open as a 4-4-2. That's not really with a view to securing a draw but to make things as difficult for the opposition whilst hoping that you can take whatever chances you get.

Manager Harry Redknapp sent us out at Wigan in a positive mood, ending his team talk as he had done for some weeks with the message: 'We can get out of this'. We played two up front as if we were the home team and that was the way we had been playing so happily away from home during our recent good run. We had been successful with the system mainly through some great work from our two attack-minded full backs Brian Priske and Mattie Taylor. This approach is OK at home but away from home, particularly with the crowd behind them, it tends to give the home side a greater attacking impetus on the counter. To play the system away from home you need to be mentally strong and it can be very demanding physically.

At Wigan Brian and Mattie were looking to go forward into attacking positions to get in some crosses from the word go, but it soon became apparent that this approach was leaving us exposed at the back. Very soon two Wigan attacks on the break had left us very exposed and vulnerable, both ending with Henri Camara in on goal with our keeper Dean Kiely having to come out desperately to foil him on both occasions. Even though we needed to win, I became increasingly unhappy with our approach to the game, thinking to myself: 'We're playing in a kamikaze way'.

10

In Wigan's midfield David Thompson, who was to join us a couple of months later, was causing us so many problems in winning tackles and getting balls forward to his strikers Jason Roberts and Camara. As seemed likely, we went one down through Camara on 34 minutes and then he 'scored' a second that was, as it transpired from the TV replay, wrongly disallowed for offside.

There were some harsh words from Harry and Joe in the dressing room at the break to the effect that: 'We are leaving ourselves too open at the back... if one full back goes forward then the other must stay back... otherwise we're leaving our two central defenders to cover their two forwards... and if there is a mistake by one defender it leaves two against one'.

Harry changed things around in that break taking off Sean Davis and putting Noe Pamarot on to play alongside me in the centre of defence, enabling Dejan Stefanovic to switch to left back and releasing Mattie to move up to left midfield. That change immediately released Mattie to attack down the left and also, with three central defenders on, stiffened things up at the back.

Now we were able to attack with more freedom and assurance and suddenly it was Wigan's turn to be chasing back. Increasingly they seemed to be running out of steam as we took control. All we needed were the goals to reward our efforts and the ground erupted with the noise from our fans at the other end when the equaliser came 18 minutes into the second half through Benjani's first goal for Pompey. It was a simple task for him to nod the ball into the net from a yard out after Mattie's close range shot had rebounded from the goal post into his path.

That equaliser ended Benjie's barren spell in front of goal that had lasted for over three months and 15 games. It was such a relief to see him score and we were so happy for him that he had scored such a vital goal into the bargain. All he wanted was to do well and score goals, but, as a club record signing carrying that huge price tag, the longer he went without scoring the more we

11

felt for him. We never said anything openly to him but, at some stage, he must have known what the press and the fans were saying about his failure to score. It's to their credit that the fans never lost faith in him however and their unique vocal backing for him went a long way towards maintaining his confidence.

We were well on top after that and had a couple of chances before Benjie's header was handled on the the line on 70 minutes and suddenly, like the previous week against Sunderland when he had scored the vital winner from the spot, there was Mattie confidently striding forward to take the penalty. I was able to watch and directed a silent prayer all the way down the pitch to Matty: *'Please make this strike as good as last week's and just convert it'*. There was no fear from Matty however, who clearly relished the chance, and slotted it home with power and confidence, even though the keeper dived the right way.

There were less than 20 minutes to play but I had no idea what the time was. I hardly ever ask or look for the time left after realising that it appears to go slower if you are counting down the minutes or seconds. You get games sometimes when you are convinced that, whatever the opposition throw at you, they won't break you down and score. That afternoon at Wigan was one such occasion. Gary might have made the game safe when he was played through but their 'keeper made a good save. That brought another ominous thought: *'Don't let that come back to haunt us or affect what happens to us'*.

That last 20 minutes or so seemed like an eternity requiring such a high level of concentration it was almost painful. You know it just takes one bounce of the ball, a mistimed clearance, a bad tackle or a missed chance: one little mistake and you're down. Then, with an awareness that the final whistle couldn't possibly be too far away now, as a team you're faced with a dilemma: we're still in an attacking mode so do we still push forward or do we sit back and settle for holding on? In such situations, with time running out, professionally teams are looking to keep the ball as much as possible and that can be achieved by taking it into the corners and wasting time if that's what it takes to win the game.

An anticipation of the final whistle was closing in on me and suddenly, after being so focused on the game all afternoon, came a sudden striking thought: *'Will this win be enough?'* We had been given no scores at half time and I realised that there had been no reaction whatsoever all afternoon from our fans to indicate that there had been any score from either side in the Birmingham v. Newcastle match. I was so curious that I began to wonder whether in some way I might be able to manage to get the score from one of our supporters in the crowd. But it's better not to know really because it can affect you and change the way you play.

I was so engrossed that I failed to even take account of the amount of stoppage time indicated by the fourth official as he lifted his board to mark the end of the ninety minutes. But two or three minutes later I was thrown on to my knees by the shrill whistle and the almighty roar that signalled a victory that, as I was to discover a further two minutes later, kept Pompey in the Premier League. In many ways my personal transformation was complete, but for Pompey things were only just beginning.

2

All the way to Charlton
1973-1992

I was born in Forest Gate Hospital in September 1973, the first child of Newton and Pauline who had originally met on the Ford Motor Company production line at Dagenham. I immediately went up in the world – in fact up to the 17th floor of 22 in a Stratford tower block in the London borough of Newham where my parents lived in a three-bedroom flat with my stepbrother Leon, my mother's son from her first marriage, who was ten years older than me. The view from the window takes you over the whole skyline of London with all it's landmarks including the Crystal Palace transmitting station and the Post Office Tower.

Even now the lifts still break down regularly. You're never sure whether they will come and if not what has happened to them. Many were the times that I had to walk down or up the stairs and, when I was with Charlton schoolboys, I can remember I would go out on my own for a fitness run and finish up by running all the way up the stairs to our flat. For some reason some of the residents used the lifts as urinals which didn't make the journeys too pleasant.

Mum and Dad are still in the flat after over thirty years, happy and comfortable in that environment and not feeling threatened.

They dream of having a bungalow with a garden and since coming to visit us on the south coast they have seen that there is more to life than London, and have recently moved down to be near us and their grandchildren. Both are now retired, after Dad had worked for Thames Water as an engineer in the sewage department.

Both my Mum and Dad had been married before and had separately emigrated to England from Jamaica and St Vincent respectively. With most of the work centred around banana production and with a high unemployment rate in St Vincent, as it is to this day, my Dad had taken the same route as hundreds of his countrymen, intending to make enough money to eventually return to the Caribbean and retire. So my Dad joined my Grandad in the rag trade in Battersea, London to train as a tailor.

Dad had left behind a big family and a 'party island' where the people worked hard, usually on the plantations, but knew how to enjoy themselves. Throughout the island the men love to play dominoes particularly in the local rum shops and on the beaches. Dad made sure he brought his beloved set with him to England which meant that from a young age I would be roped into a game when we made our regular weekend visits to my grandparents who lived nearby at Battersea.

There was no real suitable play area in the concrete jungle around the tower block and from an early age, to get me out of the flat, Dad would take me, after finishing his shift, down to Wanstead Flats – a big grassed area close to Epping Forest – to play cricket and football. By this time Mum was working as an orderly at Whipps Cross Hospital at Leytonstone.

There were very few black families in the block but we never felt threatened or marginalised. Despite the clear level of deprivation there was a good neighbourly spirit with everybody welcome in each other's flats and plenty of community parties and get-togethers.

I was a happy child but there was some sibling rivalry between Leon and me. There was a bit of name-calling – he called me 'Buckhead', something to do with the shape of my head – but he always makes me laugh, even now, with his stories. Once he had started work Leon left home and I moved into his room. But when he moved back a couple of years later I let him have his room back without making too much of a fuss, and from then we became really close. Now he was a person to whom I could talk on a fairly deep level and, to this day, we have a relationship which we had never had before he left home. He was a postman for some time, and I make sure I see Leon and his girl-friend Frances – they have a little boy the same age as my daughter Atlanta – every time I go back to London.

Being very much the baby, with such a difference in our ages, I was spoiled but not to the extent that I could have anything I wanted, and I knew that I had to wait for things. I was only too aware from my Mum's distressed state at times that there wasn't much money around. We may have been short of money but I always felt well-fed and never went without the essentials of life. Even now I don't like wasting money and it all goes back to those times.

There are few play opportunities for a child up in a flat and I had to bring plenty of imagination into my play particularly with my little cars in the front room. In fact I loved them so much I remember stealing a couple from my pre-school nursery. I had so much energy to expend that it hurt – it's no wonder I used to get so excited when I got to play outside with my cousins. To work off that energy indoors I would swing on the doors with great regularity but came a cropper one day when I went a step further and tried to climb over a bedroom door. My finger was crushed when it was caught in the frame when the door closed and now I have a disfigured finger to show for that escapade. Worse was to follow when in accidentally pulling a saucepan full of boiling water off the cooker in the kitchen I ended up in hospital for a spell as I recovered from the severe scalding I suffered.

Mum and Dad were very protective and I was often disappointed that I wasn't allowed down to the ground floor to play with other children of my own age. Not only were they conscious of the safety aspect but were anxious not to expose me too soon to a world within yards of home where glue sniffing was rife, and crime in the form of burglaries, muggings, and thieving was commonplace. As I grew up I became familiar with a rough tough environment where trouble was never far away but that just seemed normal to me.

'Don't you ever let the police come to our door because of you', Mum would say. But there was never any chance of Leon or I getting into any sort of trouble – Mum kept a tight rein on us and was fiercely proud of our good name in the neighbourhood. I remember that I was attracted to a couple of lads in my class who were often in trouble and who lived in the flats. But Mum soon nipped that in the bud and made sure that I didn't get too involved with them.

Mum and Dad brought a very disciplined approach to our home life, and from an early age I had to do some housework at weekends. It was my task to dust, clean and polish everywhere, with the big old mirror on Mum's dressing table and the pictures in the living room in particular needing special attention. In addition I would have to accompany Mum to the shops every Friday to help her out with the weekly shopping. Those were regular chores that I really didn't enjoy, even more so because I don't remember my brother doing anything of the sort.

My parents had been brought up in the West Indies with church as a big part of their lives, and from an early age I was taken to nearby St Paul's in Stratford every week. I enjoyed Sunday school, knew all the Bible stories and songs but found it difficult at a young age to sit through some of the long and boring services. I

17

found church to be a cold unwelcoming place, where you were told what you could and couldn't do, accompanied by an over-whelming sense of fear of punishment from God. But I know now that it instilled in me a very strong sense of right and wrong, and also a fear of ungodly things, a fear of the devil and a very real fear of hell's fire. At home I always said the Lord's Prayer with my father and prayed with him before going to sleep, and for many years thereafter I maintained that habit. My prayers would be for my family's health and security. Later as a teenager those prayers would often include a plea to enable me to play well, and an oc-casional 'thank you' when I had played well. However from all that upbringing I am of the belief now that a deposit was left with me which God has used to draw me back to Him. My spirit knew that I always wanted to go back sometime.

Those regular early-evening kick-abouts in the park with my Dad brought me a natural release of energy, a real love of just being out in the fresh air unconfined by the flat, coupled with the sheer exhilaration of kicking a ball around. Through spending most weekends visiting my grandparents, I had still not seen a proper game being played even out in the park, but at the age of seven came the first of the defining moments of my life, if that's not too melodramatic.

There was very little live football to watch on TV in those days but everybody would sit and watch the Cup Final on BBC. Ricky Villa's great individual strike which won the F A Cup for Tottenham in the 1981 Wembley Final struck me as simply amazing. From that moment I fell in love with football, or more particularly all the excitement, the passion, and the drama of the game. Those kick-abouts with my Dad had stirred a desire in me but seeing the game in a team context had given it life and form for me. Within days I had persuaded Mum to buy me a Spurs kit and I wore it constantly as I recreated Villa's famous dribble past three defenders and final low shot which had brought the goal which had fired my imagination. With a little sponge ball I would spend hours dribbling up and down the passageway between a bedroom and the living room in the flat. Now my mind was made up – '*I love this – I want to be a footballer*'.

From nothing more than the fact that I was always picked first in the ball games like rounders that we played at Colgrave Infants School I had an inkling that I was better and more talented than most. There was no school football team and I was restricted to the odd kick-about in the playground until, a couple of years or so after my 'Villa moment', I got to play in my very first game, one which set me on the road to achieving my dream. The Cub Scout group, based at the church, went away for a weekend camp and a five-a-side game was arranged against another Cub group in which I was up against a particularly well-known talented youngster. The boy himself congratulated me on my performance and one of the Cub Scout leaders at the game happened to be the manager of the Newham District Schools Under-11's. It all led to me being invited for a trial by the manager and within two weeks I was playing for the district team, up front as a striker or out on the right wing. I was very raw and really knew next to nothing about the game – for a start I certainly didn't understand the off-side rule.

Ironically, in the same schools team, I played alongside Sol Campbell who was in midfield. He stood out a mile, even at that age, and was clearly going to be a big star. Certainly wherever you went people were saying that he was going to be a very good player. He was already a quiet, laid-back character with an un-flappable nature and that same big smile.

When I moved to Rokeby Secondary School in Newham there was no football on offer there either after school or at weekends. Happily for me, a school friend of mine, Chris Collins, intro-duced me to a team called Pretoria which had just been formed in Canning Town by a couple of guys called Dave Wise and Paul

19

Smith, and played in the Newham Under 13's Youth League. Chris's Dad would take us to the games and very soon was telling me: 'When you are a professional footballer don't forget who used to take you to these games!' I haven't forgotten and we are still in contact to this day.

Before I signed I warned the Pretoria guys that 'it'll be difficult for me to play on Sundays' because of the family church-going, and for some time I couldn't buck up the courage to tell my Dad I had signed. At first he refused to let me go but when he was entirely happy about the company I was keeping and saw how desperate I was to play he relented and agreed to alternate Sundays only. But it wasn't long before church took a back seat and I was playing every Sunday when Dad saw how well organised it all was and, above all, how much it meant to me. Now I was really learning the game and training hard once a week. I started at left back but moved back to my old position on the right wing where I earned my fair share of goals and assists. We weren't very good though, so it was all character-building stuff and we suffered regular beatings. The club soon built some good teams and by the time I reached the Under 14's and 15's we were good enough to win those respective leagues.

I was the first black boy to play for Pretoria but by the time I left school there were seven of us in the club. I was regularly going to play in areas where there was rising racial tension but there was nothing ever said to me from within the team, even if I had to put up with the occasional comment at school. For all that I really enjoyed my schooldays and had a 'work hard' ethic learnt from my parents. Even if I say it myself, I was quite bright and particularly good at English Language, showing 'good imagination' in my writing. I loved German and French and it was only Maths that I found in any way difficult. When it came to exams I got six or seven passes at GCSE with three A's, which unsurprisingly included English Literature and English Language, so normally I would have gone on to college for further education. By the time I came to leave school however my heart was set on being a footballer and I was already with Charlton as an associate schoolboy.

Although I dreamed of being a footballer I was not one of those who can look back and say that from an early age it was the only thing I ever wanted to do. Obviously football was my first choice, and Paul and Dave at Pretoria had encouraged me to think that I was good enough to play at schoolboy level for a professional club. But, until later on, I had no real reason to think it would happen and anyway I simply had no idea how to get into the game. I had even begun to think about a career in engineering. But unbeknown to me, when I was 12, Paul was writing to the various London league clubs trying to get trials for several of his players including myself, and that led to scouts turning up to our games. If I ever got to hear of the presence of a scout at a game I was so anxious to impress and hungry to earn a trial that it hurt. I was always ultra-critical of my own performances anyway, but I remember after one disappointing display in front of a Charlton scout I solemnly promised myself never to play that badly again. Two of our lads went to Spurs to train and I remember being so happy for them and going along to watch their trial game. As it happened neither of them were taken on, and I had the same disappointing experience at Wimbledon after Paul had driven me over to play in a trial match.

I had by now sampled a few big games live with a group of us, including mates like Chris Collins, Ben Harper and David Scott, taking in about half a dozen games a season at West Ham, Orient and Millwall. The first league game I ever saw was at The Den with Millwall taking on Arsenal. But I was never a fan of any particular club although I had a soft spot for Spurs, going back to that 'Ricky Villa moment', but unfortunately their White Hart Lane ground was just too far away from us. England defender Des

21

Walker was a particular favourite of mine and I picked up things from watching him on TV. I would try and get to see him play live when his team Nottingham Forest were playing in London.

I suppose my first real break came when Charlton Athletic contacted Pretoria to arrange a game at their training ground against their associate schoolboys of the same age group, presumably with a view to having a look at us. We were walloped 6-0 and their star striker grabbed a hat-trick in the first half. I was stuck out on the right wing for that first 45 minutes, but at half-time I was moved to the centre of our defence to mark this danger man and he didn't score again. Afterwards I was one of five of the Pretoria lads who were invited to train with Charlton twice a week, and so for the last two years of my time at school I was taking the bus to Woolwich and then walking through the tunnel under the Thames up to the park where their Centre of Excellence was based.

The Charlton associate schoolboys played on a Sunday against the boys of most of the Kent non-league sides like Erith and Belvedere, Maidstone and Dover and that put an end to my happy times with Pretoria. I was conscious that I was in a privileged position having the chance to play for a professional club but there was nothing glamorous or exciting about those early days with Charlton. In fact the whole experience was a bit of a let-down and a real slog. My expenses were paid of course, but logistically it was difficult for me to get to the games and I didn't relish the constant struggle to engineer a lift each weekend or facing the constant problems with the bus connections to the Woolwich ferry. In addition the early Sunday start from home at 6 am to catch the bus with no time for breakfast meant that I was usually faint with hunger six or seven hours later by the time the match reached half-time.

It was a traumatic time and a world away from the great times and enjoyment I had with Pretoria. By now, like most teenagers in the area, at the age of 14 or 15, I was mixing with friends who were finding it easy to come by alcohol and cigarettes, not to mention cannabis. For me my parents' certain reaction was the greatest deterrent to such activities and from my upbringing I had a strong sense of right and wrong. Within a couple of years however, as an apprentice, I was drinking and smoking, with the help of the local off-licences, not to mention sampling the weed. I enjoyed the feelings, and knew it wasn't right but the peer pressure was just too great to resist, even when the older players advised against it.

I had entered a football world in which there was a great deal of falseness around and in which I didn't know who to trust anymore. I was told good things to my face but I soon realised that behind my back people were making snide remarks about me, and it knocked my faith in people. As an example, I regularly overheard comments about my ball control and first touch and found such criticism difficult to handle. Despite these comments there was no attempt to help me improve this aspect of my game. I began to wonder if it was true when people said I had played well. With so many youngsters competing for apprenticeships it was 'dog eat dog', so to speak. The parents were often ambitious and aggressive – perhaps I was too naïve but I found such behaviour alien and shocking in comparison to the quiet honest parents I was used to. With the turnover of players there was no chance to build a team spirit or relationships, and it could not have been a greater contrast from my time with Pretoria.

Very often I wondered whether it was all worth it. I was not the most confident of boys and was well aware that there were plenty of better players than me at Charlton. Everything revolved around results. I never really knew if I was good enough. I really couldn't see to where it was all leading. I was not given a great deal of encouragement or hope and felt like I was making up the numbers. It would have been easy not to bother to train or play in the matches. But somehow I found an inner desire and strength to see it through and looking back on it I can see that it was a very strong character building experience for me. I'm sure that determination came from my Dad and I never saw him show any sign of weakness, so I was shocked when he shed some tears at the passing away of my Grandad.

I was quite a skinny teenager, with no real build, and football-wise I doubted myself in several areas of the game, mainly in passing. I compensated with my speed and reading of the game, with my determination and will to win as my real strengths. Mum and Dad had by now recognised my potential and backed my dream, even coming to watch me occasionally although they didn't really understand the game and were not real football fans. Unlike some other parents there was never any pressure on me from them to succeed, and I was quite happy with that.

I was hopeful of being taken on by Charlton, but to be honest I had always rated my chances as slim. So when I had finished my GCSE exams and the time had come to leave school in August 1990, it was a surprise when they offered me a two-year apprenticeship. Not only that, a similar offer came from West Ham after a successful trial. I decided to be loyal to Charlton who had given me my first chance, even though they were exiled from their home at The Valley and ground-sharing at Selhurst Park, had just been relegated to Division Two and appeared close to bankruptcy.

I had no idea what type of player Charlton saw me as. I was in the strange position of not even having a recognised position. At the start it was a question of 'where do you want to play?', but eventually Colin Clarke, the youth coach, took a grip of the situation by taking me aside and saying: 'I see you as a centre back, that way you can see everything you want in front of you'. I respected his opinion and agreed with him when he said: 'In midfield you have to be able to have a vision of 360 degrees around you and to see a pass even before you receive the ball. I can see you are better coming on to the ball and passing it in front of you'. So the die was cast, so to speak.

Earning £27 per week, rising to £35 under the government's Youth Training Scheme (YTS), my daily routine involved a 90-minute bus and train journey to Charlton's Sparrows Lane training ground at New Eltham with training morning and afternoon and cleaning duties throughout the building in between. I was also responsible for the personal kit and boots of senior players Steve Gritt, Scott Minto and Garth Crooks. That's not to mention the youth games on a Saturday, occasional reserve team outings in midweek, and one day a week at a college near Southwick Bridge in London studying Leisure Management with the rest of the YTS lads. I hated it and found the whole subject so boring. Like the rest of the squad it seemed to be a waste of time given that we were training to be footballers. We all regularly missed classes and were not disciplined by the club which made life easier.

I was chosen as one of the two apprentices, with Jermaine Darlington, to travel over from the New Eltham training ground to Selhurst Park, before each first team home game, in a mini-bus with the boots and kit all packed. On arrival we would have the job of laying it all out in the dressing room for each individual player and it was a job that I really enjoyed. They knew that there was never going to be any bother whilst I was around and I have no doubt that my quiet, conscientious and respectful nature earned me the job. It wasn't until much later that I realised that my attitude to that job was reported back to the youth managership and brought me a lot of 'brownie points'. I couldn't help thinking that all that housework on a Saturday morning that my Dad insisted on me doing as a youngster had got me well prepared for the job.

Colin Clarke, the youth team coach, was a mad Scotsman who made us work hard but was the life and soul of the party and a joker in any situation. He could cut you to shreds with a few sharp words and initially I found that hard. With such gentle parents I took such an approach personally. Every harsh word from Colin affected me inwardly but I hardened to his approach, found a way of dealing with it, and eventually I found an inner strength such that it motivated me to produce performances to prove him wrong. Colin was held in high regard in youth football but left Charlton while I was an apprentice and I would like to meet up with him again.

Around the senior players like Carl Leaburn, Steve Brown and Anthony Barness, I never overstepped the mark by answering them back and generally kept a respectful distance. I didn't feel comfortable in the company of my 'elders and betters' at the club and lacked the confidence to speak out when around them. I found life as an apprentice both mentally and physically demanding and challenging in several ways. On the physical side I was troubled by lots of niggling injuries, possibly down to growing pains, and my body struggled with the demands of full time training and the games themselves. I just didn't have the stamina for it all, and I didn't look after myself nutrition-wise. I didn't eat well and was not going to bed at the right time, or getting enough rest. I simply didn't know how my body worked. No-one gave such advice in those days – if I had known half of what I know now then I would have made sure I got in a much better condition.

I didn't perform or shine out for the youth team. Aside from the physical aspect, mentally my attitude was all wrong – too lackadaisical and laid-back. I just didn't get to grips with how important for my future it all was, but with hindsight I was never really challenged. In fairness to myself I was never given the right advice, or pointed in the right direction. All I ever really got told was to work on the weights to make sure you get stronger. I was never going to ask for advice – I was much too shy and nervous to do that. Obviously I wanted to do well and not let anybody down, but no more than that. Little did I realise what was at stake. I just didn't contemplate failure and how hard it would be if I didn't make it. It was only later when some of my mates amongst the apprentices were shown the door, and I saw them go from club to club desperate for a contract to stay in football, that it came home to me. Put all that together and add the heavy peer pressure I experienced and its no wonder that I wasn't making any impact.

Much of that peer pressure came from the sheer weight of expectation from my friends away from football, and even from the coaches themselves. They were all looking for me to succeed. I knew that many thought a lot of me and clearly saw me as on my way to stardom. I was filled with a strong feeling of not wanting to let any of them down. They all would have loved to have been in my position, but little did they appear to realise that I might not make it.

My prospects improved when, by my second year, I was getting regular games at Welling Town's ground with a Charlton reserve side that always contained a strong youth element under player/coach Alan Curbishley. Alan was an influential figure in my career who I got on well with and who, above all, I wanted to please. I had gone up a level and found myself up against seasoned professionals. For once I felt challenged – something that was missing with the youth team. I had a point to prove in the reserves – that I could cut it in that company, that I could prove to myself and the club that I really was good enough.

For the first time I discovered that I had ability, and that if I wanted to I could raise my game to match whoever I was up against. I was still picking up injuries and in particular had a back injury which hung around for some time. I was in and out of the reserve team as I regained fitness but when I did play my performances were catching the eyes of people like Lennie Lawrence the first team manager.

Colin Clarke had been replaced by John Cartwright who was highly regarded by the FA and was later to be the England Under-

18's coach. John had heard good things about me but I subsequently got the impression that he didn't rate me and had seen better youth players. That was borne out when he began to move me from the centre of defence and try me in different positions including up front.

Despite John's obvious feelings, I had been getting indications that I might be taken on as a professional, largely based on the impressions I had made on the likes of Alan Curbishley and Keith Peacock with the reserves. But you're never really sure in such situations until it actually happens and I was on tenterhooks until that precious contract was offered at the end of my apprenticeship. Before that, with all the playing staff, I had to sit through a meeting with all the coaching staff whilst they outlined their plans for the next season. When that was all over the apprentices, one by one, were called by John Cartwright into his office to learn of our futures. I gathered there were four opinions canvassed about me, and the result was 3-1 in my favour. Of the five apprentices from my year only two of us stayed on – myself and Jermaine Darlington. It was only a one-year contract but I was so very happy at having achieved my goal and now the target was to break into the first team. The football career that I had set my heart on had begun in earnest.

3

Shown the door 1992-1994

It wasn't long before I got an insight into the world of professional football after I had signed a contract at Charlton for £350 per week in May 1992, which included an allowance of £100 to enable me to cover the cost of my rent and upkeep to my parents as I was still living with them rather than going into digs. When I received my first pay packet in August my wage was shown as £250 per week, and there was no sign of the additional amount agreed. I queried it but as evidence the club somehow managed to produce a different set of forms to those that I had signed three months earlier. There was nothing I could do about it – it was my word against theirs. I was only a young lad and I had just achieved my dream of a professional contract so there was no question of 'rocking the boat' now. Besides I didn't have the 'bottle' or the sort of strong assertive character to challenge them over it, despite the loss of pay to which I was entitled. For the first time I realised what the football industry was all about – that the clubs demand your loyalty and commitment but that it works to suit them and the players are mere commodities in the business.

The club was getting on its feet again after years as real paupers struggling to survive on low gates at Selhurst Park. I was always conscious that money was short – as apprentices we had worn the old first team shirts and much of the kit, including match balls, was recycled from one year to the next. The season started with a short spell ground sharing with West Ham at Upton Park, but a return to a rebuilt Valley was imminent. As a young professional I got to watch the first team regularly and soon realised the enormous commitment and dedication involved for them. It wasn't just a matter now of playing football and enjoying yourself – this was a high pressure job, a means of earning a living, of paying the mortgage.

I was leading a double life – during the day as a footballer with all the discipline that entailed, and at night out and about in the pubs and clubs with my friends away from football. I was still not the most confident of people but I found my confidence was higher in and around my friends away from football born of the sense that, unlike most of them, I was taking my first steps towards fame and fortune. Most of them weren't as fortunate as me and had a limited outlook on life, still at college unsure of what they wanted to do or resigned to labouring in the building trade. For me that 'good life' with the midweek late night drinking sessions and the smoking was a release from the pressures of professional football. I was still living at home but my Mum and Dad had no idea of what I was up to or the type of company I was keeping.

At the club for me it was goodbye to all that dirty work cleaning the boots and the floors. I was a fully-fledged professional playing regularly at centre back in the reserves and occasionally travelling away with the first team squad. Charlton's reserve side was still mainly made up of youth team players and the games were usually uphill struggles against experienced senior professionals. We took our share of beatings but I enjoyed those games partnering Steve Brown and playing in the stadiums of the major clubs in and around the London area.

I got on well with our reserve team manager Keith Peacock who was very enthusiastic and disciplined with himself and his players. He was like a Sergeant Major with us but managed to earn the respect of everyone. Keith really believed in me, was always ready to encourage and cajole, and made me feel as if I was a real 'son' to him. Unlike some clubs, who, to this day, don't really take reserve team football too seriously, Charlton saw it as a grounding for the first team. I saw at first hand that there were mixed attitudes amongst the first team squad to the prospect of a run-out in the reserves however. Some would take it as a punishment, sulk and not bother. Others were more positive and worked hard to regain their form and confidence to get a recall. For others it was a chance to regain their fitness after injury.

I had got through the rigours of pre-season well fitness-wise and stayed injury free through the autumn of 1992. My reserve team displays must have attracted some attention because word reached me that the new joint management team of Alan Curbishley and Steve Gritt was thinking of giving me a chance in the first team. I largely discounted it thinking that, having just turned 19, it was far too soon for me.

I got some real encouragement however when I travelled with the first team squad to Sunderland, just for the ride and the experience, although I had to work hard helping to clear the dressing room after the match. What did shock me that afternoon was the noise coming from the Sunderland fans at Roker Park despite our 2-0 win up there. Up to that time, I had become used to the tepid support from the small cluster of Charlton fans who travelled over to Selhurst Park for our home games.

I was still in the squad, on the fringes really, a few weeks later in November 1992, when, out of the blue, a string of injuries led me to make my debut against Birmingham City at Upton Park in a televised Division One game on a Sunday. I caught a bus to the game, not able to afford a taxi and not owning a car, and made my way to the dressing room an hour before kick off to sit in on the team meeting as a silent bystander just enjoying being part of it all. It was strange to be in what was supposed to be Charlton's

31

home dressing room surrounded by a sea of West Ham's claret and blue – on the benches, on the wall, and even decorating the sunken communal bath. The players were laughing and joking around me as usual, with no idea, like me, that I would be playing.

So it was a shock when Alan Curbishley came in to read out the team, and proceeded to preface that with an announcement, with a telling sideways look in my direction, that 'someone will be making their debut this afternoon'. With both central defender Simon Webster and his understudy Darren Pitcher injured I was playing and up against David Speedie, a wily old fox of a striker who I knew had a fiery reputation and a decidedly physical approach to the game. Curiously I remember that immediately I was not in any way fearful or nervous about playing – in fact with my confidence sky-high on the back of my form in the reserves I couldn't wait to get out there. There was only a small crowd of 5-6000 and little atmosphere, with, yet again, very few Charlton fans travelling across London for the game. My parents were in the crowd, and must have been surprised to see me out there warming up when they arrived. I was such a stranger to the rest of the first team lads that I warmed up by myself with no partner having been allocated to me.

The lads rallied around me with the usual standard advice to debutants – 'just do the simple things' and 'just enjoy it' - and defensive partner Steve Gatting talked me through the game which was goalless and drab. For all I cared it could have been a 10-0 win or a 5-0 defeat – all that mattered to me was that I was playing first team football. Speedie and his strike partner Louis Donawa didn't give me too many problems and Alan Pardew alongside me even encouraged me to go up for corners: 'go on, make yourself a hero'. In fact I almost scored the winner with a header which flew over the bar. Afterwards the TV pundits voted me as their Man of the Match and I was wheeled in to do the obligatory interview.

I was pleased and excited with an overwhelming sense of amazement that 'I had arrived'. In the taxi home the elation I felt was enough to wipe out the mental exhaustion which was creeping over me. As I went to order the lift up to our flat a mate appeared from nowhere and jumped on my back in celebration.

Three days later, on the following Wednesday, we were at home again, this time against Leicester City, and I knew, with their injuries still keeping Simon and Darren out, that I would be playing again. But this time it was all so different for me. I was so very nervous and those nerves got the better of me such that I was trying too hard. I put too much pressure on myself to reach the same level of performance as I had three days earlier. It was like a weight around my neck. I had set a standard for myself on my debut which was now making a high demand on me. It was the story of my life – I just couldn't accept and relax in the knowledge that through playing well on my debut I had proved that I was good enough. I had to go on proving it to myself. We won 2-0 but it was nothing like as good a performance from me. Within myself I didn't feel so good afterwards – it was all such an anti-climax after the previous Sunday.

But on the following Saturday I retained my place at Griffin Park against Brentford who ripped us apart in a 2-0 defeat. I struggled against Marcus Gayle, the former Wimbledon striker who was a very strong, physical player and in a 'purple patch' at the time. Soon he was outpacing me on the ground with his powerful running with the ball and then outjumping me in the air with his tremendous leaps. Others might have felt I did OK but, for me with my expectations and high standards, it wasn't good enough. I felt low afterwards again and even the usual 'you done well' from the managers was not enough to lift my depression. That sort of comment in defeat was meant to give you a lift, but it took me back to that falseness which was around in my days in the youth team when you knew that you had only really done well

33

when you had won the game.

So three games in a week and in that short time I had gone from the heights of complete elation to the depths of total despair. I was still in the squad when Simon Webster returned the following weekend against Newcastle, but I was disappointed not to stay in the team and felt I had done enough to get another game. It left me thoroughly disillusioned with a strong feeling of rejection. I know only too well now that however good you are you're always going to be passed up some time. I certainly didn't have any appreciation of a 'pecking order' and my obvious place in it. I didn't share my feelings with anybody at the club – it would have been seen as a sign of weakness. So I had no sort of explanation from anybody, and when you're a teenager pitched into such a situation you badly need to know what's happening. I certainly don't recall any of the management or coaching staff being in any way sensitive to my feelings. A few words along the lines of 'don't be upset, you will get another chance' wouldn't have gone amiss. I was learning fast what a hard world I had got myself in to.

Within a few weeks everything revolved around Charlton's return to their spiritual home at The Valley for which there was so much excitement and expectation. You couldn't fail to get caught up in all the build-up and, having been through some of the years in painful exile, I felt a part of it, knowing only too well what it meant to the club and its fans to have a ground and a home again after seven seasons in the wilderness and with the club's very future often in doubt during that black period. The supporters had played a huge part by forming The Valley Party and contesting 60 of the 62 seats in the local council elections, campaigning to get permission for Charlton to move back to The Valley. The 'Back to The Valley' match itself against Pompey was a brilliant day and the whole atmosphere and emotion were incredible. There was an enormous amount of last-minute work that went into making sure that everything was ready, and there were bits of the ground that still had paint drying as the game kicked off. The fans went wild when Colin Walsh scored the historic goal, after just seven minutes, that brought a 1-0 win. I remember Pompey manager Jim Smith saying afterwards: 'It was always a match Charlton were going to win'. Untypically, the whole squad went out that night partying for all we were worth.

Amid all the excitement and feel-good factor around the club I was becoming a forgotten man. I was not involved playing-wise on that great day and at that stage was not even getting a place on the bench. I felt I had failed and had missed my chance. Through not playing I really felt as though I wasn't wanted and that my days were numbered. It upset my confidence and my reserve team performances were clearly affected. The hardest thing is to knuckle down and start working to get yourself back into consideration – it might have helped if I had been given any encouragement to do so. After that, my first year petered out and was largely stop-start through another series of niggling hamstring/muscular injuries.

All I wanted to do was to get back to my 'other life' with my friends and Trish, my new girlfriend. It was good to party and take my mind off football. I had met Trish through a mutual female friend when I was 17 and for a while we were just friends going around in the same group. I didn't have a girlfriend and wasn't really looking for one. But we were gradually attracted to each other and eventually made a date on my 18th birthday. It was not the most auspicious of starts to our relationship. Trish was working that night and the date was fixed for 10.30 pm. As it transpired we missed each other in the pub where we were due to meet up. I came to the conclusion that she hadn't turned up but she was adamant that she was there waiting for me and was upset that in her mind she had been stood up on our first date. But two days later we met up again, hit it off and we've never looked back. There had been a few girl friends previously but nothing serious and I suppose I was relatively inexperienced with girls. Trish was exciting, generous, and compassionate, with a healthy appetite for life that I found irresistible. Although her family were Arsenal supporters, she wasn't in the least bit interested in football and literally knew nothing about it. Our relationship was pretty casual to start with but soon we were seeing each other every day and Trish would be round at our flat every night. I remember my Mum would knock on my bedroom door every night to bring our evening to an end in her inimitable way – 'Linvoy, its 10 o'clock'.

Initially Trish and I were just very good pals with a great bond of friendship but within a few weeks we had grown to love each other. It upset my parents when, within a year of meeting and still teenagers, we decided to live together, and caused a real rift and more unhappiness in our family than I had ever known before. Our move together was prompted by Trish's Mum deciding to move out from Stratford to Hainault in Essex. Trish was settled in the area with a job managing a shop so was forced to live temporarily with her aunt. I had been brought up in a family-oriented environment and it seemed the most natural thing in the world to me for Trish and I to make a home for ourselves. In any case Trish needed a home and this was an ideal opportunity. The thought of our mixed race relationship did cross my mind but it never attracted any comment to our faces whatsoever, although a piece of advice that had been offered to me, when I was younger, by a lady who lived in one of the flats in the block, came back to me: 'You should stick to your own kind ...it will be easier for your children in later life'.

So we moved into a one-bedroom flat above a minicab business in Stratford and it didn't meet with my parents' approval at all. As you can imagine, they didn't want me to leave home. Trish was my first serious girlfriend and, after all my hard work, they saw the relationship as a distraction to me while I was trying to make a career in football. Looking back, my parents had been in the same situation and made the same move themselves many years before. Now, as Christians with strong morals and beliefs, our move didn't match up to their ideals, and, of course, they didn't want me to come to regret it. For the first time, in their eyes, I was out of control and for two or three years thereafter relations between us were strained as a result. But even though I knew it was hurting my parents I knew it was the right thing to do. Although I still didn't have a car I had the means to get my own place so it was going to happen at some point.

Trish and I knew how much we loved each other and how secure we were so it wasn't long before we made the conscious decision to have a child together. For my parents it was their ultimate agony. We had known each other for just under 18 months. Obviously we agonised over it – *'we're so young'*, *'we've not had a life'*, *'my future's undecided'*, and simply *'how are we going to cope'*. Those were the thoughts we had, but vowed to overcome. It was still a shock, with a surge of panic and fear, when Trish first told me she was expecting, so much so that I was due to play in a reserve game that same night but had to telephone in to drop out as I struggled to come to terms with the news. There was also the reaction of my parents to deal with. Up until then I had been the model son and had brought no trouble to their door, but now they were upset at what they saw as my rebellion. From them it was also a case of 'now she's trapped you', but they could not yet know how committed Trish and I were to each other. The thought of us eventually becoming yet another statistic – a break-up, a single mum etc – was uppermost in their minds. If we had taken the traditional route of getting settled in jobs, getting married, buying a house, etc, then they would have rested easier. As the months passed however they began to see how happy we were together and that it wasn't just a passing phase. Their feelings turned to pride and anticipation as they saw Trish blossom and

37

her pregnancy advance and our excitement grow.

By the time Nathan, our son, was born in November 1993, I was just 20 and Trish was a year younger, and by now we had moved a few streets away to rent a big, old three-bedroom house from Trish's parents, which became available after they had separated. Nathan was born in Newham General Hospital after Trish had been in labour for 26 hours all told and I was there at the birth and in fact all the way through. I was so nervous and scared that I couldn't even hold Nathan properly, but I was so proud of them both.

After my brief, tantalising, and ultimately disappointing, taste of first team football in my first season as a professional, Charlton gave me another year to prove myself. Right through that summer I was on a mission to get myself super-fit ready to make an impact in the new season. But no sooner had the campaign started then I picked up another muscle injury and, after my injury-plagued end to the previous season, I could see the coaches wondering whether I was strong enough for first team football. When I finally managed to get fit my appearances were limited to the occasional reserve team game and by now there were a number of other young players, like Richard Rufus and Dean Chandler, who were even a year younger than me, and were getting more chances. When I was picked up front with the telling explanation 'Let's see if you can play in any other position', I knew that Charlton had virtually given up on me as a central defender, and that brought the realisation that my time there was coming to an end. It just wasn't happening for me in games and it was hard for me to know what to do next. I felt utterly helpless and just hung on to the forlorn hope that my performances in that first year might see me through. It was just a case of waiting for my contract to end and for the club to put me out of my misery, but it was a situation I found hard to cope with.

Charlton took me right to the wire with their decision, as

was their custom at that time, before the joint managers Alan Curbishley and Steve Gritt called me into their office. It was all over in a few short minutes: 'It's not been as good a year as before for you... it might be best if you have a new challenge'. They didn't need to say anymore.

All I could say was 'Thank you', and I was numb as I headed downstairs where a group of players were waiting in one of the lounges – Alan Pardew, Carl Leaburn, Scott Minto and Alex Dyer. There was just time for Alan to say: 'Don't worry, when you get that big money move from your next club you will be fine' before I was out the door.

Soon after driving away in my old VW Golf I pulled over in a lay-by and began sobbing. All I had achieved had gone. At the age of 20 I was on the scrapheap, and with a family to support. In one way I felt I had failed, and in another I felt Charlton had made a mistake. I was signed up with an agent but at the time he had some personal problems, and I was largely left to my own devices. I simply had no idea what to do or what route to take. Trish and I talked it over and for a short while I contemplated giving up the game but finally decided to try and get fixed up somewhere else. Keith Peacock had said he would help me to get some trials and I had three months' pay to tide me over. I had eight weeks to find a club before pre-season training would come round again everywhere.

I kept myself fit in West Ham Park with Trish as my timekeeper and I was sometimes joined around the circuit by Wayne Paul, who was an alcoholic and someone I often saw wandering around the area. He was ten years older than me, with his little boy a few months younger than Nathan, and I felt sometimes that he could see something of me in himself. The difference being that because of his addiction he could see no escape for himself from his situation. That would drive him to encourage me:

'Don't be like me – it's an easy road to get down. You still have

39

the chance to make something of your life with your talent. You have a girlfriend, a child and your parents to take care of. You're a good lad. Don't let anybody or anything take away what you've got'.

I was invited to a trial at Hereford's training ground, organised by a scouting network, where, on arrival, I found up to fifty players like me, who having been released were desperate to find a club. Two teams were picked and every player got a chance to perform in his chosen position at some time in the 90 minutes in front of a posse of scouts. Apparently such an event is still held at Lilleshall each summer but I heard nothing further after my audition.

I turned down the chance of a trial at Crewe before Cardiff City manager Eddie May invited me there for a two week trial and it was that offer which led to Barnet coming in for me. Three days before I was due to go to Ninian Park I had a call from Barnet manager Ray Clemence with a similar offer, but I had to tell him that I had already promised to go to Wales. That prompted Ray to say that he wanted to discuss it with his Chairman and that he would call me back. Five hours later he was back on the line with an offer of a two-year contract and asking if I would come down to their Underhill Stadium to sign it. I discovered some time later that Ray had taken some advice from his right-hand man Terry Harvey who told him, in effect: 'Get in now and sign him, if he goes down to Cardiff and sees their stadium he will sign for them'.

I took my Dad with me when I went down to Barnet to meet Ray and our first sight of an old ground that harked back to their non-league days was hardly encouraging. Only one side is covered with the main stand straddling the halfway line and running barely half the length of the sloping pitch. The South Stand had been temporary for some years and the dressing rooms could only be described as basic. None of that counted for anything for me and in truth I bit their hand off – there was no haggling, no negotiations. It meant so much to me to get a contract – now I knew I would be able to look after my family and I would not have to move out of London. It was the same terms as I was on at Charlton but the money was not a big consideration. I was assured that I would be part of the first team squad at Barnet, and that gave me the chance to show that I was good enough to play professional football and to prove Charlton wrong.

Dad embarrassed me when we first sat down with Ray Clemence by recounting the story of how, as a nine-year old, I had scored three out of five spot-kicks I had taken against him in the final of a penalty competition held at my dad's workplace. Ray had of course been part of the all-conquering Liverpool team of the 1970's and an England goalkeeper before joining the coaching team at Tottenham. He had taken over at Barnet in March of the previous season after Barry Fry had left and taken a number of the players with him to Birmingham. Ray had been unable to prevent Barnet's relegation to Division Three and was committed to rebuilding the team. I was joined by Lee Hodges from Tottenham, Dougie Freedman from QPR and Shaun Gale from Pompey and there was a good mix of young and old players in a squad which was smaller than I had known at Charlton. The atmosphere was different to that which I had known at The Valley where the players were usually older than me, lived in a different area and rarely met socially. It was also good to start with a clean slate, as it were. I always felt that my history at Charlton – having come through the ranks and been unlucky with injuries – often counted against me.

4

From a boy to a man 1994-1997

It soon became clear to me that Barnet needed lifting out of the doldrums after relegation, and had become something of a laughing stock after what had gone on at the club under the previous regime of chairman Stan Flashman and manager Barry Fry. There was talk from those days of players being paid in bundles of notes brought in brown carrier bags. I was told there was even a Friday night pre-match ritual, home and away, which was intended to build team spirit, whereby players went clubbing and were not allowed in before two in the morning. But there was a good core of support for the club amongst the local community with crowds averaging 2-3000 and those fans had recently played a huge part in saving the club from bankruptcy.

I had a lot of respect for Ray Clemence and what he had achieved in the game. He was a forceful and dominating figure, with a big presence, and like many, I found him intimidating at times, although he was never a bully. Inevitably, after all his years at Anfield, he was imbued with the Liverpool mentality and was at pains to kick-start a new era at Underhill based on their very high standards. Ray would never tolerate any lowering of those standards and there was clearly a need for greater discipline both on and off the field. He insisted on good football being played but, unlike some former internationals who went into management, Ray readily recognised and tolerated players' limitations, probably because he had started his own career modestly at Scunthorpe.

With Ray there was a lot more physical training than I had been used to, and it didn't help that, after signing, I was a week behind on pre-season and struggled. Stamina fitness work has never been my strongest point and here I was finding myself bringing up the rear in the long distance running. Soon it was a standing joke that I couldn't run for very long at a fast pace over any sort of distance. It's the case to this day that most players can out-run me but I am quicker than most over a short distance.

I was on the bench for the first two games and I was conscious that the older players were already regarding me as a threat to their positions. Centre half Mark Newson was unfortunate to go over on his ankle in the second game at home to Leyton Orient and I came on for the last ten minutes or so there, and kept my place for the trip to Scarborough the following Saturday. That full debut for Barnet must rank as the worst performance of my career. It was an absolute shocker. If someone had said to me afterwards, or indeed to any of the 1500 or so fans who had witnessed it, that I would play in the Premiership in twelve years' time, let alone play for Barnet again, no-one would ever have believed it. It was a bit of a culture shock to play at the McCain Stadium with its solitary stand and a bumpy, divot-littered pitch but my biggest problem was that I was paralysed with nerves. I wanted so badly to do well and prove myself to the rest of the team and, of course, repay the faith that Ray Clemence had shown in me. Simply, that old fear of mine, of letting everybody down, had come to plague me again. I was simply weighed down by the burden of expectation.

The tension of the occasion crippled and drained me. I have never been so nervous in all my life. I just could not relax, was trying too hard and fifteen minutes into the game I was hyperven-

43

tilating and blowing for air. There was no power in my legs and it must have looked, for all the world, as if I had never played football before. I couldn't read the game, couldn't pass the ball, make tackles, head the ball cleanly, and was completely off the pace. What Alan Walker, my defensive partner, or indeed Ray, made of it all I never got to find out. Post-match I got the silent treatment from the players who were at pains to avoid me although inevitably I knew they were talking about me, and unfortunately I even overheard one telling remark – 'the worst player we've ever had at Barnet' - which probably summed up the general feeling in the dressing room. Happily the 1-0 away win meant that my performance did not have any great bearing on the result, otherwise my great sense of disappointment would have been even more acute.

I had recovered my composure, and got a proper focus and desire not to let myself down again, by the time we played at Leyton Orient in the League Cup three days later. My earlier performance at Scarborough was largely ignored and presumably seen as a 'one-off' by Ray, who was struggling anyway to put a team together with such a small squad and a number of injuries to contend with. It was a relief to put in a decent display, in front of my parents and some friends, in our 1-1 second leg victory that put us through to the next round against Manchester City. Generally however my early performances for Barnet were shaky, so much so that my team mates dubbed me 'Shinners' because so many of my passes were flying off my shin. That nickname followed me to Reading when Terry Bullivant later took me to Elm Park. I wasn't unaware also that there were a few unpleasant comments coming at me from the Barnet fans.

When we went away to Hartlepool at the end of August all the anxiety I had experienced a few weeks earlier on my debut returned on arrival at the hotel on the morning of the match. I had to tell Ray that I felt really sick and wouldn't be up to playing, so he ordered me to bed. An hour or so before the team were due to leave by coach for the ground, Ray's assistant Terry Bullivant came to see me and got me to agree to get up and walk with him to the ground to get some fresh air. It was soon clear that he knew what was at the root of my problem. As a former player at Fulham, Terry told me how nervous he used to get before games and how he never came to terms with it. But we talked it through together and Terry told me how important it was not to worry, but to enjoy the game and to take things as they come. As we got to the ground I felt OK and mentally ready to play and as it turned out I had a good game. I knew by now that I was, in my heart, a perfectionist who set himself high standards of performance, who asked too much of himself and was riddled with doubts about his ability. It helped considerably at that time that Ray and Terry were aware of my agonies, and were happy for me to talk it over with them and bring it all out in the open.

Even later in my time at Barnet, when I was one of their best players, I was still so short on confidence in my ability, and before games I would pray – first the Lord's Prayer, as I had been taught, followed by a request to God to help me to 'consistently play well'. I was so nervous that I couldn't sleep the night before a game and to calm myself down I got in the habit of having a couple of strong drinks before going to bed. Once or twice a coach became suspicious the next morning, presumably because they smelt drink on my breath, and would say something like: 'Do you like a drink, Linvoy?' which brought a denial from me. As I said before, players would never show any form of weakness. Even when I played well, not only could I not accept that my prayers had been answered, but I was still ultra-critical of my performance in some way or another.

For all that I was happy and settled at Barnet from the word go and there was a good spirit and a bonding amongst players who were on the same level financially, and usually, like me, had a young family. The socialising would start in the club bar after the games where the wives and families mixed, and we would often have get-togethers for birthdays or at restaurants for Sunday lunch. Trish and I hit it off with Dave McDonald and his wife Keely in particular, who had a little daughter. But that family life didn't stop me going out with the single lads to clubs in London and Essex.

Dave McDonald was known as 'Smacker Macca' for his habit of slapping his hand across your face as a form of motivation before a game. That aggressive approach was matched on the pitch with tough tackling and he was often sent off, much to Ray's disgust. As an Irishman he liked a night out at an Irish pub and he took me out on my first real serious drinking session after we had got back to Barnet on a Saturday night from a game in the north of England. I had never drunk so much in my whole life and was much the worse for wear, with Dave still as right as rain. When at 3 am I said I was hungry his reply was: 'Eating is cheating, have some more real food', and promptly put another pint of Guinness in my hand.

There's always a clown at every club and it was Mickey Tomlinson who gave us most laughs in the dressing room particularly with his speciality of acting dumb during team talks. During one half-time talk the coach was going through a sequence of play and asked Mickey: 'If Duggie plays the ball back to Carl Hoddle what do you have to do?' Mickey paused for five seconds and said, as if he didn't know the answer: 'Kick it?' The coach, looking for him to say: 'Move into space to receive a pass', replied: 'What do you mean?', and Mickey replied: 'Kick it', by which time we were all in fits of laughter.

Facilities and resources at Barnet were a world away from the Premiership in those Division Three days when money was obviously tight. There was no gym at the training ground but in a corner of a dressing room you could find a few old plastic weights, donated by a supporter after he had no further use for them, that

46

needed sand placed in them for weight at regular intervals. We would even have to clean our own boots and take our training kit home to be washed.

There was a great deal more intimidation around at that level too as I found out when we went to Doncaster and their midfielder Gary Brabin – an uncompromising, tough tackler – had clearly heard about my performance at Scarborough. 'He's crap. He'll give us the ball back, just you see...' was his opening gambit to his team mates within my earshot in an attempt to intimidate me. With my fragile self belief, each critical remark directed towards me, like 'He's so nervous, look at him', tested my confidence. But on that afternoon it only served to increase my silent determination to rise above it. I proceeded to mark their forward out of the game, determined to prove Brabin wrong, concentrated on 'doing the simple things well' and avoided going forward with the ball, as I had so often been told. It was another brick in the wall of self belief I was trying to build.

Striker Dougie Freedman, who had signed from QPR in the summer, was really making his mark, scoring four against Rochdale and then the goal by which we beat Manchester City 1-0 at Underhill in the first leg of the League Cup. After a hatful of goals for Barnet it was no surprise when Dougie moved to Crystal Palace for £800,000 at the end of the season. He was a very confident lad who we socialised with but who had an edge of anger to his personality with a real chip on his shoulder. The second leg at Maine Road brought the biggest test of my career to date with their big striker Niall Quinn, not to mention his partner Paul Walsh, for me to contend with. I took a great deal of confidence from my display that night against Quinn, particularly in the air where he was so dangerous. We ran them close and the final 4-1 scoreline flattered City. We equalised their early goal but simply ran out of legs late in the game.

There was plenty of drama that season in the FA Cup when we

47

had a home draw against nearby non-league Woking in the first round. We fought back from being 3-0 down at half-time to earn a replay with a 4-4 draw and then proceeded to lose the replay in front of the Sky TV cameras. Ray really lost it in the dressing room afterwards, something I had never seen before. When he launched into his scathing attack on our display he just happened to be holding a hot cup of tea. His uncontrolled anger led him to squeeze the plastic cup and we could only sit and watch as the hot tea burnt his hand while he pretended not to notice. His anger climaxed with a tray of sandwiches being thrown at us and smashing against the dressing room wall behind. Defender Alan Walker sat for a few minutes with ham and cucumber on his head too frightened to move. Some of Ray's frustration was probably directed against the new Chairman Tony Kleanthous who, a few days before the game, had threatened to switch the players to part-time to save money, which according to Ray was 'not the best preparation for a cup tie'. The threat didn't really bother us anyway once Ray had moved quickly to assure us that it simply wasn't viable.

Referee Uriah Rennie, with whom I have crossed paths many times since, took his first league game that season when Barnet visited Preston at Deepdale just before Christmas 1994 and marked the occasion by sending off two of our players. When a clearance from one of our players hit him the ball fell into the path of a Preston forward who ran on to score the only goal of the game, so he managed to get an 'assist' into the bargain. Rennie mystified us all that afternoon, and often still has the same effect on me to this day, by turning down any number of our penalty appeals, and afterwards Ray was firm in his opinion that 'he will never make a top flight referee'. I certainly felt he would struggle at that level on that performance.

It was an unremarkable season with Barnet seemingly stuck in mid-table but, after a heavy 4-0 defeat at Walsall on Boxing Day,

Ray was adamant that 'some of you had too good a Christmas' and, to our dismay, promptly stepped up the fitness training. Monday mornings brought what we named the 'Circle of Death', which was a gruelling form of circuit training built around several progressive stations. In fairness to Ray it did pay off and, a couple of weeks later, a 4-0 win over Hartlepool put our season back on track although we were still very inconsistent.

I have often thought that I grew from a boy to a man during my time at Barnet and one incident that first season brought home to me that it was about time that I shed my diffidence and stood up for myself more. I had been down with flu and had not trained all week but Ray was desperate for me to play in the home game on the Saturday against Darlington. Naively I told him that I would try and play, but after ten minutes I was physically out on my feet. I struggled through to half-time, by which time we were 2-0 down, to be met in the dressing room by Ray who was clearly placing all the blame for our performance at my door, and accusing me of making too much of my sickness: 'You've only got a cold not f*****g malaria'. I didn't say anything, came off at half-time but was very disappointed with his attitude. Terry Bullivant called me at home on Monday morning – 'Ray asked me to call you' - to see how I was, and when I returned to training Ray called me in and apologised but added: 'Be a man in future, and tell me if you're not strong enough to play'.

When my first season of league football was over I was runner-up in the Player of the Season voting and I felt I had made some progress towards proving Charlton wrong in their judgement of my ability. I harboured hopes of bettering myself particularly as I was often voted Man of the Match and felt that I was playing comfortably within myself with plenty in reserve. Although I was enjoying my football the wages were still poor, despite a new contract, and not enough to support my family. So we had to take loans to get by and rely on my mother to pay for most of our

shopping, including Nathan's supply of nappies. I can remember
Trish and I trying to scrape some silver coins together to buy some
bread and a bag of potatoes to make some chips. It hurt my pride
to think that I was still reliant on my parents but we had nowhere
else to turn. They would never express it of course, but I could
sense their continuing disappointment that Trish and I were un-
married and were struggling with a young child.

Dougie Freedman left for Palace to be replaced by Sean Devine
who was to become equally successful up front. During the close
season Barnet signed goalkeeper Maik Taylor from non-league
Farnborough, buying him out of the Army for £800. As a fellow
keeper with whom he had a strong affiliation, the youngster was
soon Ray's blue-eyed boy, particularly when it became obvious
that Maik had hunger and ability aplenty. If anything however
Ray was even harder on him and he was quick to make his feelings known when on Maik's debut we went down 4-1 at Hereford
and he was at fault for three of the goals: 'Don't start thinking you
are f*****g Grobbelaar, just do the simple things'. That outburst
surprised me at the time, knowing how highly Ray rated Maik,
but it was clearly an attempt to get him to cut out any attempt at
showmanship. Eighteen months after moving to Underhill Maik
moved to Southampton for £500,000 and has since become a
top keeper at Fulham and Birmingham, not to mention Northern
Ireland.

We had a disastrous start to the season with only one win in
eleven, although we were playing good football, and Ray came
under fire from the fans. In fact the chairman of the supporters
club went right over the top on one occasion and directed a whole
load of abuse towards Ray's daughter. As you can imagine it
didn't take long for Ray to get that gentleman into his office for a
reading of the riot act. Temporarily things didn't improve and a
defeat at home to Plymouth in mid-September 1995 took us to the
very bottom of the Football League. That night some of us went

to a party at the Spot night club in Covent Garden. As was usual we were recognised as a group of footballers and were asked who we played for.

Our prepared reply was: 'We play for the strongest team in all the leagues', which drew the response: 'Why?', and then came our punch line: 'Because we're holding up all the other clubs'.

It was Ray's lowest point as manager and his biggest test, although amongst the players there was the feeling that we were doing the right things, that it would come right and that it was too early in the season to worry unduly. Ray had been given the dreaded vote of confidence from the club's new Chairman but we knew that the pair did not see eye to eye and that Ray's days were probably numbered, particularly after a subsequent disastrous 4-0 home defeat by Rochdale. The lads liked Ray and didn't want to see him go, but by the time we travelled to Northampton a week later we were only too aware that it could turn out to be his last match in charge.

Players will often pull together to save a manager they want to play for and I could sense such a mood at the Sixfields Stadium that afternoon. A 2-0 win was the happy outcome for Ray, and I spent the afternoon in the sort of physical battle I relish, this time against Northampton striker Gary Thompson which ended up with me being carried off and taken to hospital with a suspected socket fracture after he had elbowed me in the eye. It was hardly accidental and, in those days, strikers were permitted to use their arms to obtain some leverage to climb for the ball in the air, which meant that they would often lead with their elbow. Unlike these days it was not seen by referees as a foul. Heavy bruising was the diagnosis and I was fit enough to play the following week.

That win triggered an 11-match unbeaten run in the league and a Manager of the Month award for Ray but that run came to an end at Colchester despite my neatly lobbed goal. Any chance we had of making the play-offs that season was ruined by our inconsistent home form, matched by my own form overall. Despite that I was runner-up to Maik Taylor as the Player of the Season, and there was paper talk of QPR being interested in me. I always had a move in mind, deep down I was confident of being able to play at a higher level, and couldn't bear the thought of playing out my days in Division Three. Financially Trish and I were worse off than ever and still in no position to get our own place. It was having a negative effect on me and affecting my confidence. Ray must have sensed that because he put me, and Micky Tomlinson too, in touch with a sports psychologist called Jazz Karim to try and help us fulfil our potential.

Jazz immediately put my inconsistency down to my personal worries, my lack of confidence and diet. I had to write down all my worries and out of that he got me some financial advice and persuaded the club to give me a loan. There were plenty of tips on diet to help me, and he seemed to understand what I was going through, on and off the field, and that enabled me to improve my performance. Jazz's biggest contribution to my cause was to get me to believe in myself and my ability. At Barnet, just as I had experienced at Charlton, we were judged collectively with the result being the sole yardstick, so if the team was losing games then inevitably you felt as if you were not playing well enough. There was no reassurance or feedback on individual performances, unlike today where there is plenty of information available thanks to the ProZone data analysis system.

From a young age I had always been immune to the street crime and drug culture in the Stratford area, but it was about this time that Trish and I had our first experience of that scene when we were burgled and, in fact, it was someone we knew. The drugs had always been around me in the neighbourhood, but in the background. It was the way people got their release and, with my friends, I developed an interest in the rave scene and began to visit clubs and parties around London and Essex at weekends in the close season, but not with any other players. We would listen to the pirate radio stations and get to hear of the location of any all-night rave parties which were usually held in old used warehouses or hastily erected marquees. Drugs were in demand, rather than alcohol, from sellers at the parties and that led me to have a little dabble of my own when I was offered and tried ecstasy and LSD. I didn't enjoy either, and, in a way, the feeling they brought, a sense of being almost completely out of control, frightened me, and that was a blessing because I very soon didn't want any more of it.

At the clubs I was only interested in the music and never went out looking for anything else. There was no drug testing in football in those days, but I was well aware that taking drugs could seriously jeopardise my career. In my naivety I knew little then of the effect drugs could have, but now, as I have come to know more, I am only too aware of the problems that can come from such experimentation with drugs. I have known friends who were addicted to cocaine, whose lives were centred on it, and I have seen how it controlled and changed their lives.

Like most footballers in those days I would go out and get drunk on a Saturday night, and I enjoyed the feeling, whether with or without Trish. It was part of the football culture, and some of the senior professionals would drink socially during the week in addition. Jazz was tolerant of the habit as long as it didn't come to rule my life, realising that I needed the release the drinking brought.

Looking back I was a typical footballer, with their built-in selfishness. Everything revolved around football, with my needs paramount in the family. But increasingly I felt there was something missing in my life. I would try to find it through drinking, and for a few hours I would be happy, but the next day I would find that nothing had changed.

Paul Wilson, the Barnet skipper, was my first real role model in football – someone who, despite being six years older than me,

53

I could relate to and ask for advice. Paul always gave all he had every day of the 12 years or so he spent at Underhill. It was Paul who got me fitter and stronger, and consequently less susceptible to injury, by encouraging me to take up extra weight training with him. He was not the most skilful player around but was an inspiring figure with his single-minded, professional and focused approach that meant he looked after himself and his family carefully off the pitch, and then went out and gave 100% on the pitch.

There was considerable upheaval during my third season at Underhill and the first day brought a big shock when Ray announced that he was leaving, having accepted an offer from England manager Glenn Hoddle to join him with the national team as goalkeeping coach. 'Look lads, it's an opportunity I just couldn't turn down' was Ray's explanation to us, but we were also only too aware that he was continually at loggerheads with the chairman. Terry Bullivant took over the managership but he lasted for only six weeks before bidding us farewell after a disagreement with the chairman. Terry Gibson, the former Wimbledon striker and youth team manager at Underhill, had a brief stint as caretaker but was effectively replaced after just two weeks when the former England and Tottenham midfielder Alan Mullery, a friend of the Chairman who had been appointed as Director of Football two days earlier, arrived unexpectedly in our dressing room at Colchester to announce that he would be giving the team talk that afternoon.

Alan had been working in the media for ten years or more as a pundit reporting on games at the top level, since managing at Palace and QPR, and was clearly out of touch with modern players, and more particularly the lower leagues. So inevitably we felt our performances were being compared with the likes of Manchester United, for example. I had no problem with Alan but he couldn't hide his lack of respect for many of the senior players. He wanted them out and soon a power struggle developed which did little for team spirit. He was clearly uncomfortable in the job and the dressing room, became increasingly nervous in his team talks, and you could see that the stress of it all was just too much for him.

By the time he resigned, with half a dozen games left in the season, only Sean Devine's goals were keeping us afloat and we were in real danger of relegation back to the Conference. We took matters into our own hands as far as a new manager was concerned and a deputation of senior players persuaded the chairman to re-appoint Terry Bullivant in the job. Terry had been black taxi-cab driving in London for a living since walking out earlier in the season. 'It's the only way we will stay up', was the message from those senior players that brought Terry and his black cab back to Underhill. An immediate 2-1 away win at Torquay went a long way to taking us to eventual safety. It's amazing what teams will produce for a new manager in a crisis – often in the short term however.

During that season we had lost our star goalkeeper and I was really pleased for Maik Taylor when he got that big money move to the Premiership with Southampton on New Year's Eve because I knew that, with his young family, he was in an even worse financial situation than me. Despite our position, in which we were continuing to rent Trish's parents house, we had planned to have another child and our daughter Atlanta was born in April 1997. A few weeks later, as the season closed, I was offered an improved contract taking me up to £500 per week, and I felt as if I was on decent money at last and could perhaps support my growing family properly. After being named Player of the Season, there was a lot of pressure on me to sign a new contract and I began to feel that, in the face of media speculation that one or two Division One clubs were lining up bids for me, Barnet were working to get me to stay. I had played 46 games that season, had got much fitter and stronger through regular weight training and had well and truly put my old injury-prone days at Charlton behind me.

Things got interesting when Terry Bullivant left Barnet to manage Reading in the early summer and then soon Alan Pardew, who I had played with at both Charlton and Barnet, joined him as reserve team manager at Elm Park. As soon as I heard that Terry was being linked with the vacant Reading job I had an idea that there might be a chance for me to move there with him. I got on to Alan about the possibility of a move and I got a strong hint from him: 'Just keep your phone switched on, that's all'.

The former Peterborough manager John Still, who I knew to be a strict disciplinarian and good organiser, took over at Barnet. He had contacted me three years earlier when I left Charlton, had verbally offered me a contract at Peterborough but had then left me disappointed when I heard nothing further from him. As pre-season training got underway at Underhill he appointed me as captain as an indication that I was well and truly in his plans for the new season. But my heart wasn't really in it and I was waiting by that switched-on 'phone, hankering after a move to join Terry and Pards at Reading.

5
Tears of Frustration 1997-1998

The eventual move to Reading I craved got off the ground in the most unexpected way, and introduced me to the murky world of transfers and agents, with a call from an agent called Mark Curtis, of whom I knew nothing, telling me that a Division One club was interested in me and would I like to meet him to discuss it. I was already contracted to the Stellar Sports Agency so this approach from another agent placed me in a very difficult position. On the one hand I was anxious not to do anything that would prejudice a possible move to Reading, but equally I was concerned about breaking my contract with Stellar in getting another agent to represent me. Mark had also spoken to my Barnet team-mate Lee Hodges in a similar way so we decided to meet him, agreeing that 'This is our big opportunity'. I still had a feeling that what we were doing wasn't right, and that feeling was reinforced when, on meeting at a hotel, Mark made it clear that 'the only way this deal will be done is if you do it through me'. When I pointed out that I was already with another agency, Mark assured me that he would sort it out, and so, rather apprehensively, I signed with him, fully believing that he would speak to my present agency and explain the situation.

Mark did later tell me it was, surprise surprise, Reading who were involved but the Barnet Chairman Tony Kleanthous, with whom I got on well, turned down their first bid and I was persuaded by Mark Curtis to put pressure on the chairman by approaching him to stress how keen I was to have the opportunity to play at a higher level. In the event, two weeks before the season started, Reading upped their bid to £500,000 with my value being placed at £400,000, but the first I knew that things were happening at last was that, on the day of the game, Lee and I were taken out of a first team friendly match. Little did I know, in my excitement, that, typically, such a big move was going to be fraught with stress and upset along the way.

Lee and I had to meet up with Mark at his house on the Monday where we spent two hours waiting for the go-ahead from Reading to travel over to discuss terms. When that came through it was Lee who had to drive, with Mark a non-driver. None of us had been to Elm Park before and we couldn't find the ground so we stopped to ask for directions and came across a lady in shorts with not only the hairiest legs we had ever seen, but the longest hairs too. We just screamed with laughter, the situation releasing all the tension we felt, and leaving us wondering 'what sort of place is this?' When we finally arrived at Elm Park to be met by the Chief Executive, Secretary and manager Terry Bullivant, they went into the process of selling the club to us, which included the viewing of a model of their proposed new Madejski stadium. There was really no need for any of it, with Lee and I just ready to sign without any further delay.

Lee went into the office first with Mark and there were some comings and goings before a deal was finally agreed. At one stage Terry came out and worried me with his whispered comment 'You need him to go easy here otherwise the deal will be off', in a clear reference to Mark's demands. When it was my turn Mark was adamant that I should aim for a figure of £1500 per week plus appearance money, particularly as he had come across a 'piece of paper' in their office which referred to a starting figure of £1000 per week over three years. But Lee got me confused saying I should push for more: 'You should get more as a £400,000 player'. But I didn't like confrontation so I settled for the £1500, without a signing on fee, and was just glad to sign and, in effect, treble my wages.

At the outset, compared to what I was getting at Barnet, I was obviously well pleased with the deal, but, when I became familiar with the wage structure at Reading, I realised that I could and should have been offered more money. My lasting impression was that Terry and the Reading club felt that they were doing me a favour and I couldn't escape the feeling that they exploited my nature and desire to improve myself.

The transfer set off a chain of events which not only upset and scarred me in some ways, but for a while left me financially worse off than I was at Barnet. In fact the day after signing I had a call from David Menasah from the Stellar Sports Agency asking for details of my new deal, reminding me that I was under contract to them and owed them money out of the transfer. All I could do was put him in contact with Mark who had said he 'would sort it out'. Mark himself soon came on to me asking for his fee in the region of £8000, suggesting that I could borrow the money if it proved difficult to raise all at once. So we asked Trish's Aunt to lend us the money to enable us to pay Mark, and that meant we had to pay her back by instalments. The situation between the two agencies was not resolved by Mark, and I found myself being sued by the Stellar agency. The matter was settled out of court, for £500, one week before I was due to make an appearance, with some assistance from a PFA representative. Two years later I ditched Mark as my agent.

Initially at Reading I found myself taking my turn for the two-hour drive each day from London in the company of four others in the squad – my mate Lee Hodges, Darren Caskey, Trevor Morley, and Ray Houghton – and we would stop off on the way for coffee each morning at McDonald's in Watford. I never really felt totally at ease in their company - it was probably my insecurity showing through. It was nothing they ever did to me. I simply felt intimidated by them. They had all been at big clubs, had good pedigrees and would openly, in the car, express their superiority over the other players. It would often leave me, as a young player with humble origins, wondering what they felt about my ability. Darren and Trevor were close friends and both in fantastic positions financially, with really good lives and the big houses and cars to show for it.

Ray Houghton, in particular, had an aura about him from his days with Liverpool and Ireland. As player/coach he was in the habit of speaking down to people giving out the impression that he too was better than most of the other players. I know the rest of the squad shared this view and found it discouraging. It seemed to us that that we were continually being rated against the level of ability to be found at Liverpool during his Anfield days.

Reading made a really shocking start to my first season there and their last at Elm Park before the move to the new Madejski Stadium, with just one point from the first six games with only two goals scored. From a personal angle I played well from the word go, in partnership with fans' favourite Keith McPherson, and I could tell the crowd were appreciating me. Terry attempted to stop the rot by taking us clubbing in midweek with a view to building team spirit amongst a squad who had not really got to know each other by virtue of all the late new signings. It was a dangerous move by Terry – running the risk of being spotted by the fans out on the town with all the bad publicity that would generate. The outcome was a 2-1 home win over Oxford, with Carl Asaba, a record signing from Brentford at £800,000, getting the opener.

Carl was an aggressive physical striker but, off the field, his quiet, mild mannered nature completely belied his image amongst the fans. He was a brilliant lad, very genuine, not one for social-ising but happy just to play with his model racing cars, and to dote on his cat called 'Fluffy' of whom he carried a picture in his wallet. Carl was a dedicated professional, who had a chequered career with several clubs, and who was so conscientious that he over trained at a gym away from the ground sustaining injuries in the process. He was a financial wizard, looking after his money so carefully that we joked that he must have set up his own Carl Asaba Bank to ensure it was secure.

A week later we travelled to Tranmere and lost 6-0, and we got off lightly given that we were five goals down at half-time. What a horrible Saturday, with Keith and I being given the run-around by David Kelly and Gary Jones. A real reality check for me – welcome to Division One! Terry was simply stunned after-wards and his assistant Ron 'Chopper' Harris did most of the shouting in the dressing room. The players seemed to like Terry as a coach but didn't totally respect him, on two counts – both his humble playing background and previous managerial experi-ence at lowly Barnet. Player power was coming to the fore at the club and, as often is the case, it was players who were bought by previous managers, and who found themselves left out, who were sniping away in the background at the under-performing of the newly signed players and generally undermining things. It was all a far cry from the team spirit and harmony I had found at Barnet. Despite that Tranmere fiasco I was still playing well and that was down to the advice I received from Jazz Karim, who I was still see-ing in London once a month as a life coach at my own expense. He got me to focus entirely on my own game and to take no no-tice of what was going on around me as far as the team's results, other player's performances and club politics were concerned.

As I have explained, while I was at Barnet I carried a fear of not being able to play at a higher level. I was regularly plagued by a dream in which I was falling from a high building and, as I got close to hitting the ground, I would wake up in a fearful state. As my successful last season at Barnet ended, the dream was repeated but this time it had a different ending. This time I stayed in the dream after falling, rather than waking up in fear of landing, hit the floor, wasn't hurt and went through the surface with ease. The significance of that last dream came to me soon after I arrived at Reading and I really believe that it signalled a breakthrough in that the fear had gone and was no longer holding me back. A mental barrier had been removed. I had landed in Division One, felt comfortable and confident there and there was no need for me to be scared.

My first visit to Fratton Park found Pompey in even worse shape than us and they obligingly let us escape with a 2-0 win. I remember that there was no Fratton end, with a new stand still under construction, and no real atmosphere and that really didn't help Pompey's cause at that time. We followed that Fratton win up with a 4-0 home win over Sunderland with Carl Asaba grabbing two goals, but then came five successive draws during which I encountered Paul Dickov for the first of many battles over the years. Paul is a fiery, aggressive, but honest opponent and we have developed a mutual respect over the years. It was no co-incidence that I had to come off with a cut head in that goalless draw at Maine Road. That winless run also included a 3-3 draw at Nottingham Forest in a Friday night live Sky TV game. Forest were a strong side with the likes of Van Hooijdonk up front and Steve Stone and Nigel Quashie in midfield, but had Dave Beasant in goal sent off. I had a very harsh penalty given against me but managed to redeem myself with a header for our third goal.

Early in December 1997 came the game I had been waiting for ever since I had signed for Reading – the visit of Charlton and my opportunity to prove that they had made a mistake in releasing me and that I could play at that level. I did see it as a personal thing between myself and Alan Curbishley. I saw Keith Peacock beforehand and he knew only too well what I was setting out to do that afternoon. I was very nervous beforehand, but put my focus on not trying too hard, being relaxed and determined to enjoy myself. In our 2-0 win I didn't put a foot wrong and was a happy man afterwards. After the game I briefly saw John Robinson, one of my former Charlton colleagues, and just gave him a smile that I knew said it all. I had achieved one of my main goals and put all that hurt behind me. But in truth it didn't give me the satisfaction that I thought it would.

I had been playing with some pain for some time and it was finally diagnosed as a shin fracture. During my couple of months on the sidelines Reading climbed into a respectable mid-table position and reached the fifth round of the FA Cup. The time had come to move house and the fact that, with my injury, I couldn't manage the driving from London every day and was stuck in Reading, apart from my family all the week, rather forced the issue. We were ready at last to finally make the break, become independent and get a place of our own - Nathan was close to going to school and Atlanta was not yet a year old. The club agreed to lend us the necessary deposit, with certain repayment terms, and during my injury break we got down to the serious business of looking for a property. We didn't know where to look but knew that Reading itself was too expensive. Carl Asaba, that astute investor, came to our aid, recommending some new houses in Didcot, just 35 minutes out of Reading. Before long we were excitedly moving into a four-bedroom detached house. Another of my goals had been achieved and in our eyes and everybody else's we had finally made it. We had got out of London, I was established at a Division One club and all those struggles whilst I was at Charlton and Barnet were now behind us. There was even paper-talk about then Premiership sides Leeds United and Barnsley being interested in me.

Football was the be-all and end-all in our lives. It could provide the answer to everything. I was driven by the belief that money and what it could buy, and how it could settle our debts to the club and Trish's Aunt, would solve our problems. I believed that if I did well in the game and earned more money then I would be able to give my family everything they needed. So our whole focus was on football and my career, on the basis that if we were financially secure then we would find happiness. But for now there was still something missing and an emptiness in our lives.

In the New Year 1998 things went horribly wrong for Reading with injuries costing us dear. Influential figures like Lee Hodges, Phil Parkinson and Carl Asaba had to be replaced by young inexperienced players and we lost 15 of the last 17 games, failing to score in 11 of those. Morale was desperately low and it was no surprise when Terry resigned in mid-March with eight games left. The fans had never really taken to him and were never behind him – knowing his other profession they dubbed him 'the taxi driver' and were only too pleased for him to go back to that business. I admired the dignified way he left the club, and he meant it when he said 'I'm going to take the pressure off the team'. Terry's strength was in coaching and he didn't like confrontation and upsetting players so the management role never really suited him. Alan Pardew took over for one game and the players liked him. We were keen to do our bit to get him the job but promptly lost 2-0 at home to Huddersfield to ruin any chances he might have had. The former Scottish international and Celtic manager Tommy Burns took the job at the second time of asking, having been Reading's first choice in the summer before turning it down which led to Terry's appointment.

As you would expect from his background Tommy was very professional in everything he did and there was no lack of respect from the players for his methods. He immediately installed new forms of discipline, with a strong emphasis on fitness training and regular meetings, and he would spend hours out on the training ground coaching us into his ways. Training was long and hard with a great physical intensity, on the basis that 'we train as we play'. Tommy's aim was to ensure that we were physically fitter than most teams and for him that was all it would take. In fairness to him he did insist that we play ourselves out of trouble. So there was often a slow patient build-up out of defence but although we were great in possession we could be easily outmuscled. Tommy's arrival brought no upturn in our poor form and the problem, as I see it now with hindsight, was that we had taken too much out of ourselves on the training ground and were simply too tired. Our game was played at one pace, but physically we just couldn't manage the sort of thing, like a sprint or change of pace, that would take our game to another level.

One particular memory I have of Tommy during this period gives an insight into his Catholic faith and his desperation not to lose any key players like myself whilst the results were so poor. One night in a hotel before a game I was unwell and went to bed, but, whilst half asleep, I became aware that he had come into my room. He stayed with me for about 45 minutes without speaking to me, but I believe that he was praying for me and my recovery. As it happened I did manage to play the following day.

On transfer deadline day in March, in desperation at Reading's league position, Tommy must have set some sort of record in signing seven players, all Scottish-born, apparently with a view to giving the squad a boost. Far from a boost, all the arrivals got us bemused as to how bringing in mainly reserve team players from clubs like Newcastle, Kilmarnock and Celtic would improve things. As is often the case with a new manager at a club in crisis, he brought in players he already knew. Most had not played first team football for some time and those same players had been par-tying and drinking whilst in the reserves at other clubs. When they followed that same lifestyle whilst in Reading's first team it meant Tommy's understandable gamble had no chance of paying off.

Such a massive influx of new players led to a feeling of 'them and us' in the dressing room. The newcomers naturally latched on to one another and sat together apart from the established players who were by now very occupied with thoughts of what their futures might be. There was no chance for us all to get to know each other, and it was not conducive to creating a new team spirit. Tommy had also established a new wage structure to accommodate these players which was to cause some resentment. There is a well-used saying in football: 'Winning is a habit, and losing is a habit', and, despite all those signings, there was no sign of the losing habit being broken.

One or two of the new players with what the fans saw as high price tags had difficult times. Jim McIntyre came from Kilmarnock for almost half a million pounds apparently to join the attack and score the goals to get us out of trouble, but he promptly admitted to the local media that he wasn't really a goal scorer which led to him getting a lot of stick from the fans.

With Reading due to leave Elm Park, and move to the brand new Madejski Stadium the following season, the pressure to stay in the Division One was immense. We went to Nottingham Forest in the penultimate match and it was a 'must-win' last chance saloon game for both sides on the promotion and relegation fronts. We had to win to give ourselves any chance of staying up, and, after our meal in the hotel the night before the game, Tommy laid it on the line to us, saying: 'I will never again put this on to you, but everywhere you go, as you sleep, as you go to the toilet, think of this game, nothing else from now on'. We were missing several key players due to injury and I had Phil Parkinson as a stop-gap central defender alongside me. We lost to a goal from Chris Bart-Williams three minutes from time.

The realisation that we had been relegated brought tears to my eyes that afternoon. Tears of frustration and failure, but also of relief that all the pressure of the previous weeks, in which all the focus for every waking minute had been on getting out of trouble, had been lifted from my shoulders. Until it happens, players don't realise what relegation means, not only to the supporters but also to everybody in the town. Reading is a close-knit self-contained community, unlike Charlton and Barnet whose identities are somewhat submerged in the London area. I felt responsible for all that pain and disgrace the town felt – well that was my experience anyway. I cared for the club and I always desperately wanted to win for the fans. Even if I played well, and perhaps even got a Man of the Match award, it meant nothing to me if the fans were disappointed and let down by the result. Perhaps it was an unnecessary level of responsibility that I took on every week.

The following week, already relegated, we played the last game of the season, and the last at Elm Park before the move to the new stadium, and lost 1-0 to Norwich in what was intended to be a special sentimental occasion for the fans. There was a real 'no show' from the players that afternoon and luckily the Chairman, Mr Madejski was abroad and not there to see the performances of the players who were going to grace his brand new multi-million pound stadium in the next season.

Tommy went mad after the game: 'The fans deserved more than that. Some of you have played your last game for Reading today'. As I sat there part of me couldn't help wonder whether perhaps I might be one of those who would inevitably be released, and whether that might be something I would actually welcome. There had been talk during the season of Leeds being interested in taking me in exchange for their Scottish winger Andy Gray but there was no question of me seeing Tommy and making my feelings known.

Once that dreadful relegation season was over Trish and I couldn't wait to spend the summer back in London close to our families and friends, where we still felt we belonged. In Didcot we felt that people only wanted to form friendships with us because of the football connection, and because they were Reading fans. That meant that whenever we were invited to anything we soon found ourselves being dragged into conversations criticising the club and other players. One night we were invited to a party and, as we arrived outside, we could see through the windows that many of those present were wearing Reading shirts. That was enough to make us turn around and head back for home.

Throughout the season we had been going back to London every weekend for our home comforts, and each time on our return journey Trish would break down in tears. Our dream move to a lovely new house, with an equally lovely car, had turned sour. Trish had become homesick, and, as a non-driver, she felt trapped on her own all day with two young children in a wealthy area with people out of her age group to whom she just couldn't relate. Trish has an outgoing personality but she was finding it difficult to make friends outside football and I was becoming concerned that she was getting really low. What friends she did slowly make were depressed themselves, and it became clear that the number of our neighbours who were on anti-depressants was unreal. The word 'depression' was not in our vocabulary before but Trish was changing from the carefree girl she used to be, and it was clear that she too needed to see a doctor and get treatment.

I had no experience of depression and we had no-one close to speak to. It was certainly something that you couldn't share with anyone at a football club. I had never known anyone, even family, have the condition and I admit I didn't understand it. I tried to put it at the back of my mind. I would tell myself that it would go away eventually, that we would get through it. It seriously entered my mind to make it a reason to get a transfer back to a London club. Half of me would have loved to have gone back, but the other half reasoned that we had a beautiful house on a beautiful estate out of London and we had to get over it. It didn't affect me playing-wise and I was still picking up regular Man of the Match awards, but, with Trish's condition, it gave me no satisfaction. As the situation continued I found myself picking up a number of minor injuries which I put down to stress.

After the relegation the words of the Barnet Chairman from nine months earlier, after he had reluctantly agreed to my move to Reading, had come home to me: 'You will regret this move – you will go down, and we will go up', although he was only half right as Barnet missed out on promotion to Division Two. It seemed like a throwaway, idle threat at the time but I certainly never envisaged having to drop down a division, or that it would bring us such unhappiness.

6

'It shouldn't be like this...'
1998-2000

After the relegation, our move to the new Madejski Stadium in the summer of 1998 brought a lot of expectation of getting back to Division One and you also couldn't escape the feeling that the club was clearly geared up for the Premiership. All the facilities were there but there was much to do to get it right on the pitch if the gamble of building such a stadium was to pay off. Some significant investment in the team was called for but the not so astute purchase of a Liberian striker called Mass Sarr for £150,000, and a winger from York called Graeme Murty for £700,000, were the only major arrivals, to add to a goalkeeper Peter Van der Kwaak and a defender Elroy Kromheer from Dutch clubs for free. A series of niggling injuries meant Graeme made little or no impact that season but amazingly he's still at Reading, having been converted to full back, and as skipper led them to the Premiership and has earned a full Scotland cap.

Tommy Burns was under pressure from the start, but, probably because of his reputation in Scotland, the fans were seemingly prepared to give him one last chance.

If anything the fitness training in pre-season reached a higher level of intensity than ever before under Tommy and at one stage we went 30 days without a day off including weekends. Continuous fitness testing and examination of the resulting data told me what I already knew – that I was OK on short sprints but, with my stamina levels, I was never going to be in the leading pack of the long distance runs. On our two-week pre-season tour of Holland we would do a series of sprints and runs at our training base before games which usually meant that we were all falling asleep exhausted on the coach to the ground. After one particularly gruelling morning session I fell asleep in my room and the coach to the game went without Mass Sarr, my room mate and me who had to get a taxi to the Dutch ground. That brought a galling £100 fine, which Trish and I couldn't spare so I didn't ever tell her. I knew it was small change for Mass who was on much bigger wages than me.

Finally I was adjudged to have reached the required level of fitness but went down with a thigh strain three days before the season opened and missed the three away games as the stadium had not been finished in time. I recovered in time for the opening game at the plush Madejski Stadium late in August and it was great to play there. Unfortunately it was soon clear as the weeks went by that neither the home team nor their modest Division Two visitors could provide the quality football to match the magnificent stage. In fact invariably the opposition would be lifted by the stadium and its facilities and raise their game. It didn't help that we were being somewhat tactlessly reminded of the club's past glories by the continual screening throughout the stadium and its lounges on match days of action from four years earlier under joint managers Jimmy Quinn and Mick Gooding when Reading came so close to being promoted to the Premiership.

The struggles under Tommy continued in the lower division with only one win in the first eight games and I was competing for my place with a young Dutch lad called Elroy Kromheer who had been brought in on very good wages. Elroy was unable to handle the English game both mentally and physically and that was never more evident than in an embarrassing 0-6 home defeat to Bristol Rovers. In an amazing game all the goals came in the second half with Jamie Cureton grabbing four, and Jason Roberts, who out-muscled Elroy all afternoon, getting the other two.

Tommy displayed ruthless tendencies towards those players who were not in his plans, and there were several of the 'old bri-gade' in that category, having played under three or four previous managers. It's often the case with clubs that such players move to the sidelines, and sit out their contracts when they should re-ally move on. New managers have different styles of play which sometimes doesn't suit those players who were brought in by earlier managers to play in some other roles. Tommy's method of dealing with such players was to get them to report for training at different, often deliberately awkward times to those of the rest of the squad. So players like Andy Legg, Gareth Davies and Jason Bowen were training with the youth team and having no contact whatsoever with the manager and the other players. Those players would tell us that: 'They were treated worse than lepers', but the only winner is the manager and it's all part of the plan to make life as uncomfortable as possible for them. In effect to force them to ask for a move and thereby forfeit the balance of their contract.

We climbed to the edge of the play-offs at one stage in that sea-son but fell away and finished tenth, with just one win in the last eleven games, five of which I missed through injury. I had been playing regularly and felt that I had done well so my aim of get-ting a proper level of wages when my contract ran out in a year's time was largely on track, or so I thought. By now there was no doubt in my mind that in the last two years at Reading I had been left well behind financially. Not only did I get little satisfaction from playing well but there was the added bugbear of not being rewarded properly. When I went to the club the highest earner was on about £2000 per week which was fairly low wages for

Division One. I signed for £1500 per week and now I knew for certain that since Tommy Burns had arrived the wage structure had been revised. I had watched as a stream of new signings had secured up to four-year deals on twice the wages I was being paid and I had seen the lifestyles they were enjoying.

After the last game of the season Tommy wanted to speak to us all individually. I rarely had any contact with Tommy on a one to one basis. He saved that for the players he had signed or his favourites like Darren Caskey. Managers generally tend to have their favourites – players who have their ear or are taken into their confidence - and it makes it difficult for the rest particularly if you have any pressing individual concerns with which you have to approach them. It usually leads to a 'meeting' which can take on a formal nature.

For myself I felt, with Tommy, that he was always looking to replace me and that nothing I could do would ever be enough to keep my place in the team. So I wasn't prepared for what came out of that short meeting. Tommy first asked me: 'How do you think you've done this season?'

To which I answered: 'I don't feel that I have had a good season, and been consistent enough'.

I was really shocked by his response: 'You've been one of the successes of the season for me'.

I had seen how he was with his favourites in praising them up to the skies but never expected him to come out with something like that to me. He had never ever given me the impression that he rated me so highly.

By now I was represented by the Professional Footballers Association (PFA) and I knew that they had spoken to Tommy about a new contract. So when he finished our little chat by saying: 'Your agent has rung me, and we'll sort out a new contract in the summer', I wasn't too surprised. The Bosman ruling had just taken effect and at that time the clubs were more fearful of the consequences, as far as players being able to leave at the end of their contracts without the club receiving a fee, than they are now.

I was a happy man through that summer break. Not only had I pleased the manager but it appeared that a new contract was on the horizon, so perhaps at last Trish and I could begin to address our problems. I spent the summer chasing up the PFA constantly to see if there was any sign of an offer from the club, but nothing arrived. I might have known.

Trish and I were married that summer, on 9 June 1999, in a small, family, low-budget affair at a Didcot registry office. We were a real family now and we always had in mind to get married, not just for the sake of the two children. It felt right to put the seal on our love at that time. We couldn't afford a honeymoon, and up to that time we had never even been on a family holiday.

Reading's prospects were boosted by the big money signing of striker Nicky Forster from Birmingham but once the new season got under way I found myself sidelined as a regular sub, despite Tommy's words of praise for me in our conversation at the end of the previous season. There had been no mention of a new contract and I began to feel that I was on my way out. Alan Pardew lost his job at the club when the reserve team was scrapped but before he left I spoke to him about my situation along the lines of: 'I get the impression that Tommy doesn't rate me', to which he replied: 'Don't worry when you get your chance again you will stay in the team'.

After only one win in the first seven we were just one off the bottom of the league and I wasn't the only one who felt that Tommy's days at Reading were numbered. One or two of the senior players were asked by the Board if he was the right man for the job and their feelings can be summed up as: 'We think he is a good manager, but we don't think he can turn it around'.

Tommy had been a Board appointment, against the players'

preference for Alan Pardew at that time, so when he was sacked the board asked us who we would like this time. Pards was the unanimous choice again, having earned even more respect during his time as the reserve team manager, and so he was given the job until the end of the season, bringing in former England coach John Gorman as his assistant.

I wasn't too unhappy, in a selfish way, to see Tommy go, knowing that under Pards I would have a good chance of playing. From being one of the senior players I looked up to at Charlton a few years back, now here he was as my manager. Pards certainly had a rather special way about him. He created a relaxed atmosphere with plenty of banter and jokes, but equally you could come in for some stick from him and he could be really cutting at times. Players knew where they stood with him though – if you didn't perform then he would very soon let you know.

When I got my place back in the side it soon became obvious that I was desperately unfit. I was not getting any games having previously been on the bench for some weeks, and, with no reserve team football either, my fitness had clearly dipped. The source of the problem became apparent when I was unable to complete one particularly hard first team training session. I just couldn't do anymore – I was 'gone', as they say – and it drew a torrent of abuse from John. That upset me because it was obvious I had a problem, and it wasn't pleasant to have the coaches mistrusting me and mistaking my motives. When I later reported that I had no energy in the last half-hour of games the club sent me to a nutritionist in London who concluded that I was not taking in enough carbohydrates. The trouble arose because I had been eating less to ensure that I didn't put on any weight during the period when I was not playing. So I was ordered to take on plenty of jacket potatoes, bread, pasta etc to build up my energy levels. It soon did the trick and before long I was back to my best, even if the results didn't improve.

If anything performances and results under Pards got even worse and at Christmas we were in the relegation zone after going 13 games without a win at one stage. It was the same squad of players that Tommy Burns had struggled with, gates were down to 6000 odd in the new 24,000 capacity stadium and there was no shortage of tension in the dressing room. One particularly heated exchange involved John Gorman who threatened to quit over the direct type of football we had adopted: 'We need to play more football, there is just not enough football being played out there'. As it transpired John jumped ship early in the New Year to rejoin Glenn Hoddle, with whom his career was entwined at this time, at Southampton.

Pards brought in Martin Allen as first team coach, who had previously worked at Portsmouth as reserve team coach, and he had a reputation as a hard man from his playing days at West Ham where he was known as 'Mad Dog'. Martin had an affinity with Reading through his father who had played for the club, and it soon became apparent that he was a very strong, enthusiastic character who was there to instil a winning mentality in what was, by now, a demoralised squad. He immediately impressed me as a coach, and I well remember a double session in his very first week in which he spent a couple of hours working with us on set plays with free kicks both for and against. The way in which he got us organised to both attack and defend at free kicks was absolutely spot on and a breath of fresh air. In all my time in the game, up to then, I had not had that sort of intensive coaching, not even from Tommy Burns.

Martin's training methods were, to say the least, unusual; crazy, outrageous, mad at times, and you had to have a strong mentality to meet his demands. He would constantly be looking for ways to physically challenge us whilst having fun and building team spirit. Soon after joining he had us back in the afternoons, twice a week, for intensive fitness work on various madcap routines. As a regular feature he would have twelve of us crammed in a small changing room to work on a circuit of weights to build triceps. The hot showers were turned on throughout with plenty of steam filling the room thereby ensuring that we worked up an enormous sweat. The circuit involved 30 seconds on each set of weights and at the end of his exercise each player had to let out a loud, mad animal noise, say roaring like a lion.

Another instance of his antics came on the morning of a home match against Bristol Rovers during our usual warm-up running around the pitch. This time, in an empty stadium, we were ordered to run up the steps one by one to the top of the main stand and then along the concourse to the closed burger stand, where we had to queue and each pretend to buy a burger. Then we had to take our places in the seating and each sit, for some time, continually shouting abuse at the non-existent players on the pitch to mimic what had been directed towards us previously.

Martin was always looking to change routines and, as an example, for one midweek game at Blackpool we went up early on the day before, had a slap-up fish and chip supper and then a night out at the cinema. Whether the fun we had from those simple pleasures contributed to the vital 2-0 away win is difficult to tell but the team was bonding as a result.

I remember that we had a difficult away game at Preston, where David Moyes was then manager, and Martin was determined to get a psychological edge and ruffle their feathers before kick off. So he got us out on the pitch early and took us to the end of the Deepdale stadium where the home side would usually warm up in front of their own fans. That really upset them and we were greeted with a chorus of booing. Before long the Preston team, with David Moyes, came out and joined us at the same end so that there were 28 players warming up in the same half of the field, with two goalkeepers in the same goalmouth. Preston were very angry at our stance and the two managers were soon at each other's throats, such that the police had to get involved and order us to the other end before matters got out of hand. Even then Martin ordered us to walk very slowly to the other end as if we didn't care, just to antagonise them even further. We got what was a very good 2-2 draw out of that match. How much of that was down to Martin's pre-match antics I am not sure.

The impact of such an approach can only last for so long and be of a short term nature. A few of the players didn't take to Martin or his methods and either couldn't handle it or were offended by his often personal remarks in their direction. He wouldn't tolerate anything less than 100% in training at all times and I remember one particular bust-up with a senior professional in the squad who he accused outright of cheating on a run. You couldn't argue with the big impact he made in just a few weeks as far as team spirit was concerned and that was shown in the results which got us out of trouble in the last two or three months of the season.

My new contract was obviously uppermost in my mind as the season rolled on but now that Pards had taken over I was confident, given that he knew me so well, that he would see me right. In fact when he was reserve team manager in the previous regime, Pards had actually advised me not to accept any new terms Tommy Burns might offer but to 'wait and see', on the basis that he 'didn't have my best interests at heart'.

It was the Friday before we were due to play at Oldham when Pards handed me the club's written contract offer. To say I was shocked and upset at the derisory offer on the table is a gross understatement. Immediately I couldn't escape the overwhelming feeling that they were taking advantage of my good nature. There was no anger initially – that was to come later.

Three years earlier I had signed a contract at £1500 per week and now the club were offering me another £15,000 a year, an increase of slightly less than £300 per week to £1800 per week. Given that I knew that the pay structure at Reading had improved significantly during Tommy's time and that the highest paid player in the first team squad was earning over £4000 per week and the lowest over £2000 per week, it was nothing more than an insult. The first person I spoke to, after receiving the offer, was my good friend Lee Hodges and he was mortified for me.

The following day at Boundary Park, Oldham brought my worst performance in a Reading shirt. Despite that we won 2-1, but I was just in no mood to play. My head was full of all these powerful negative messages: *'It doesn't matter what you do for the club... you give your all for the fans... you give everything for the town... and this is how the club reward you... it shouldn't be like this'*. I began to question what it was all about and whether there was any meaning to my life: *'We've moved here... we've not made any real friends... is life just about making as much money as possible from football... and then dying and giving it all to my kids?'*. At times like that I hated football and all it stood for.

I knew that all this uncharacteristic bitterness and questioning came out of what I saw as the lack of recognition or acknowledgment for what I had achieved, at the complete lack of equality with the rest of the squad, and at the way in which the club, and more particularly Pards with his knowledge of my personality from our days together at Charlton, were seeking to take advantage of my good nature.

It was not a question of being greedy. Trish and I knew that this was a lot of money I was being offered and that it was a great contract in worldly terms but in the footballing world it simply did not come up to scratch, and certainly did not match the existing wage structure at Reading. I was relying on this new contract to sort out all my problems. At 26 years of age I was approaching the real peak of my career and this was vital to my future.

For John Polston, a fellow defender and a very good friend at the club who, with his wife Jo, had given Trish and I some valuable advice on financial planning and housekeeping, there was no doubt: 'What you want is what you should get. There are four or five players at the club who are not playing who are getting more money than you are being offered'.

'I spoke to the PFA representative at the weekend and that conversation left me very disillusioned. It seemed to me that they didn't want to be at loggerheads with the club over the issue, which seemed illogical when they were supposed to be representing me. Very soon afterwards I told them I didn't want them to represent me any longer. Sean Evers, who was in dispute with the club at the time, put me on to John Mac, who had originally been my agent at the time when I left Charlton.

Pards spoke to me again the following Monday and asked for my reaction to the offer to which I replied: 'Very disappointed'.

He seemed surprised: 'Why?'

To which I replied: 'I know what other players are on at the club'

To my astonishment Pards then offered me what he clearly expected me to accept as an explanation: 'Strikers invariably earn more than defenders because they score the goals that win games'.

That argument just didn't wash with me and I said: 'I'm not happy with that, even if it's true, and I want a better offer. I'm not asking to be the highest earner but I want a better offer'

The conversation was effectively ended when he replied: 'There's no way we can offer you what you want'.

When Pards later confirmed that the Chairman had refused to pay me any more, I began to believe that he had convinced the club that he could get me to settle for such a low figure. Then, after about a month's stalemate, the club came back to me with a new improved offer taking me to just over £2000 per week rather than the £1800 originally offered. A £10,000 signing on fee was also included in the package, but I would still have been one of the lowest paid players in the squad. By now I had made up my mind that I wouldn't settle for anything less than £2700 per week, knowing that such a figure was well within the pay structure, and that it would enable me to manage my debts.

I had another meeting with Pards and this time we had a good discussion. I was able to explain the situation at home with Trish and the level of the debts I had built up in the early days while I was still struggling to manage. I was able to explain that my contract had been unchanged for three years but that not only had the cost of living gone up but so had the wages paid at the club and in the game generally.

From that Pards got to know my side of the argument, so it was really disappointing when later, as the press reported that contract talks had stalled, he was quoted as saying that I was 'being greedy' and that 'we've made him an offer which we believe is good enough for him'. As it stood I knew that in the eyes of the fans I was one of the better players and one of their favourites – I had been a runner-up in their most recent Player of the Season poll. Clearly Pards was trying to get the fans on his side in case I did leave the club, and I suppose that was understandable. For my part I never went to the press to air my grievances or to make a case for being treated fairly.

Other than that Oldham game I was able to put my off-field feelings behind me on the field and my performances were unaffected. I suppose it was a sign of how much I had matured that I was able to be so professional in that respect. When I missed a number of games due to a back problem, the injury was not made public by the club, and, with them insisting that I continue to travel away with the team, the fans were being led to believe that I was being left out because I wouldn't sign a new contract.

It was probably totally wrong of me but, as the season drew to a close, I was building up real resentment to the club and the manager. The club made it clear there would be no more offers and I had already reconciled myself to leaving the club. So we made a decision to sell our house in Didcot and rent a house in Reading from a former player. The house was sold in a few weeks. We made a good profit and it was sufficient to pay off all our debts.

I felt increasingly in need of some inspiration from a higher power and found myself thinking about going back to church. I did ask the neighbours about the nearest church but to make it happen I needed someone to hold my hand and physically take me there. But in my heart I felt compelled to go to the Bible for answers, so I found myself buying one. At the same time I came across one of Norman Vincent Peale's self-help religious books 'The Amazing Power of Positive Thinking' which was really inspirational. The book's closing words in particular stayed with me: 'We may never meet in person but in this book we have met. We are spiritual friends. I pray for you so live and work successfully'.

I'm not sure that many of the Reading fans really believed I would leave, although before and after the last game of the season at home to Stoke, many of them greeted me with the same message: 'Don't leave, Linvoy'. On the day I felt disappointed to be leaving. If it had been purely down to sentiment I might have changed my mind and stayed. But I told myself that I had given everything to the club, the supporters, my family and indeed to myself, and that I had to take a stand on this. My performances over three years spoke for that.

Given my nature, a throwaway remark in my direction across a crowded hotel room from Martin Allen: 'We'll be in Division One in a year's time, you know', was all it took to raise doubts in my mind and severely undermine my fragile self-belief. I consoled myself with the news from John Mac that the likes of Southampton, Barnsley and Charlton had expressed an interest in me. All I needed now was one of them to actually get in contact and make me an offer.

We had our first family holiday and during those two weeks in

Spain I hardly slept a wink. Would I have a club to go to on my return? I was racked with worry. I knew nothing else but football. I wasn't equipped to do anything else. The other players had told me that 'you can always get a club somewhere', but what would I have to settle for? How would it affect Trish and the family if we had to go to the other end of the country?

I was technically a Reading player, still under contract and being paid until the end of June, so when it was time for the club's customary mid-summer fitness tests I surprised everybody, including Pards, by turning up for the day. He called me over, saying: 'What's going on?'

I said: 'I haven't got a club yet'.

Pards' response was: 'There's nothing left to offer you'.

My last words were: 'Well I'm not going to break the rules of my contract - I'm still a man of my word'.

As pre-season training drew closer I was becoming more and more worried but then, out of the blue, I had a call from John Mac to say Luton were interested and offering £2400 per week. Even though it was less than I had wanted from Reading, it proved to me, once and for all, that they were wrong in saying that no club would pay more than the £2000 or so per week that was their final offer to me. So John and I met up with Luton manager Lennie Lawrence, who I knew from my Charlton days, at Kenilworth Road. I was just happy that there was a club prepared to take me and we shook hands on a deal, on the basis that Lennie just had to get board approval before it could be completed. That didn't stop Trish and I immediately finding a house in the area which we could afford.

We were happy that this deal would leave us financially better-off, but there was just a tinge of disappointment amongst the feeling of relief that at last I was fixed up. I remember saying to Trish: 'All this battling just to end up with a club on a par with Reading and in the same division'.

The next day I took all the family to a Pizza Hut for a celebratory meal and after 20 minutes in there I had a phone call from John Mac. I couldn't quite hear him over the din, so I slipped outside to make out what he was saying:

'Lennie has been sacked – there's been a takeover with a new owner, and they want to put someone else in as manager. So the deal's off.'

I felt as if my whole world had collapsed. It had been my only offer. We were shocked – and at first Trish just didn't believe me. We decided to go on another holiday, somewhere different, this time without the children – if anything to make up for not having a honeymoon when we were married. The idea was to try and switch off from all the stress and uncertainty – perhaps even to get our heads right and think clearly about our future. We chose Malta but we didn't enjoy it at all. But I did come back determined to keep myself fit and in shape – driven by the thought that it would enable me to get signed up by somebody.

It was a phone call from Pards, of all people, that finally provided the breakthrough, presumably after he had heard that I wasn't fixed up. I was taken aback when he said:

'I don't want to see all that you have achieved go to waste. You've got too much talent. I will speak to Tony Pulis at Portsmouth. I'll tell him it would be worthwhile for him to have a look at you, that you might not start in his team, but once you're in he won't be able to leave you out'.

I was grateful obviously but could only mutter: 'Thanks mate for that. I was disappointed that we couldn't agree anything. All the best, mate, for the new season'.

It wasn't long before I had a call from Tony Pulis: 'We've started back three days a week. Do you want to come in on Monday for a week and have a trial with us'?

Of course I jumped at it. But I was a disappointed that it only amounted to a trial. I felt I didn't warrant this and that I had proved myself at Reading. But I knew it was only my pride talking, and Trish and I decided that I simply had got nothing to lose by going to Portsmouth – perhaps even a lot to gain. Who could tell?

7

All change at Pompey 2000-2001

I had the route to their Eastleigh training ground explained to me but Portsmouth seemed like the end of the world to this London boy. As for the club, I was aware of the recent financial difficulties, of all the players being put up for sale and then warming up in T-shirts indicating their 'price', of the arrival of Milan Mandaric to save the club, and of the 'great escapes' over the years. I was well aware that the club was renowned for its heart and fighting spirit.

John Mac's words of encouragement went with me: 'Remember the usual bits... the positive handshake... show yourself to be keen... just like starting a new job'. I was so nervous at the outcome. I was a complete stranger and didn't know anybody at the club. I could barely name more than one or two of the players. I knew that nobody would recognise me. I waited around sitting in the car for somebody to turn up in the car park and it was a relief when the manager Tony Pulis arrived in his BMW. Out I got to greet him:

'I'm Linvoy Primus'.

'Good to see you. Big Kev the kitman will show you where to go'.

I soon recognised people like Justin Edinburgh, Aaron Flahavan and Lee Bradbury.

Darren Moore, who I had played against during my Barnet days when he was at Doncaster, made me feel very welcome and I immediately felt really comfortable with him. Straightaway I knew it felt right at Pompey. All my nerves just melted away and I felt completely at ease in the environment. However my heart sank when I realised that a large part of the first week was going to be taken up with running sessions, and I was back to long distance again for which I was just not prepared. Even the lads who had got fit from the previous weeks' fitness training were struggling. The lads did realise my plight and gave me a round of applause when I finally came in after my first three and a half laps of the training ground, happily just within the 25 minute limit set. Luckily the Pompey fitness coach recognised my limitations long distance-wise and I was soon limited to the shorter distances.

It soon became obvious that a 'him and them' situation had arisen between Tony and the players who hadn't been signed by him. I sensed that the likes of Steve Claridge, Adrian Whitbread, Andy Awford, Guy Whittingham and Scott Hiley were trying to exert some sort of 'player power'. For me it was a reversal of the situation which had arisen at Reading – now I found myself on the other side of the fence as one of those new signings who was a threat to the old brigade, rather than the other way around. But, unlike those Reading days, that generated no resentment amongst the players whatsoever, and in fact there was a great togetherness in the squad that made me feel very comfortable.

I knew that at the end of my first week the squad were going down to the West Country to play three friendlies in five days, whilst based at Woodbury Park Hotel, Golf and Country Club in Devon, owned by Nigel Mansell. I knew that if I could get on that tour and play one or two games it would give me a better chance to prove myself. At the end of my week's trial I bucked up courage and spoke to Tony: 'How am I doing?' He replied: 'I'm pleased with what I've seen so far. Dave (Kemp) and

Lindsay (Parsons) have been impressed. Now we need to see you in some games'.

I roomed with Darren Moore at the hotel and partnered him at the back in the first game at Dorchester and I found the going really hard – being absolutely shattered both during and after the game. In particular my breathing - shortness of breath, out of breath, whatever you want to call it – was just not good, and I knew, like a number of the players, that I hadn't recovered from all that work in the previous week's training. But I stuck at it and fought my way through, knowing how much my future depended on that performance. Darren had a different reaction to the training, having to come off with a hamstring problem.

The following day, after a light training session, I was back in our room when Darren came rushing in to join me, with some news: 'I've spoken to the Chairman. He's impressed with you and wants to sign you'.

I thought *'Yes-s-s-s'*, and later when Darren had left the room I jumped up and down with joy, fell over, and broke some springs in my bed, which luckily went unnoticed subsequently. I phoned Trish with my great news, with no mention of the bed of course. John Mac was cool on the news saying: 'Let's wait and see if Tony wants you, nothing's done yet'.

One thing that did impress me about John was that, knowing that I wouldn't be covered by the club's insurance against injury whilst playing for them during the trial period, he negotiated such an insurance for me during that period. It struck me that he was putting my interests right to the fore in all of this.

On the Wednesday night we played at Exeter and I was pleased with my showing. Players were dropping like flies, breaking down with injuries brought on by all that intensive training. It was hard for me too, but the football was going well. I had jumped to Division One and I felt confident, almost arrogant about my ability in that company. The atmosphere I had found myself in had helped – I was sure of that.

My mood got even better when John phoned to say that Barrie Pierpoint, Pompey's Chief Executive, had confirmed to him that they were prepared to offer me a contract. In my impatience to get it completed, I went to find Mr Pierpoint who, understandably irritated, said: 'You'll have to wait for a bit, but we'll get it sorted out'.

But it wasn't long before I was gripped by fear again when I heard that the club had been linked with two central defenders, Steve Butler of Gillingham and Marc Williams of Watford. So despite the Chairman being so keen to sign me there were now two other centre halves in the equation.

Mercifully Mr Pierpoint called me over on the Friday morning, the last day of the West Country tour, before we set off for Plymouth for the final game. I could have kissed him when he told me: 'We're going to sign you'. I had no idea what had caused the delay but that was now of no concern to me. I had got the result I wanted so much, and was so happy that at last it was about to happen.

I played the whole 90 minutes at Plymouth and then we faced the long haul back to Portsmouth by coach, arriving back in the early hours of Saturday morning. According to the players, the match at Plymouth, the furthest away from Portsmouth, was deliberately planned as the last of the tour so that none of them would have time, on their return, to go out on the town. I was well aware already that I had joined a club where, unlike Reading who were a thoroughly sober bunch, there was a drink culture around. I had soon got to hear of some of the exploits from as recently as the previous season when Rory Allen and Aaron Flahavan had been involved in a fracas at a bar.

At the weekend Trish and I made plans to look for houses on the south coast and John Mac gave me some idea of the terms he would be looking for from Pompey. We knew that I was not in a strong position bargaining-wise, and that it was almost a 'begging bowl' situation on my part, so desperate was I to get a club after 'burning my bridges' with Reading.

The following week I duly signed for the almost £2100 per week on offer – almost exactly the amount of Reading's final offer but without their £10,000 signing on fee and less than Luton's offer. Neither the Chairman or the manager were around when I put pen to paper in club secretary Paul Weld's office and the transfer could not have been more low-key, even if I was not expecting any sort of fanfare. There was no announcement from the club but the news did reach my friends and family in the Reading area through their local paper.

When it was all over John was frank with me: 'I sense that they're still not sure of your ability and whether you can handle it at this level. They haven't paid a fee so from their perspective they're not taking a huge chance with you. I just feel that if you do really well then we can go back in after a year and ask for an improvement'.

Despite the lingering disappointment with the wages, this was still a fresh and exciting start for us away from Reading and Didcot, with no debts and with the added satisfaction of having found the deposit for our house ourselves. We felt positive about the move and it was already clearly benefiting Trish. Her depression had lifted and it was great to see her occupied and focused on our new home. We didn't want to repeat the mistake we had made previously in Didcot where we had found ourselves too remote and detached from the local community and the shops. We were now looking for somewhere no more than 20 minutes from a town centre, although we were conscious that house prices were generally higher on the south coast. We had strong recommendations from Justin Edinburgh, Darren Moore and Lee Bradbury about Whiteley, an out-of-town development near Fareham, and it really fitted the bill particularly with a good local junior school there for Nathan.

With Darren Moore as an automatic choice I found myself in direct competition with Adrian Whitbread to partner him in the centre of defence, but was hopeful of starting the season in the side. Before that I had a potentially serious moment in the last pre-season friendly at Woking when I was knocked out and taken to hospital after fellow defender Dave Waterman accidentally caught me with his elbow. A ball was knocked over the top by Woking and, with their forward going after it, Dave and I both gave chase, back towards our own goal, with our eyes firmly fixed on their player. On reaching the ball together Dave got his head to it but at the same time caught me with his elbow. I was out cold before even hitting the ground and woke up in the dressing room on a stretcher with a split lip. There was a hole in the lip through which I could touch the tooth that had been forced through it by the impact. Dr Nigel Sellars, who was later to become the club doctor and was at the match as a supporter, came to the dressing room and offered his advice on treatment. Kev McCormack, our kit man, drove me to hospital where I had eleven stitches, seven on the inside and four on the outside. It meant that when it was time for the photo shoot a couple of days later I was parading a big fat lip in the official team picture.

I was in the team to start the season at Sheffield United but on the morning of the game Darren was doubtful with a hamstring injury. I was keen to strike up a partnership with him but Darren wasn't confident that his hamstring would be strong enough and he went and told Tony of his doubts. That was a surprise and a big moment for me – pointing to the fact that I had gone into a more mature and professional environment. I had not been used to players being able to discuss and give an opinion about their fitness to play directly with the manager – it was always something between the physio and the manager with the player somehow not considered mature enough to be involved in the decision mak-

91

ing. As it happened Tony decided to take a gamble with Darren's fitness and it paid off.

I was up against a big, strong lad in Marcus Bent at Bramall Lane and rose to the challenge and felt confident throughout what turned out to be a first day 2-0 defeat. I did slice the ball into my own goal for their second and felt for a moment that the ground would swallow me up, particularly as it was in front of all their fans at the home end. It didn't knock my confidence or take away my feeling that I had played well. A number of the senior professionals like Guy Whittingham and Scott Hiley were frozen out, left behind and didn't travel with the squad, but it was to their credit that on the following Monday at training I felt a strong sense of acceptance, rather than any form of resentment towards me. They were asking me about such things as my family, the children's schools, what made me leave Reading etc, when I met up with them again.

A 1-1 draw with Grimsby in the first home game didn't go down well with the Fratton Park fans who booed us off at the end. Striker Lee Mills and midfielder Nigel Quashie made their debuts but there was clearly unease amongst the fans that had carried over from the previous season, with the absence of any big name signings in pre-season being taken as a sign of the club's lack of ambition. From my perspective I felt that it was a strong squad, with a number of very good players. Playing in such company had definitely rubbed off on me and taken my game up to another level.

I was still commuting from Reading but a few of the lads went out to a night club after the match, and Adrian Whitbread was attacked and 'glassed'. The subsequent press reports on the incident didn't help our image with the fans, and Tony called a squad meeting on the Monday. After discussing the game, he said: 'We had a problem after the game, as you know, with Adie being attacked. After a performance like that it really wasn't a good time to go out on the town. I am going to have to fine all of you who went out, and try to stamp it out'.

Tony challenged a number of players over their social activities, and I sensed an air of animosity towards the manager out of his attitude towards them. Going out on a Saturday night didn't break any club rules, and I didn't think he handled it too well. My feeling was that he would have been better advised to have urged the players to 'use their common sense' over such outings, at a time when the fans were unhappy.

The next home game brought a great 3-1 win over Wolves – our first three points of the season – and at last Fratton Park came alive with a good atmosphere and a buzz about the place. There was more vocal singing support than I had known at the Madejski Stadium and with the Fratton crowd closer to the pitch it seemed even louder to the players. Wolves had enquired about me before I left Reading and I wanted to prove to them that they should have taken me. I often found in my career that having a point to prove, from one angle or another, was a useful form of motivation in approaching a game. Wolves were the big boys in the league and favourites for a Premiership place and our performance that day made me realise what we could achieve as a team, particularly at home.

It was Steve Claridge's first start of the season and what an influence he was on the team with his maximum effort and non-stop running. I could see why he was such a fans' favourite. I had already been impressed by how hard he worked in training. Steve was a very personable and popular character who got on with everybody. He was the busiest person I ever met with what appeared to be a million things going on in his life and his mobile phone ringing non-stop.

I spoke to my old mate Lee Hodges at Reading in the week after the Wolves win. He told me that one of their coaches had seen the game and had rated me as Pompey's star player. That they could see not only what they had lost but also that I was good enough for Division One gave me a great deal of satisfaction.

There were some very good players at Pompey and I was impressed by the performances of the likes of Shaun Derry, Justin Edinburgh, Darren Moore alongside me, and Lee Bradbury. Shaun was one who I rated highly - he had good feet, was a good passer of the ball, had a great attitude, and was a good man to have in the dressing room with his jokes and breakdancing to the music from our 'ghetto-blaster'. His tendency to pick up silly bookings let him down but I always thought he was potentially someone who could have done well in the Premiership. Justin and his wife Kerry became very good friends of ours, and he was a down to earth sort of guy, despite his success at a big club like Spurs. He brought plenty of big-time experience and was a good leader who gave us plenty of laughs in the dressing room. Lee Bradbury was another who became a close friend and was a level-headed family man, with good integrity, who really impressed me with his range of skills and high work-rate.

However there was never going to be a real sense of togetherness whilst there was still that now familiar mix of 'them and us' in the team – 'them' being the Pulis signings like myself, Justin Edinburgh, Lee Mills, Ceri Hughes, Shaun Derry, Russell Hoult, Nigel Quashie and Kevin Harper, and 'us' being the old guard, like Adie Whitbread, Thomas Thogersen, Jason Crowe, Scott Hiley and Stefani Miglioranzi from the pre-Pulis days. The latter group would find themselves left to train separately knowing that they would never be a part of the team.

Darren was a big strong solid presence, a great leader and communicator, who gave 100% week in and week out. We were great pals with a close relationship, still are, and partnering him at the back filled me with confidence. Our catchphrase was 'no frills', with the aim of doing the simple things well. Darren is such a positive guy and he earns so much respect, wherever he plays during his career, from the other players who often phone him for advice. What I admire about Darren is that even if he has a slight injury he is prepared to carry it and play through it. It takes something serious to force him to come off or miss a game through injury. Darren is up there with Sol Campbell, Arjan De Zeeuw, John Polston and Keith McPherson, as one of my best defensive partners.

I enjoyed training with Tony and got a lot out of the work he did with us in defence. You knew exactly what was expected of you in your job as a defender as far as discipline, tasks and duties were concerned. What did scare me and certainly kept us defenders on our toes was his habit of nominating an opposition player for you to mark during set-pieces in real games. The snag was that if your player scored then you were fined with the money going into the players' pool. It meant that as a defender you were really accountable and if your player scored then the blame fell well and truly on your shoulders. Happily I was never fined so didn't ever have to face Trish's wrath on that score.

Tony was a great believer in team play in training – that is 11 v. 11 games in order to get a shape and discipline instilled. It was unusual and, whilst I could see the theory behind it, the key to keeping players sharp and interested was to vary the training routines week by week. The problem with the continual use of team play was that the older players could see it wasn't working where it mattered out on the pitch on match days. That led to a sense of disillusionment creeping in amongst the squad, and in addition Tony's tactics were increasingly being questioned by the players amongst themselves. Tactically it seemed as if teams knew what our strengths were and were able to prepare adequately to prevent us playing in the way we wanted. I felt Tony was a good motivator but, like many managers up and down the country before and since, he had a problem with several of the players he had inherited, like Scott, Steve and Adie, who he clearly didn't rate or want in his team, and his success or failure depended on how he dealt with such senior and influential figures.

I noticed from very early on that Tony never travelled on the coach with the squad on away trips which was unusual for a manager, and something I had never come across before. Presumably he had his own good reasons for his habit of making his own way to and from games, but it seemed to me that he was always noticeable by his absence and that it didn't contribute to bonding with the squad.

We moved into our new house at Whiteley during the week before the next home match against Watford. I had been having my pre-match meals early in a hotel prior to that, but the first in our new home was taken late at 12.45 pm. The result was that I felt thoroughly sick during our warm-up running on the Fratton Park pitch. I found myself throwing up in front of the fans, but luckily Bob Jones, the groundsman, was close at hand to quickly cover it up with sawdust. It wasn't the best preparation but I immediately felt OK with my stomach happily light of the meal.

A 3-1 defeat that day, a subsequent home defeat by West Brom, and away draws at Burnley and Stockport increased the pressure on Tony, and the senior players were adamant that the formations were not getting the best out of the players. By now we were playing a narrow midfield of four with no real width. Lee Bradbury and Lee Mills were strikers who relied on crosses, and there was a sense that it was not the sort of system that suited Steve Claridge. That meant that Steve was yet another senior player who was being sidelined and seen as a threat by Tony.

Mladen Rudonja, a Slovenian international winger who many players felt had been signed by the Chairman, was being ignored by Tony highlighting the problems it can cause when a player is foisted on a manager in that way and he doesn't subsequently fit into his team-building plans.

There were rumours around the club that if we didn't win at

lowly Stockport the Chairman was ready to get rid of Tony. By now it was noticeable that his team talks had lost their power and that he was lacking his earlier drive in training. The run of bad results that had brought no improvement on the previous season, coupled with the continual rumours about his position, the hostility of the fans towards him and the animosity from the senior players appeared to be taking their toll. He was a different man now to the one I had met on arrival at the club three months or so earlier. The atmosphere in the dressing room had got noticeably quieter with none of the laughing and joking you come to expect.

At our next training session after the Stockport game we went straight into a very hard running session, and the immediate reaction from the players was: 'Is this his way of punishing us before he goes?' We knew that Tony was due to see the Chairman after that day's training. His subsequent dismissal was a disappointment to players like Darren, Justin, Shaun and Ceri Hughes, but it was obvious that it would be difficult for him to turn things around without the support of the fans and the Chairman. When we heard that Tony had been given 'leave of absence' to fight his lawsuit with Gillingham it was a bit of a surprise, but it was obvious that something had caused him to change over the previous couple of months.

Steve Claridge had made no secret of the fact that he would like the manager's job and within a day or two it soon became apparent to us that he was likely to be given his chance. So it was no surprise to the players, at least, when Chairman Milan Mandaric called us in to a meeting to announce his appointment, even if it was a bit of a shock for the supporters. Steve was asked whether he wished to be known as 'Steve or Gaffer' in the future, and caused some amusement, and a bit of a shock, with his answer: 'Gaffer'. The day before he had been our pal and very much one of the lads; now here he was as manager. It was an early indication for me that it might be an uneasy situation.

I was pleased for Steve and I knew that he had the respect of the players which gave him a head start. By now, after my experiences at Barnet and Reading, I had become used to managers coming and going, and clearly, as always, only time would tell if it was the right decision. However I never got the impression that Steve's appointment was permanent, even if he may have thought it was, and it seemed to me to be more of a stop-gap with a view to seeing how things went that season, and perhaps even, to saving some money on a replacement. Certainly you would expect a new manager to be given a two or three year contract as some sort of vote of confidence.

Steve had a good knowledge of the game, he was enthusiastic and was a players' player – one who led by example on the pitch. He listened to the players and knew only too well how they should be treated and what their needs were. He was a good communicator who was not over-aggressive in the dressing room, but inevitably the many friendships he had made amongst the players made things difficult for him when it came to decisions on selection and the like.

Tony's style and approach in training had been very regimental and latterly had become mundane and rarely challenging, so when Steve announced that he was going to 'bring some life back into the players' it was the spark we needed. Guy Whittingham took the training sessions and had responsibility for the team talks and tactics generally, both pre-match and at half time, with Andy Awford taking a scouting role. But the final decisions were down to Steve, and I was impressed with his coaching expertise and organisational ability. Steve also made it clear that he would bring players 'in from the cold' and that it would be 'a fresh start for everyone'. One immediate beneficiary of that was Scott Hiley who was installed at right back and became a big influence in the team with his vast experience.

Temporarily there was a real turnaround in the atmosphere, which is something you often get with a new manager, and three wins on the bounce certainly helped. The third of those at Crystal Palace – a 3-2 win, coming back from two down – seemed to signal a new dawn, but that was followed by four consecutive draws. Soon we were hovering on the fringes of the relegation zone after only one win in fourteen put the pressure back on. Steve looked drained, both physically and mentally, from the demands of the dual player/manager role – there was no getting away from either. I'm sure he didn't realise how intense it was being a manager. For me his strange decision to drop goalkeeper Russell Hoult, after just one mistake at Barnsley, was one sign of his increasing desperation.

Steve would take it personally when he got letters from the fans complaining about the performances. While we were getting changed ready for training he would read them out to us, for example: 'They want to know why we are drawing so many games?... how can they say that?... we are still collecting points, aren't we?'

Steve's answer to our bad run was to get us doing a lot more running in training, rather than playing football, in an effort to get us all fitter. Steve was a fit lad himself, but for the rest of the squad the new regime brought a string of stays in the treatment room for various muscle pulls and strains. The loss of one or two key players to such injuries didn't help and the Chairman's reluctance to back his new manager's judgement with funds for new players led to rumours that Steve was being forced to identify players in our squad who could be sold for a decent fee to enable such funds to be available. That reluctance was highlighted when Steve wanted to sign full back Jamie Vincent from Huddersfield and the transfer dragged on for so many weeks that Jamie didn't actually move until a day or so before Steve was sacked.

The Chairman would regularly come into the dressing room

pre-match and make a speech to the squad about 'doing it for the fans', 'making sure you can look in the mirror afterwards and say you've done your best', etc, etc. It was the source of some amusement amongst the players but for others it left a question hanging in the air: *'Who's in charge of the team, the manager or the Chairman?'* We knew Mr Mandaric had his own strong opinions about team affairs and left the manager in no doubt about who was in charge of the club. There was an element of resentment amongst the players at his interference and assumption that he could offer more of a lift to the team than his manager. The feeling was that his place was in the boardroom and that it was the manager's role to inspire the players.

During that awful run I was sent off at then top of the table Fulham, the first red card of my career, in front of several old friends of mine from London. It centred around an innocuous challenge on Louis Saha who was taking the ball across me. With my foot outstretched I took the ball but Saha went down and immediately he looked at me and said: 'It's not your fault'. I was getting changed alone and upset in the dressing room when I heard the familiar sound of boots click-clacking down the corridor towards me and suddenly there to join me was Ceri Hughes in the doorway. 'Surely not' was my welcome to him as we started to see the funny side of two totally undeserved dismissals. We deserved something from that game but it was a dark rain-filled afternoon with a strange atmosphere that seemed to affect our fans who threw missiles at my old Barnet team-mate Maik Taylor in the Fulham goal and a snooker ball at a linesman.

A week later at Barnsley – the game in which Russell Hoult made a hash of trying to shepherd a ball out for a goal-kick and let in Bruce Dyer for the only goal – I overstretched and tore a thigh muscle that led to a four-week recovery period. During that time I was troubled by a sharp stomach pain which was diagnosed as 'Gilmore's Groin' – actually a tear of the adductor muscles, usually high up near the attachment to the pubic bone, and named after the Harley Street surgeon who discovered it. After the operation to repair the damage I was out of action for almost five months – the longest period of my career to date – during which time Steve lost his job. I watched all the home games and became the best player in the team from the stands in the course of envisaging myself out there doing things differently. At least I didn't get to feel the intense pressure that was building on the team as we slipped dangerously close to the relegation zone. The buzz generated when Steve took charge had long since faded away.

Rumours were circulating that the Chairman was unhappy with the performances and we felt, like the Tony Pulis situation earlier in the season, that some action was imminent. The message coming down to the players from the senior players, like Justin and Scott, who were close to Guy, was that 'Steve's under pressure – he's not got long if he doesn't start getting results'. Even the local paper was examining our record and questioning whether Steve was the right man for the job. So it was no shock or surprise when, in his absence, the Chairman turned up at the training ground to tell us: 'I'm relieving Steve of his job as manager'. We were more concerned about who would come in as manager next.

So Steve's managership came to a messy end and we all knew he was very upset. He always felt that he wasn't given a fair crack of the whip and had his hands tied by not being given the freedom or the money to bring in his own players, as any new manager would expect. The job probably came two or three years too early for Steve, but he loved the club and couldn't resist taking up the challenge. His inexperience did show and combining the role of player and manager proved to be too much for him.

8

'It all took some believing...' 2001

We were about to welcome our third manager of the season, and it was no wonder that the results were poor with the players unsettled by so much change and instability. We soon became aware that Graham Rix had put his name forward for the job and had been interviewed. None of us really knew too much about him, only the record of his time as a player at Arsenal and as a coach at Chelsea. A lot was made by the press of his time in prison, and we were interested in how he would handle that situation if appointed. When he was confirmed in the job, the players became aware that there were one or two on the board who were unhappy with Graham's appointment but were prepared to go along with it and give him the benefit of the doubt. For our part we were encouraged because he was a 'name' who had a presence about him, and he was recognised in the game as a good coach. So there was an air of excitement and some expectance that he could take us forward as a team.

I was working hard in the gym to get back to fitness after my groin operation and I missed out on Graham's one to one chats with each player. So I went upstairs to the cafeteria especially to introduce myself to him, and was encouraged when he told me that he knew all about me and added: ' I want you back in the team as soon as possible'.

One game into Graham's managership Darren was injured and ruled out for the rest of the season, and, in my continued absence, Scott Hiley was paired with new signing Carl Tiler in the centre of defence. Scott was a revelation as skipper that season and eventually was named as Player of the Season, after being on the verge of quitting football a couple of years earlier before Pompey gave him a chance to resurrect his career. Scott was well-liked and the life and soul of the party, with plenty to say for himself, who sometimes rubbed people up the wrong way if they were the butt of one of his jokes and didn't see the funny side of it.

Having known of Carl from his time at Charlton I looked up to him, knowing he was a good experienced defender who had played at big clubs like Everton and Villa. Unfortunately the Pompey fans didn't take to him at all, but, in fairness to Carl, he hadn't been playing league football for some time before he arrived at Fratton Park and was then thrown into a struggling team. The fans quite rightly expect every player to give everything and, through the timing of his move, Carl just wasn't able to show what he could do.

By the time I was ready to return for the home game with top of the table Fulham, after some reserve team games, we had dropped into the relegation zone with four games left in the season, after just two wins in Graham's first nine games. I was very nervous in the dressing room, bouncing up and down on my toes to stop the adrenaline kicking in, and Kevin Harper exclaimed: 'You've got plenty of energy'. Whereupon Graham retorted: 'That's because he hasn't played all season', which of course just wasn't true. I must admit that I didn't warm to that remark, in fact I took it personally and it hurt. It gave me a great deal of satisfaction to go out and do well against Louis Saha that afternoon, in our 1-1 draw.

After a 3-1 defeat at Blackburn we had just two home games left and we could make ourselves safe by winning the first, at home against Crystal Palace in midweek, and in doing so would send them down. In the lead up to the game there was a real air of confidence around the training ground that we were going to win – there was a lyric from a garage music anthem around at that time with the words 'we're going to do this' that we adopted for our dressing room sing-song and it seemed to fit our mood. I remember that there was a guy, who was employed to assist Kevin McCormack, the kit manager, who had been a Pompey fan for many years and was clearly well aware of the club's record in such situations. He was in no doubt what was going to be the outcome of that Palace game, and expressed his opinion loud and clear in our dressing room: 'I've seen Pompey blow these moments be-fore...' For myself I just dismissed such negative thoughts: 'I'm not thinking about that, we're going to win'.

Palace had to win therefore and in the days before the game their Chairman Simon Jordan sacked the manager Alan Smith and put his assistant Steve Kember in charge. It turned out to be an astute move with Steve obviously a popular guy in the Palace camp, and they were well up for it and desperate to prove that he could save the club. There was a real buzz and still plenty of confidence about in our dressing room as we prepared for the game. What we could not have foreseen, and were totally unprepared for, was how well Palace would play on the night – and it's fair to say that it was totally unexpected given their poor record of just two wins in the previous sixteen games. We went out that night convinced that Palace would not be able to live with us and when they nicked a couple of early goals we were shell-shocked – with my thoughts: '*Oh, no, that's not in the script*'.

We pulled one back almost right on half time but from the kick off the ball was played back to Carl who tried to find me with a square pass. I was standing ten yards or so to his left but my old Barnet team mate Dougie Freedman closed me down, stole the ball off me and sprinted away to make it 3-1. Graham usually left the half time shouting and bawling to his assistant Jim Duffy but this time, for once, even he joined in. When we went 4-1 down in the second half a crescendo of boos, and chants of 'You're not fit to wear the shirt', echoed around Fratton Park, the like of which I have never heard before or since. Worse than that, a Pompey fan came on to the pitch from the Fratton End and offered his replica shirt to Lee Bradbury – the sort of thing I had never seen before.

It was the lowest point of my career. I was demoralised, shattered, and so disappointed. When it was all over, all Graham could say to us as he walked out of the dressing room in disgust was: 'You got us in this mess, you sort it out'. We heard the next day that the defeat had increased the murmurings about Graham's managership in the boardroom – with a typical unidentified reaction being: 'I knew it was a mistake to take him on as manager'.

Just to rub it in, when I opened the front door at home the next morning I was greeted by a chorus of 'going down, going down, going down' from the builders across the road. It wasn't quite all over however – there was nothing for it but to dust ourselves down, prepare to beat Barnsley at home four days later and hope that results elsewhere went our way.

We were due to play Barnsley on the Sunday afternoon and the day before we trained at Fratton Park. During the session Scott Hiley, as captain, came up and told me: 'Graham was going to drop you tomorrow'.

Immediately a sense of anger and grievance gripped me, knowing that I was no more to blame than anyone else for the Palace defeat. Scott quickly added: 'I've convinced him to play you. But now you have to prove me right'.

With so much resting on the game for the club and myself the tension was such that I had three successive virtually sleepless nights before the game and when I did doze off I would wake up with a start thinking for a few moments that the game had already been played and lost. Before the game the dressing room was quiet and there was a high level of nervousness after the performance against Palace a few days earlier. No one was more focused than I was after what Scott had said to me the day before. Unlike Palace, Barnsley had nothing to play for, didn't really want to be there and couldn't have been less motivated for what was the last game of the season. The Pompey fans had clearly forgiven us for the Palace capitulation and were up for it as if it were a cup final. Our comfortable 3-0 win ensured safety after a brief tortuous wait post match to confirm that Huddersfield had lost and were relegated instead. We were persuaded to do a lap of honour around the pitch as if we had won something and afterwards someone said to me that you shouldn't be celebrating survival. But it was more a sense of relief amongst both players and supporters, and that feeling was even more acute for me after having experienced the pain of relegation at Reading.

A few days after the season had finished I went to see Graham in his office – and it's unusual, almost unique, for me to be driven, let alone find the courage, to seek out and confront a manager. In fact I was so nervous that, on arrival, when I first went to speak, that the words just wouldn't come out of my mouth. I swear it was 10-15 seconds, with Graham staring expectantly at me, before I was able to utter a sound. I could hear a little voice inside urging me: 'Just say it, for goodness sake'.

When it finally came out I said: 'I was very disappointed to hear you were going to drop me last Sunday. I didn't feel I was worse than anyone else'.

In reply all Graham would say was: 'I felt I had to make a change'.

By now I was really up for it: 'Carl Tiler was as much at fault as anyone else'. There was no time for Graham to reply before I hit him with the big one: 'Have I got a future here?'

His reply was: 'Yes, I want you here, but I have to make such decisions – it's part and parcel of football'.

For me that was inconclusive and it didn't fill me with confidence. I certainly didn't feel that I could trust him anymore. In fact it wasn't until Graham had left the club that our relationship was repaired to any extent.

For Trish the buzz of a new house had worn off and she was beginning to feel lonely on an estate that was underdeveloped and still looking like a building site. It was different for me with my focus on football but when I got home I was conscious that Trish was pining for her family and friends in London. It was hard to make friends away from football and those we had in football had lifestyles we couldn't afford to follow. We were still finding it hard financially and were conscious that friends like Lee and Darren had been set up financially through big money transfers earlier in their careers, and Justin had benefited from his days with a top club like Tottenham.

Before we left Didcot Trish had taken riding lessons at a farm where the owners liked to have riders help out in the stables in return. She really enjoyed it and it had given her an interest and sense of purpose. Before that Trish had become obsessional about cleaning around the house to fill up the time, but riding and working in the stables had enabled her to forget her problems and given her a completely different perspective. So it seemed sensible, to avoid a return to her depressive episodes, to find similar stables and riding in Hampshire. For a while Trish rented a horse which entailed a significant financial commitment but it was worth every penny for the pleasure it gave her to go to the stables. After taking the children to school and nursery, she would spend four hours or so there during two visits a day looking after and going out with the horse.

After the experience of having to care for and feed a horse Trish naturally wanted one of her own, and she pressed me to buy one but I was worried that the cost of stabling, food and general up-keep would sap our money. Then while we were mulling it over a cheque for £1000 arrived out of the blue from a family member in repayment of a long forgotten loan we had made that was not supposed to be repaid. The timing was unbelievable and it seemed right to use it to pay for a horse, knowing how happy it would make Trish.

The change in Trish was really satisfying. She had found real happiness in owning, riding and caring for her own horse. It was not something I could relate to at all. I'm not into animals at all and was happy to watch from the safety of the car. I couldn't even stand the smells from the stables finding their way into the car. But the therapeutic value to Trish was priceless and soon she became a confident rider through regular hacking. Not only that she was starting to make non-football friends with other horse owners with whom she shared the mucking-out duties and caring for each others' horses. Rather than rushing back to London at weekends Trish could be found at the stables on a Sunday morning, so it had the effect of loosening our ties with London.

Unfortunately it transpired that, in the world of horses, it was not always the idyllic world we first imagined. We were aware of the backbiting, envy and jealousy that exists when people compete over horses and equipment, and the way they looked after them. Up to now Trish had not been on the receiving end of any of that. Soon, it started happening to her, and it led to an edgy atmosphere which left Trish somewhat depressed.

It became unbearable for her, and it was no surprise when she came home one day, and said: 'It's time I changed to another stable'. A very good friend of Trish's wanted to move with her so the search was on to find some stables with a decent field for their horses at a price we could afford. After a couple of weeks, in the spring of 2001, an ideal place was discovered at double the rent, but it was so right that I just couldn't stand in Trish's way. A very professional, clean set-up with schooling facilities and some lovely friendly owners was just what the doctor ordered, and all our previous worries were behind us.

By the early summer 2001 however Trish was slipping back into a depressive mode and even her riding couldn't mask her problems. I just didn't know how to help her through it, and so, very reluctantly, it was back to the necessary medication. We were still finding it hard financially and the new contract with Pompey hadn't put us where we wanted to be. Here we were again; trapped in a material world, now under all that peer pressure to live up to the image of a professional footballer with the lifestyle, the designer clothes and the big cars. Everybody expects footballers to be a certain way. Driven by the thought that to be happy we needed to be like my friends Justin and Lee - both finding themselves financially in the sort of position we longed for, whom we saw buying everything they wanted.

Trish became friendly with Keith and Sam, the stable owners, and they told her, in the course of conversation, that they were Christians. Trish knew nothing of Christianity and had an open mind to what they were telling her of their faith. My first reaction to was to say to her: 'Don't get too close to them... they'll try and trap you... they'll be bible-bashing with you soon... they'll take money from you for it'. I really rubbished them in the hope that it might put a stop to any ideas Trish might have had of getting even friendlier with them. A couple of hours later, thinking about it, I couldn't believe what I had just said – I hadn't been brought up by my parents to make remarks like that, in fact quite the opposite. Suddenly I felt really guilty about putting these people down without having given them a chance.

Little did we know that Sam, the stable owner's wife, had sensed Trish's unhappiness and was praying that Trish would open up to her so that she could be of some help. Our experience at the previous stables had made us both more guarded about getting close to any non-football people, and we were back to putting up barriers. But Trish was, as a one-off, prepared to open up to them about her depression and let them try to help her. One evening she came back from the stables to tell me that the stable owner and his wife had invited us all to their church. I was a little worried but Trish made it clear that she was desperate to accept their invitation, saying: 'I've tried everything else, why not try this?'

I left it for a couple of days and on further enquiry Trish was adamant that she wanted to give it a go. I was prepared to go for her sake and finally it was a case of *'Well church is the last place we'd go, but why not?'* Then I said we ought to go for six weeks otherwise it wouldn't be a fair trial. I was also concerned that Keith and Sam would think badly of us if we only went once. The way I remembered church there was always plenty of gossip and I didn't want us to be talked about and cast in a bad light.

So it was that one Sunday we got the family ready and then drove over to the farm to meet up with Keith and Sam and follow them through the country lanes down to their church. We were all very quiet in the car during the drive, and I was pre-occupied with a sense of foreboding of what might await us. I had visions of an old and traditional grey brick building with a spire and stained glass windows, with the vicar in flowing gown waiting outside to greet us. As we turned into the packed car park I could see that I could not have been more mistaken – here was what looked like a brand new modern church marked with bright red and yellow bricks. I was still wary, and muttered to myself: 'This doesn't look like the sort of church I remember'.

We moved towards the entrance, trying to avoid eye contact with several smiling people who were looking to greet us. That brought another word of caution from me in Trish's direction: 'These guys are up to something, they want us and they want our money'. As we got inside I noticed the absence of any pews and rows of individual chairs. It was all so laid-back, and there was what appeared to be a leader at the front in a t-shirt and shorts.

I was surprised to see a guitar band at the front ready to provide the music, with an overhead projector providing all the words for the service and the songs. Later a preacher, again in casual clothes, spoke and everybody was immediately drawn by what he was saying. I wasn't bored at all and I could see that the kids were enjoying it. I felt comfortable during the service and from early on felt a real sense of warmth covering me like a blanket. As we drove home in the car afterwards I turned to Trish and said: 'That felt really good', and she replied: 'Let's go back next week'.

I knew that Darren Moore, my room-mate, was a Christian and in the past I had seen him reading the Bible and other inspirational books and leaflets before going to sleep, but he had never spoken to me about his faith. Now I told him of our church-going, how much we were enjoying it, and that I had come to believe in Jesus. Soon Darren was telling me of his journey in faith over the odd hour or so, but he would never pressure me and would wait for me to ask him questions or instigate the conversation. I know now that it must have been a real temptation for him to persuade and encourage me but his way of dealing with me was a lesson for the future for me in dealing with people when they came to me in the same way.

The West Country tour brought me a foretaste of the aggressive banter, which occasionally bordered on intimidation, which I would have to deal with in the coming months. Darren had been sharing his faith with two of the other players before we went away to Woodbury Park and now over the dinner table at the hotel six or so of the other players turned on him: 'Stop trying to convert everybody with your bible-bashing, and forcing your ways on them'.

To which Darren replied: 'Actually the guys approached me and asked me about it'.

I shied away from the conversation, but then two of them turned to me: 'You're going to church, aren't you?'

111

Timidly I said: 'Yes, but mainly because of Trish'.

'How do you find it?'

'It's peaceful and I enjoy it'.

Back came the retort, with a glance at Darren: 'Oh, no, you'll end up like him'.

'No, because I don't know enough about it. I just know that I enjoy it and will be going back again'.

So ended my first encounter with the reactions in the dressing room, in its various forms ranging from simple mickey-taking to outright hostility, that I would have to handle in that male-dominated world if I was to take the same road as Darren. For now that was all something that he had to deal with – I had not yet made Jesus the centre of my life.

It was at Woodbury Park that Trish 'phoned me on her return from church, and immediately I could tell from her voice that she was excited and full of life: 'Lin, it was as if the pastor was talking to me today, me alone. It was as if I was the lost sheep and God is looking for me'. I was just so happy for her, that she had received some form of revelation from God. I knew that it was not forced or manufactured, that it was genuine, and her own personal moment.

When I came off the 'phone I told Darren and he was so thrilled, although he wasn't aware of Trish's history of depression. I remember him telling me: 'When you read the Bible it's a living word that you experience. You will find stories that relate to your own life, and the answer to every question can be found in the Bible'. That didn't make sense to me then – it was just a book of stories that weren't relevant to what I needed. I had no idea about how much wisdom you could gain from reading it.

For the first time, in Keith and Sam, we had found a couple who were not interested in football and in my profession but in us as friends, pure and simple. When they came to dinner one night we got round to talking about God, and I shared with them something that had been on my heart for a long time – 'whether there was life after death?' and simply 'what does it take to go to heaven?'. Somehow I believed in judgement and a reckoning of our good deeds, but was unsure of the form it would take. I imagined, perhaps, your life being played out on a big screen in front of you.

But Keith was firm in his reply: 'That's not right. The only way to be saved is to call on the name of Jesus and accept Him into your life'. To back this up he showed me the appropriate passage in the Bible and said 'This is what we believe'.

I really couldn't believe that it was as simple as that, and argued with him for almost half an hour: 'Is that all there is to it?... surely you had to earn the right?... how can saying a few words be enough?' Despite Trish's assertion that I was delving into it too deeply, my questioning to Keith became more intense when we were left alone by our wives, as I tried desperately to trip him up. But the more I asked the more Keith's answers appeared to have a strong ring of truth about them.

I became convinced in my mind that Keith was right, but such a fear overtook me. I was so wary of commitment and my mind was filled with fear. I conjured up all sorts of thoughts to stop me believing in it: *This could be a cult thing... something demonic... what could they do to us?'* Then I came to my senses with the realisation: *'What have I got to lose? I've got it all to gain.'* So I said to Keith: 'What do I have to do to be saved then?' To which he replied: 'Just merely say a prayer of salvation – why don't you say the prayer with me now?'

By now Trish and Sam had rejoined us, so I turned to Trish: 'Why don't you say the prayer with me too?', and to my surprise she instantly replied: 'I already have!'

I stared at her in amazement and listened as she explained that she had been away to Butlins holiday camp in Bognor Regis the previous week with the children and had been studying a

Christian booklet entitled 'Why Jesus?' which invited readers to pray such a prayer of salvation. 'How do you feel?' I asked Trish, and she replied: 'I felt good and for the first time at peace, without any darkness over me'.

That did it for me: 'I'm in for this'. So I closed my eyes and Keith led me through it, with me repeating his words of the prayer. When it was quickly over we embraced each other but immediately I couldn't understand why Keith was so excited. I had been waiting for the fireworks, for something spectacular to happen, and was disappointed when nothing occurred. I thought: *'That can't be it, nothing happened'*.

When Sam exclaimed: 'The angels in heaven are celebrating now', my thought was: *'What's she on about?'*, but she insisted on showing me the appropriate passage in the Bible that confirmed that when one person comes to the Lord the angels celebrate. It was all so difficult for me to understand, coming from a world full of 'wind-ups' and 'mickey-taking', always being around people with a cynical attitude to anything spiritual or non-factual that couldn't be proved scientifically. The Bible was not literal to me and I had no realisation yet that God's word could be true and real.

The following day I casually picked up the Bible and read from John's Gospel. Suddenly there was something different about it, just as I had been told would happen. To my surprise there were little bits of text that I understood, that I hadn't come across before, and that had meaning for me. I was conscious that the words were making sense, rather than just words that passed into and out of my head almost immediately as before.

I also told Darren that day, just as he was about to go out to train. All I needed to say was: 'I've done it'. The smile on my face said it all for him and he knew what I meant. All Darren had time to say was: 'I can see it in your face. It's the best thing you've ever done, for you and your family'.

114

A couple of days later I told Stefani Miglioranzi, our Brazilian-born midfielder, who was an evangelical Christian, and, like Darren, he was just as excited as Keith and Sam had been. That prompted Stef to tell me how a miraculous healing of his baby brother had led to him and his family becoming believers, although since coming to England he had never felt comfortable in a church here.

Later I 'phoned Richard Rufus who had been a team-mate at Charlton and who I knew to have been converted. I remember the sense of amazement I felt a few years earlier when I heard of Richard's conversion, knowing what sort of life, as a typical footballer, he had led. I could feel his joy coming down the 'phone, and immediately he said: 'Now you've got to feed your spirit with good things, and I will send you down some material'. Within a few days a pile of books, videos and DVDs was delivered to my door, and I was soon poring over them. When I came home from training I was no longer switching on the TV for the sports news. I just didn't realise how interesting it all was – but I still had a lot of doubt and questions that needed answering. The thought struck me: 'Was this really the Christianity I had known as a child – when the church seemed full of meaningless words and insincere people?'

I had never seen people so happy for me and I knew the joy and pleasure I saw in their faces was something different than I had ever experienced before. Inside I was very happy, but it all took some believing and my head was full of the recurring thought: 'Is this really true?... am I really a Christian?'

'Leave all your worries with Him because he cares for you'
1 Peter 5.7

115

9
'Whatever you want me to do...'
2001-2002

So I had become a 'Christian' but thus far I felt I had only scratched the surface and I was desperate to get to the core of it. Keith and Sam had to put up with a good deal of questioning and I would have them up to the small hours as I tried to catch them out with questions about the after-life, world suffering, prayer, healing etc. They would patiently show me the answers to my questions in the Bible but the words still weren't real to me so I couldn't wholly believe what was being said. Trish was urging me to relax, not to be too questioning, not to try and work it all out yet.

I still didn't know what was supposed to happen to you when you became a Christian, so I came out and asked Keith there and then. What he said in reply frightened me: 'When I was a young boy of 7 or 8 I said the prayer of salvation, and I began to speak in foreign tongues'.

'What's that?' was my obvious question.

Keith replied: 'It's a heavenly language that enables you to speak directly to God'. Little did I know then, but finding yourself speaking in such a way was a familiar and well-known phenomenon experienced by some Christians. I then remembered that I heard my Aunt speak in a strange language when my grandad died. I was 12 at the time and I remember being shocked and a little frightened at what sounded like a ghost. When I later asked my Dad what had happened, he said: 'Your aunt was taken by the spirit'.

So it was that I finally made up my mind, based on all that I had heard and in an effort to get some closure on this question which was vexing me, and told Keith and Sam: 'I will believe that I am a Christian when my knee is healed and I speak in this heavenly language you told me about'.

Keith was keen for us to pray together there and then for my knee but after ten minutes or so I felt some peace and warmth but nothing happened with my knee. It was the same when, in church after a service one Sunday, a few people prayed intensely over my knee. I only went along with it to humour them and was very sceptical about the outcome, thinking: 'I don't think it will work'. So when they asked me afterwards if my knee felt any different I said: 'Not really', and I wasn't surprised.

One day Darren said to me: 'I've got these two guys I would like you to meet. They'll help you to read the Bible, will answer your questions and teach you what it's all about'. Darren had previously been introduced to them and had been meeting them on a regular basis for mentoring to help him with his faith. But I was still apprehensive about meeting them and didn't know what to expect, but agreed on Darren's say-so: 'OK, I'll hear what they've got to say'.

I was very sceptical beforehand of meeting them, wary of letting them into my life or my family, and had made up my mind that they only wanted to know us because we were footballers or because they wanted our money. As Darren and I drove to the outskirts of Portsmouth I was well into my normal defensive mode on meeting people, typically: *'What can these guys want from us?'* We were met at the front door of Mick Mellows' house, where he lived with his wife and teenage children, and greeted by name

117

and with firm handshakes. I was introduced to Mick, an assistant chaplain at the football club and a former Pompey player and teacher, and then to his friend and fellow Christian Mick O'Brien, an ordained minister in the U.S.A. Darren embraced them warmly in a way that made me think that he must trust these guys.

All my questioning of these two guys brought very much the same answers as I had obtained from Keith and Sam, and I just couldn't catch them out. So much so that I began to think about the possibility of a conspiracy: *'Perhaps they're all part of the same cult?'* So I had to pose the question: 'Do you know Keith and Sam?', but that was quickly denied to allay my fears and leave me thinking: *'This must be another form of Christianity'.*

When we left I told Darren that I had enjoyed their company and wouldn't mind seeing them again. What impressed me was that they made it clear immediately that they wanted nothing at all from me, and weren't looking for the usual tickets or signed shirts.

During that summer of 2001 I had kept fit with a great deal of cycling but unknowingly I aggravated a knee condition that had given me problems at Reading. This problem was then exacerbated by the extreme rigours of pre-season training which were all down to Jim Duffy who felt that we needed to be 'beasted' in our first week back, i.e. to run to the maximum limits. We had been found a different training ground that season at the naval base at HMS Collingwood near Fareham but the pitches were found to be unfit so we were working in the establishment itself. We changed in green khaki tents before embarking, to our amazement, from the first day onwards on a series of long runs timed over unbelievable distances. Immediately, despite a good level of fitness, the players were picking up all sorts of muscle strains and all the tents needed were some Red Cross flags on top to resemble a scene from the 1970's TV series 'MASH' (Mobile Army Surgical Hospital).

Managers and coaches were very anxious to get the squad fit as quickly as possible in pre-season as there was so little time for it once the season started. Once the games get underway no manager wants to be accused of having players who are not fit enough. But things have changed in the game in the last few years however with the advent of sports science and it's universally accepted that you have to build up to fitness gradually. In fact if you reach full fitness too early you can peak too soon, and overtraining can mean that when it comes to games the players are tired and have nothing to give. It's not match fitness in any event - that comes from playing games.

As I've mentioned before, long distance running has always proved difficult for me. My body just isn't built for that sort of running, but that doesn't mean I'm unfit. In fact I can compete with the best on short sprints. However I managed to get through that first horrific week, but all that overtraining came home to roost when I started to feel my knee during the second week's ball-work. I didn't want to report the injury, having spent half of the previous season on the sidelines, but it got worse and before we were due to travel to Woodbury Park Hotel for our customary West Country tour I had to reluctantly go and see the physio Gary Sadler about it.

It was whilst I was anxiously awaiting the results of a scan on my knee to establish whether an operation was necessary to repair the damage that Darren and I went back for more Bible study with Mick Mellows. This time Mick O'Brien, now aware of my concern about my injury, suggested that we pray for my knee. Mick Mellows got me to sit on a chair with a high straight back, with my back hard against the back of the chair, and to raise my feet together parallel to the floor with my heels pressed together and the toes apart.

With my legs in that position a difference in the lengths of each leg could be clearly seen, so Mick O'Brien held my feet in his

119

hands and said he would pray, in the name of Jesus, to correct the imbalance. I chuckled inwardly at the prospect but nevertheless closed my eyes whilst Mick prayed. When he had finished the first thing I heard was an exclamation from Darren: 'Lin, did you see that. Your leg grew!' I said: 'No chance'. But when I looked down it was there for all to see, my left leg was now the same length as my right.

Mick O'Brien then said that all three of them would pray for my knee. I put my feet down, and with Mick Mellows' hand on my knee, they prayed over me for healing. Soon I felt what seemed like waves of electricity going through my knee, and my immediate reaction, with my eyes still closed, was that Mick must be using clown buzzers fixed to his hand to give those electric shocks. 10-15 minutes later it was all over.

Mick asked me: 'How does it feel?' To which I replied: 'I don't know what you've done but I felt electricity going through my knee'. He said: 'Why don't you get up and try it'.

I got up and gingerly started going through a series of leg exercises – things that would have caused me pain before – stretching my thighs, bending my knee and taking my foot back to my bum, then squatting on my haunches (something I just couldn't do before), and finally standing up quickly with all the strain in the knee involved. There was just no pain whatsoever, and I was simply blown away by it. I remember muttering: 'It must have been hypnotism', but Mick retorted: 'You weren't hypnotised Lin'.

The three of them encouraged me to stay standing on the spot whilst they prayed for me again and before long, when one of them put their hand in front of my forehead, I just found myself falling to the floor. I should have hurt myself but it was like falling into a feather-bed. I had lost all power in my body and lay there unable to move, whilst they continued to pray over me. I was filled with an overwhelming feeling of peace, although still wide awake. Nothing else mattered, all was perfect. I had no problems, no worries. I was encased in a bubble of love. I would not have cared if the world had come crashing down at that moment - I was at peace with a total reassurance. My past, my future, it all seemed insignificant.

As they continued to pray, I found myself, in my head, joining in with prayers for Trish and the children. Then I sensed that my lips were moving and I was trying unsuccessfully to speak normally, but a completely different sound was coming out of my mouth. In that moment it felt perfectly normal, perfectly natural – I felt no fear and it didn't frighten me. It seemed like gobbledygook and a strange language, but I didn't want to stop it. It went on for about two minutes, and when it was all over I was instantly taken back to my conversation with Keith and Sam when I told them: '*I will believe that I am a Christian when...* '. I had challenged God and He had met me.

It went quiet in the room, and I was thinking: '*These guys here don't know that God has met my demands... that I believe now*'. Then I found myself making a promise to God in return: '*God, whatever you want me to do I will do, and I give it all over to you.*'

It had seemed to me that I had been on the floor for no more than 15 minutes, but Darren told me it had been almost an hour, and added: 'Did you hear yourself speaking in tongues?'.

I still felt peaceful as we bid our farewells, then looked at my watch to see it was 4.30 pm and realised that I was due home at 4 pm for an important meeting with our financial adviser. As I went to drive home Trish 'phoned me on my mobile to chase me up, and I said to her: 'If you knew what had happened to me you would realise that it doesn't matter anymore, because all will be taken care of'. Trish knew that I was worried about our finances so for me to say that she must have realised something significant had happened. On my way home I was filled with an overwhelming sense that everything would be well.

121

I was desperate to tell Trish when I arrived home but had to contain myself in front of our financial adviser. It was in fact a meeting to consider our very first investment and our first positive move to secure our future even though it meant that we would have to be careful with our spending from then on.

That night I told Trish what had happened that afternoon and naturally she wanted some of it, having not yet experienced an encounter with God. We went to bed and as I was laying there I prayed to God to help me to speak in tongues again. Soon I felt as if the tip of my tongue was being rolled back and as though I was unconsciously trying to form an unknown word. I began to emit two syllables repetitively and Trish told me that it all sounded strange. After some time she dozed off but the sounds kept coming in the same repetitive way and I had no wish to stop them. By now I was feeling a warm pressure, and the room was filled with a peaceful presence. It lasted for almost an hour and a half, before I feel asleep. The next day I was so eager to tell Mick O'Brien of my experience, and his reaction was: 'You were in God's presence, and were speaking directly to Him'.

Besides Trish, Darren and Stef were the only people I told of these experiences, but one weekend I found myself relating it all to a couple who were neighbours of ours and by now good friends, mainly through our regular barbecues together. I had no trepidation telling them but it really surprised them and I could see the look of shock on their faces. I could envisage them thinking: 'What on earth have they got involved in?'

Nevertheless some time later, I invited the husband of the couple concerned, who I knew had been having work problems, to come to a 'Men's Breakfast' that Darren, Stef and I had agreed to attend at a local hotel to hear a Christian speaker. Despite not being a believer he agreed to come and when it was all over I was surprised to see tears in his eyes. On arrival home my neighbour, still clearly amazed at his experience, said to me: 'That speaker

122

this morning was talking directly to me into my heart. I've never had an encounter like that before'. That was a source of great encouragement to me – learning that God is ready to help everybody – and it reassured me that He does speak into your heart.

Mick Mellows had previously said to me that at some time Darren and I ought to consider some form of evangelism together – perhaps an invitation 'beer and curry night' at a local restaurant with Darren and I giving our testimonies. My reaction was: 'No way, I could never do that. I just wouldn't have the confidence to do it, and anyway it doesn't feel right for me'. Mick's reply to that was: 'God will know when it's right for you. I know you will be such a figurehead in the city because of your allegiance to God'.

I was downright sceptical at this extravagant claim for me from Mick. Football was full of big talk, with managers and chairmen coming up with promises, plans and ideas that didn't come to fruition. I had heard plenty from managers of how they would build a team, push for promotion, make you a great player etc, etc. In another example Trish and I had only recently been persuaded to join a 'Pyramid' scheme in which we were led to believe that we could earn a lot of money. In the event we got our fingers severely burnt.

I was still only about six to eight weeks into my Christian journey when I was invited to a Full Gospel Business Men's Fellowship meeting where again I had an extraordinary experience of God's power. Keith and Sam, with some of their family and some of our friends from their stables, were there and, after a dinner, Mick Mellows got up and gave his testimony. Seeing him up there was a source of great inspiration to me and demonstrated to me that if you let God's power work in you then you can do anything. After a subsequent prayer time I collapsed to the ground when I was prayed over, which shocked a few people. Not that it hurt me because again it was like falling into a feather-bed. Afterwards people came up to me and said: 'You're not embarrassed to fall, are you? You must have great trust in God's power'.

I didn't tell Gary Sadler, the Pompey physiotherapist, who was treating my knee injury, of my healing, and was still carrying out the new exercises he had prescribed. In his eyes they were having a positive effect and a week later we went to see the orthopaedic surgeon to discuss the results of an earlier scan taken before my healing. The surgeon told us: 'There is damage behind the knee cap that can be dealt with surgically. We can go in and do the work that will keep you out for a further three to six months'. At this stage I was so confident that I had been healed, and that God's power was at work, that I resolved to ask for another scan if he was adamant that an operation was needed.

As it was, his subsequent examination and tests on the knee brought no pain, to which he responded by saying: 'Are you sure it's not hurting?' Gary's conclusion was that the exercises had strengthened the muscles behind the knee which explained why there was no pain when pressure was put on the knee. So it was decided to continue as we were with the rehabilitation work with a view to a possible return to light training, but the surgeon made it clear that the knee would give further problems and that it was only a matter of time before I would be back for the operation.

Before all that however, that early 'beastliness' in training to which the squad were subjected in pre-season had a bad effect on the whole squad and they felt as if they had been overworked in an unstructured way just for the sake of it. There were plenty of moans and groans amongst the players and, although they had got through it each day, they were obviously struggling, with the tell-tale sign of not feeling as well as they should the following day. When it came to the tour it was also reflected in the lethargic performances against non league opposition at Yeovil in a 2-1 defeat and at Tiverton in a goalless draw. Despite it only being pre-season we knew those results mattered and that the alarm bells were beginning to ring with the Chairman and the management.

We knew also that it was being reported in the local paper back in Portsmouth that the Chairman was unhappy and there was a feeling in the camp that things weren't right.

The sound of those bells prompted the calling of an emergency meeting by Graham and Jim in the hotel, to which Darren, Justin and Scott were called, and which, to his great surprise, came to signal the beginning of the end for Darren at Pompey. It started with the usual 'how can we solve our problem?' but soon it became clear that their thoughts were centred around the three at the back, which was Graham's preferred defensive formation. Darren was obviously playing in the centre of the three but before long he was in no doubt from the tone of the meeting that Graham and Jim didn't want him there anymore and preferred to see Scott, with his better passing ability, in the role rather than on the right. When it was all over Darren came back to the room I shared with him and told me that he was being made a scapegoat for our current problems. He had played in the central role throughout his career and simply couldn't understand why suddenly, because of a couple of results in friendlies, he didn't appear to measure up. Obviously football is all down to opinions but this came as a shattering blow to Darren.

Through all this I was out of action and working in the gym on my rehab. I got to know our striker Rory Allen really well during my time in treatment as he recovered from a string of injuries which included the breaking of both ankles. I discovered what an intelligent guy he is, one who had a lot more interests than football, chiefly politics and cricket, and who held deep views on life. When he turned his back on football, reportedly to join the 'Barmy Army' in Australia supporting the England cricket team, there were a few eyebrows raised but when you are injured and unable to play for a very long time it affects you psychologically in that you come to have not only doubts about your ability but also whether you're strong enough to cope with the demands of

125

the game. For Rory there must have been a real worry about being tackled in the future given what he suffered. Playing is also a habit whereby you become accustomed to doing certain things well and you get immersed in the pattern and flow of the game. If you don't play for a year or eighteen months then you find yourself having to re-learn how to play, in a manner of speaking.

Rory was in a difficult place emotionally with so much uncertainty over his future. His decision to give up football was seen as crazy by some but it got to the point where he had to make a decision. He could have just hung around for 6-8 months and seen out his contract, and I admired his honesty and courage in grasping the nettle. When he wrote to Peter Storrie the Chief Executive requesting his release he said that he felt he had nothing more to offer the club. In doing so he gave up a lot of money wages-wise so I was pleased that it worked out well for him and he is settled in another career.

The appointment of Harry Redknapp as Director of Football made everybody sit up and take notice. The feeling amongst the players was that at last this club means business and perhaps we can wave goodbye to all that rubbish of last season and before. For me it meant even more because Harry was manager of the team I used to watch as a boy. However wherever you went there was one overriding feeling from the players and fans alike: 'He's here to be manager'.

When I introduced myself to Harry he immediately made me feel special with the words: 'I know who you are son'. My reaction was: *'Hi, he knows me!'* and my mind went back to the last time I met him - as a youngster at Upton Park thinking about signing on for West Ham as a schoolboy.

We were always conscious of Harry's presence at the club, despite him having no apparent involvement in the playing side of things. The word was that he was behind the signing of the young defender Alessandro Zamperini and I was understandably wary of the Italian's arrival given my contract situation. It was Graham who was instrumental in signing striker Peter Crouch however, and, once again, the players became aware of murmurings from the boardroom, this time about Crouchie's arrival on the lines of 'he's not good enough for us'.

The signing of the legendary Croatian international Robert Prosinecki made a huge impact in the dressing room too – the feeling 'why has he come to little old Portsmouth' just about summed it up. Like many of the players I was stunned by his arrival – you dream of playing with people like him and when it happens it's difficult to take in at first. Once I had got to see him in action I knew I had never seen ability like his before. We knew that he was not a Rix signing but politically Graham had to show he was happy with his arrival. There was nothing big-time about Prosie who worked hard in training, even if he was a chain-smoker, albeit in a discreet fashion. There was a feeling that the rest of the players were accommodating him into the team, but with his magic on the ball and what he could create going forward we soon realised we had gained a top man from an attacking standpoint, even if he offered very little when we were defending. His class was there for all to see – at his age all that was missing was the energy and the 'legs'. Now the only question to be answered was whether he could handle the physical rigours of Division One, particularly through the winter months.

It was the day after our last pre-season friendly against Leicester when everybody was hit with a shattering, stunning blow. As it was a Sunday I was, as usual, at church with the family and during the service I became concerned at the number of calls that were showing up on my mobile phone. Finally I took a call from Warren Hunt, a young reserve team player, to get the terrible news that our keeper Aaron Flahavan had been killed in a car accident during the previous night. An incredible numbness came over me and I couldn't get my head around this unbeliev-

127

able news. I had been with him a few hours earlier at Fratton Park where he had watched the game from the stand. Not knowing what had happened I was imagining different scenarios. I rushed round to Justin's house and together we watched Sky Sports News with film of the wreckage and the area where the body was found. Such accidents always involve someone else, not someone you know.

All the players felt compelled to come together that Sunday afternoon and 15-20 of us met up at a Portsmouth pub where we sat quietly together just spending time in his memory. Film of Aaron was shown on the TV in the bar and the accompanying music triggered a flood of tears from all the players in the bar. Not knowing the circumstances we really struggled to make sense of it and, as a newly converted Christian, I wondered why it had to happen. I knew one or two of the players would ask me to explain it and that I would be lost for an answer. We all went into training the next day in sombre mood and Graham offered us the option of going home instead. It was not the best way to prepare for the start of the season on the following Saturday.

Aaron was a flamboyant, happy-go-lucky guy, and the life and soul of the party. He was liked by everybody and I will always remember his wry smile that would appear despite any disappointment or anger he was feeling. I think he felt let down by the sport he loved in that he was regularly denied chances to play and show his ability, whether it was through injuries and illness, regularly being dropped or simply nobody having enough confidence in him. There were hundreds at his funeral and I, for one, didn't realise how many friends he had outside football. Andy Rimmer, our chaplain then, conducted the funeral and Darren read a passage from the Bible, which must have been a hard thing to do and something I could never have done.

As the season opened it was common knowledge that Graham was anxious to bring in striker Mark Burchill from Celtic but the impression we had was that the transfer could only be author-ised if the funds to pay for it were raised by selling someone. We knew already that Graham was prepared to let Darren go and I was made aware that I was seen as cover for his departure on my return from injury. Darren was club captain, an integral part of the team and only halfway through a four year contract, but the club knew he was in demand and, as such, he would command a decent fee.

Darren didn't really want to leave but he was told in no uncer-tain terms that he would never play for any Pompey team, even the reserves, again. When West Brom showed an interest it gave Darren a chance to go back home, close to where he was born and near his parents, and to play football again. It was a test of his patience when there was a delay of five weeks or so whilst the clubs sorted out a deal. Darren eventually moved but being so close to him I felt strange about it, particularly as I was seen as his replacement.

Burch's arrival meant that Lee was on the sidelines and it was difficult for me, knowing how my good friend felt about not play-ing, but it's something every footballer has to go through sometime or another. As it happened Burch soon suffered a serious training ground injury that put him out for the season, and put paid to Graham's hopes for him. He had already impressed with his fin-ishing and quickly formed an effective partnership with Crouchie so it was clear he would have been a key player. During a training ground game his studs had got caught in the turf and his body had still turned with his foot stuck in the ground. The weight of his body went through his knee, causing cruciate ligament dam-age, mirroring exactly the accident and injury that would befall Todorov two years later. Lee was quickly back in the team and, by now, we had made an encouraging start in the league, sitting in the top ten, with Prosie providing rich entertainment, particularly at Fratton Park.

Prosie's passing was brilliant, the delivery and accuracy of his set-pieces were unbelievable, and, for good measure he was now scoring outstanding goals. With the ball he was magical, but without it he didn't do as much defensively as we needed in a team that was not playing well. Away from home you need everybody pulling their weight work-wise in what was a tough and physical league. As winter wore on the pitches got heavier and the ball didn't move so freely and that plainly didn't suit his style of play. Also the demands of the English game and its conditions took its toll and his influence waned as he began to suffer physically.

Crouchie benefited from Prosie's regular assists in those early weeks of the season and ended up with 19 goals in a season in which he really made a name for himself after suffering rejection at both Spurs and QPR. He was still only 20 years of age and a really nice well-mannered lad who showed a lot of character to ignore the amount of stick he took from away fans over his height and build – we used to hate it when those chants of 'freak, freak' started up with great regularity. With his all-round technical ability - his good touch, eye for goal and strength in the air – I could see him playing in the Premiership eventually although I never imagined, at that stage, at his age, that he would graduate to international status. The Pompey players were really pleased for him when he moved to Aston Villa, at a time when Premiership clubs were increasingly ignoring players in the lower leagues.

With my knee having fully recovered and feeling strong, it was soon time for me to return to action and I was ready for a reserve team game at Fratton Park. By now I had developed a strong desire in my heart to share what had happened to me. The night before the game I just knew that I would play well, be interviewed by the press afterwards, and take the opportunity to reveal my healing. I went to bed and went to sleep but woke up with a voice from within me saying, with great conviction, over and over again: *'This is the power that raised Jesus... this is the power that raised Jesus...* '. Soon I felt a strong sensation like an electric current running through my body as I lay on my bed. It was the best sensation ever – natural, joyous, devoid of fear and simply every good feeling you could ever imagine. That was followed by a sensation of being lifted, from my middle, off the bed which was momentarily scary before it soon stopped. By now Trish was awake and I turned to her: 'How could this be going on? Did you see what happened?'

As I lay there, I was reminded of Demos Shakarian's book 'The Happiest People On Earth' in which, after being lifted out of his body, he looks down on the earth and sees all these unhappy faces looking up at him. With this comes the message: *'If you give up, all these people will not get to know me. If you continue to work for me, then this will be the result'* and he turns to see the all the same faces are looking up at him smiling.

Then I thought of Ezekiel in the Old Testament who, after being lifted up out of his body, was called by God to go to Israel to be a prophet. The thought of such a modern calling frightened me: *'Is that sort of thing going to happen to me?... will I have to give up football?... am I going to be a vicar?'* All Trish would say, when I tried to discuss it, was: 'You're weird', before I eventually got to sleep.

'Do not conform yourselves to the standards of this world, but let God transform you inwardly by a complete change of mind'
Romans 12.2

10

'I alone know the plans I have for you...' 2002

My spiritual experience the night before the reserve game in which I was to give my knee the ultimate test – a 90-minute game at Fratton Park for the reserves – filled me with an even greater conviction to honour God, speak about my healing, and start to tell my story. Most players, me included, would approach such a game, after a serious injury, full of trepidation as to whether such an injury would recur. But I was confident all day that my knee would stand the strain of the game, with no fear whatsoever about the outcome, and I got through OK with no problems.

As I left the dressing room after the game there was a reporter, Dave Kemp from the local newspaper 'The News', outside waiting for a player to interview. His first enquiry to me was: 'How do you feel?'

My reply was: 'Before I start, I've got something I want to share with you, I'm a Christian...'

Dave interrupted me before I could go on: 'So am I'.

I was not altogether surprised by his revelation given what had happened to me previously. It was even as if God had placed him there to ensure that everything was reported correctly. Dave didn't appear to be shocked at the story of my healing, but merely said: 'I will give it to the paper to use'.

The outcome was the story was featured all over the back page of the newspaper under a big headline: *'God healed my knee'*, and I had well and truly come out, so to speak. It coincided with my joining the squad having been selected to make my return to the first team to play at Rotherham. I was shocked at the ridicule I received from several of the players. They came at me like a pack of dogs on the attack, with Shaun Derry and Justin Edinburgh leading the way with their laughter. I expected some flak but not to that extent. I've never dealt with criticism well but this was something else and it hurt. In effect they doubted my integrity.

It got worse on our return to training the following Monday, after the defeat at Rotherham, when I had a group of about ten players coming up to me. Before I knew it I was being hit with all sorts of comments: 'You've lost it... you're mad... if there's a God why do kids die?... why did 9/11 happen?' etc, etc. I tried to hold my hand up and say I didn't know but they wouldn't let me speak and kept cutting me off. I was shocked by how severe and vehement their reaction was. In the end I found myself getting angry.

It was Jamie Vincent who bailed me out on that occasion by standing up for me. A group with such a mentality has a strong voice, particularly in the confines of a dressing room. I'd never heard Jamie say anything about religion and it took some courage for him to go against the group, but he didn't shy away from it, saying: 'If that's what happened to him, you have to respect him. He hasn't done anything wrong. If that's what he believes then I haven't got a problem with that.'

Nevertheless from then on, at least twice a week, one or two of the players would start on me with the same theme: 'What makes you believe?', with questioning covering all sorts of thorny issues. But, whatever answers I came up with or even confessed that I didn't know, it would always turn into the group being united in putting down God in a big way. That would hurt me inside in a big way, in the same way as it would if they were insulting my Mum or Trish. It was painful in a way I had never experienced before. If I spoke to anybody at the club, there would be a chorus in my direction of: 'Don't try and convert him, leave him alone'. I really did wonder what I had let myself in for.

Trish was sympathetic and tried to help by saying: 'But you've got to tell them about God'. Mick Mellows gave me a piece of scripture: 'When you are persecuted in my name you will be blessed'. I would hold on to that in my head during all that ridicule in the dressing room and suddenly the hurt would be lessened.

Playing that 90 minutes at Rotherham without any ill-effects was the ultimate proof of my healing, and afterwards God spoke to me in my heart, with the command: *'You're going to give your appearance money for this match to the Lord'*. As it happened there was an appeal at our church for funds to supply a mini-bus for the use of a children's charity in Africa, to which I donated my appearance money. I had learned to be obedient to God and the lady from the charity was overwhelmed by my response.

The Japanese international keeper Yoshi Kawaguchi had arrived a few weeks earlier and we had heard that he was a legend in Japan with a huge following. The move was heralded as having huge commercial spin-offs for the club with the World Cup due to be played in Japan in 2002. Graham was quite happy with Dave Beasant in goal and Bes was playing well so he felt no need to change his keeper. However before the game against Wednesday at Hillsborough it became clear that Yoshi had to play, with the pressure for him to appear reaching breaking point. There were conflicting stories around the dressing room as to the consequences of his non-appearances like: *'a TV deal with Japan might be pulled'*, *'a shirt sponsor would pull out'* and *'it will cost Pompey a lot of income from spin-offs'*. So our 3-2 win that afternoon marked his debut and the stories that we let Wednesday score in the very first minute as a protest at Dave's dropping for Yoshi are simply untrue. It was just the way it happened on the afternoon.

Amongst the defenders it's true to say that we did feel a nervousness at Yoshi's presence borne out of a lack of confidence in him. It was mainly down to his decision making, in particular coming for the ball on crosses. Yoshi's catching generally was also a concern and the feeling amongst the players was that through his lack of physical presence and unfamiliarity with the English game he was ill-equipped physically and mentally to handle the challenges he would have to face, particularly from set-pieces. Graham didn't ever criticise him but in any case there was a big language problem, and before each game we would rehearse him on the various commands he would need – 'keeper's', 'mine', 'away' etc – if he was to communicate with us defenders effectively. For a few weeks it seemed not to matter whether we won or lost, Yoshi just had to play.

Soon after my return Lee suffered the most dreadful injury at Millwall following a horrendous challenge. We all knew how serious it was when untypically he went down and stayed down. The outcome was a potentially career-threatening cruciate ligament knee injury which led to Lee spending over a year out of the game. I really felt for him- no player was so honest or ever worked so hard for the team.

Things came to a head for Yoshi when his obvious handling errors cost us two goals at Grimsby in the space of five minutes, leading to a 3-1 defeat which put us perilously close to the relegation zone. Now it was totally disheartening for us all and clear that it couldn't go on. We couldn't bring ourselves to have a go at him because we knew that in truth he shouldn't have been playing.

The following Saturday – a disastrous 4-1 third round home FA Cup tie defeat against Leyton Orient – proved to be Yoshi's swansong in a game where just about everything went wrong for us. Orient had obviously noted our poor form beforehand and came to Fratton Park with some belief that they could cause a shock. They were proved right and we contributed to our humiliation with a poor attitude and a complete lack of confidence. For my part I knew full well what to expect from Orient, having been in the same position myself with a lower league club.

The Pompey fans were understandably upset and gave us some deserved abuse. The first person we had to face as we arrived back in the dressing room was the Chairman, who had marched straight down from his seat in the Director's Box, to express his disapproval, even getting there before Graham and Jim. We just sat round, still in our kit, as he let rip in an emotional outburst: 'I am totally embarrassed by your performances... I'm upset for the fans... this is my lowest point in football... I can't protect you from all of this... you all need to take a really good look at yourselves' etc, etc.

It was the most embarrassed I have ever felt after a match. I met Mr Mandaric at a children's Christmas party the next day and he was clearly very unhappy – so much so that I barely got a 'hello' from him. To rub salt in the wound the game featured prominently on BBC TV's Match of the Day as a much heralded giant killing. To add to my personal discomfort one of my friends 'phoned me later that weekend and was at pains to tell me that someone he knew who had watched the match had expressed the view that: 'Linvoy Primus had looked like a carthorse'. That made me so angry – just to add to all the other emotions I was feeling.

A subsequent run of just one win in seven included an amazing 4-4 draw at home to Barnsley that not only included a sublime hat-trick by Prosie and one of my rare goals but a sending-off for me, my first ever 'straight red'. I was marking Chris Morgan at a corner and he was both grabbing me and holding my shirt in a successful attempt to restrict my movements. My reaction was to try to push his hand away to loosen his hold on my shirt. When that failed I swung my arm round rather more forcibly in an attempt to get free from his grip. Immediately the referee blew up and told me: 'I'm sending you off for throwing a punch'.

Not only was I angry and disappointed with the unjustified red card, but, with the score at 4-2, the referee awarded a penalty for my alleged 'punch', which was converted to put Barnsley right back in the game. They then equalised in stoppage time which Graham, not to mention Prosie and the rest of us, found very hard to take given his increasingly tenuous position at the club. Graham came into the dressing room after the game and immediately launched into an attack on me; 'Because of you we lost two points'.

I shouted back at him: 'Just have a look at the video, which will prove that it should never have been given'.

I was so frustrated and upset with Graham's accusation and that I couldn't convince him of my innocence. It didn't help my cause when the incident didn't show up in the video of the game so there was no footage to back up my claim that I didn't throw a punch. On the Monday afterwards I knew I had to go in early to apologise to Graham for shouting back at him. I was hoping that it would end on a good note by him apologising to me in turn, but that wasn't happening. I was disappointed that he wasn't prepared to give me the benefit of the doubt, and all he would say was: 'I won't fine you - we have to put it behind us and move on'.

I found this incident hard to take, and it got me asking questions of God. I was as angry and frustrated as the next man, but thankfully Mick Mellows sent me a text: *Jesus was innocent and he knew he was innocent, but he was still hung*. At that stage I still had a lot to learn.

That bad post-Christmas run culminated in a disastrous 0-5 defeat at West Brom – as it happened, both Darren Moore (having moved to The Hawthorns of course) and I missed the game with hamstring injuries. I went with the family and couldn't believe what was going on out there as I watched us get battered. The Chairman was so upset by the performance that he withheld the players' wages. In fact the squad first heard of it from 'Sky Sports News' on TV but didn't take it too seriously until the month's wages didn't show up in our bank accounts.

Finally Peter Storrie and Graham told us of the decision formally and there was a great deal of anger and no little embarrassment amongst the players, with the overall feeling: *'How could he do this?'* Through the national press headlines, and with the whole country following developments, we felt belittled by the whole episode. There was a bit of a revolt, with the matter being referred to the Professional Footballers Association. The biggest worry for a number of the players was how the mortgage was going to be paid with the due date of the wages normally coinciding with the mortgage payment due date. When an overdraft situation ensued there was talk of making the club responsible for the bank charges incurred. Fortunately the matter was quickly settled before the FA and PFA could get involved on our behalf, but the Chairman had not exactly endeared himself to the players with what we interpreted as a publicity stunt. We understood how embarrassed he must have been by the West Brom result but publicly flexing his muscles with a big show in that way, to demonstrate what power he had over us if we didn't perform, didn't help the situation.

We got to hear of the whispers in the boardroom and knew that, despite the votes of confidence for Graham, football is a results business. We always felt that Harry was a threat to Graham, mainly because of his success managing in the Premiership, and, although we had little or no contact with him, he was a hovering, watching presence in the background at the games and at the training ground with the Chairman. You couldn't escape the feeling that Harry was lined up to replace Graham, and to us it wasn't a question of if but when he wanted to take the job.

Looking back now, Graham did well to disguise any feelings he had about all this and if he had any personal anxiety about the situation he certainly didn't convey it to us.

It became obvious that Mr Mandaric wanted someone who shared his ambition of Premiership football whilst Graham had gone on record early on as aiming for 'mid-table mediocrity'. He was a realist who knew only too well that the squad he had inherited wasn't good enough for those heady heights. There was no doubt that Graham was a good coach but, for me, there was always some doubt whether he was strong enough mentally to be a manager – there were times when he looked unduly stressed. He was a good motivator, and certainly was at his best in one-to-one situations where he was always encouraging and trying to build you up. Coaches tend to get closer to the players, and in that respect Graham was more of a coach than a manager. But then, in fairness, I suppose that's the sort of thing one would say if a manager is unsuccessful.

Graham had a good relationship with the players, some would say too close, but his style was to be up close and personal, which unfortunately didn't work for him at Pompey. Everyone wanted to do well for him, but when things were not going well he didn't show that essential element of hardness and would shy away from having a go at us, leaving that to his assistant Jim Duffy. He would be the one to criticise and point the finger if you were not playing well. The players would react to Jim with an equal measure of respect and discontent; the latter on the basis that some players find personal criticism hard to take and out of it develop a dislike for the coach. Occasionally all eleven of us would be on the end of it and I remember, in particular, we went to Gillingham on Boxing Day, lost 2-0 and were simply awful on an icy pitch that we all clearly didn't fancy. While Graham stayed silent, Jim had a real go: 'That was terrible... not one of you earned your pay today' etc, etc.

Pompey's best eleven was good enough at home to beat most teams but there was no real depth in the squad. If we had a few injuries then we were never the same threat. Generally there was also a lack of experience in the squad, with only Lee Mills having won promotion elsewhere. Graham leaned towards potential rather than experience in giving young and up-and-coming players like Courtney Pitt, Neil Barrett, Steve Lovell, Alessandro Zamperini and Lewis Buxton their chances. I also sensed that there weren't too many of what sports people call 'seasoned winners' around.

In a similar situation to that I had experienced at Reading, there were a number of players in the Fratton Park squad, who had played reserve team football for a couple of years previously at Pompey and elsewhere, who found it hard to step up and meet the higher demands of first team football. These were players who were determined to enjoy life, as it were, but again it proved that you can't be out partying and drinking and perform to a high standard on the football field on a Saturday. They thought they could live that sort of life and get away with it, but something has to give, you can't do both. Such behaviour is frowned upon in the modern game with its greater professionalism, even though it's still down to the individual how they behave. In 2001 however such behaviour was still part of the football culture – it was changing but only slowly. At Pompey the players were being treated like adults and trusted, and Graham would never physically stop people going out. I must say that, when you're in training, you can always tell if someone has been out the night before.

We were all but safe from relegation by the time things came to a head for Graham, after a goalless draw at home to Sheffield Wednesday, half a dozen games after that West Brom disaster, with just five games of the season left. The writing had been on the wall a couple of weeks earlier when his assistant Jim Duffy had been sacked. I was still missing through injury and unbeknown to me, after getting wind of the Chairman's intentions, four or five of the senior players had decided to form a deputation to plead Graham's case with him. Scott Hiley (the spokesman as captain), Shaun Derry, Nigel Quashie, Kevin Harper and Peter Crouch went to the boardroom, with the other players' unanimous backing, and argued that Graham was worth standing by on the basis that he was a good coach who had been unlucky with injuries. They came back and reported: 'He listened carefully to what we had to say... we feel positive about it all'.

Twenty-four hours later the deputation's efforts were shown to have been wasted and Graham was sacked, which many of us thought was somewhat harsh. Despite the almost inevitability about Harry's immediate appointment as his replacement you couldn't help feeling that perhaps at last here was a real 'name' in the game with a high profile as an established Premiership manager.

While all these tumultuous events were taking place at Fratton Park, my own spiritual shake-up was happening too. I had no idea of the effect that the newspaper story of the healing of my knee would have on the Christian life of the city of Portsmouth and surrounding areas. Wherever I went out in the community meeting people in the course of fulfilling functions for the club it would be mentioned. It was soon clear to me what a great encouragement it was for local Christians to have me 'coming out' like that.

Then, out of the blue, I received a letter from a young Pompey fan that was so timely and gave me such a boost. He sent me a verse from the Bible (Jeremiah 29 v.11), with a brief note saying: 'I believe this scripture is for you', which read: 'I alone know the plans I have for you, plans to bring you prosperity and not disaster, plans to bring about the future you hope for'. I was stunned by this verse which gave me so much hope, and it reinforced my strong belief that my life was really going to be taken care of. But I knew that God still needed my co-operation and that it was up to me to do everything to the best of my ability to ensure that His plan was fulfilled. I needed to be sensitive and obedient to what He was guiding me to do, otherwise I could end up making the wrong decisions and being in the wrong place.

After a few weeks there was a level of acceptance of my beliefs in the dressing room which was replaced by a curiosity about what went on at Mick Mellows' house during our meetings. By now a number of the players had met and talked with the club chaplain, Andy Rimmer and Mick Mellows, his assistant, during their regular visits to the club and training ground, and that enabled barriers to be broken down. I even found myself being bold enough to say to players with injuries: 'We will pray for you if you want' and they would reply: 'OK pray for me at your next meeting and I will come to your meetings if I find I can train the next day'. Out of that I got in the habit of praying for individuals at the club and the team itself.

Then one day Mick told me that somebody had raised the possibility of me giving a talk with my testimony, and 'did I fancy the idea?'. I had never had the urge or desire to do such a thing, and initially all I could think of was how hard that would be for me, but I trusted Mick, particularly when he stressed the likely impact it would have, coming from a footballer of all people. So I gave my first testimony before about 100 people at the Oasis Church Centre in Portsmouth in the form of a question and answer session in company with an interviewer. I felt comfortable and came through OK. I was worried and nervous beforehand but, once I got started, it really flowed and I felt the presence of God carrying me through it. Trish was there and she recognised the joy and happiness that I gained from doing it.

For three years Mick had been praying that Christians would come into the football club which he saw as being at the centre of the life of the city. For Mick a prominent role model from the club was essential – someone who could go into areas of the city where the established church couldn't go. Darren Moore had arrived to fulfil that role, but he had moved to the Midlands, and I came to see how important it was to Mick for that role to be continued.

About three months later Mick organised a 'Curry Night' in a local curry house and it was advertised as an event at which there would be food and drink and I would speak about becoming a Christian and my faith. The idea was that non-Christians would feel happier in such a location rather than being intimidated by a church venue. Lee and Haley Bradbury, our neighbours, came along and again I felt a peace over me whilst I was up there speaking. I often wondered what the bigger attraction was - me talking or the chance to meet a footballer and have a chicken biriani and some beer all for a fiver.

It was the first of many such events over the following six months or so, but Mick taught me that there was no pressure regarding the numbers attending, whether it was one or a million. I was happy to rest in the knowledge that God would call and bring the people who he wanted to attend.

During this period I regularly started to see pictures during my prayer time, and one such vision showed streams of paint pouring from dozens of upturned paint pots into long grass. Rivers of paint were heading towards an invisible barrier where their progress was halted. I mentioned this vision to Mick who remembered that a few days earlier a story, which I hadn't seen, had appeared in the local newspaper describing the interception, by drugs squad officers, of a ship at the Portsmouth ferry port and the discovery of a haul of cocaine concealed in paint pots. As part of our regular prayers for the city, we had recently prayed that God would break the chain of drugs being supplied to the community.

When I prayed for somebody in particular I would see pictures that I later realised were symbols of the circumstances in their lives at that time. I remember praying for a lady at the request of some friends and seeing bees in a jar that were angry and desperate to be released. Suddenly the lid of the jar came off and the bees flew from the jar. At the time I told her friends of my vision and later, when I met them again, they said that their friend had felt suddenly that all her bottled-up frustrations and anxieties at work had been released and left her.

I developed a voracious appetite for reading the Bible and Christian literature. At last I felt, after all these years, I was beginning to learn what it was all about. I wanted to know more and more, and would become very frustrated if there was anything I didn't understand. That meant I was speaking to Mick every day, and I was fortunate enough to get not only plenty of encouragement from him but also desperate pleas to relax into it. I know that Keith and Sam, thinking of my welfare, had some concern about the, by now, strong influence of both Mick Mellows and Mick O'Brien over me, and the possibility of me being exploited, but, once they had met them, shared their beliefs, and been to one of their meetings, they had no worries over our close alliance.

I could be myself with 'the two Micks' – their passion for Jesus matched mine. I felt I belonged with them and I could be myself. I had never before really let people into my life, but now, for the first time, I had close friends, who were trustworthy and reliable and who knew the real me.

You build only acquaintances in football – in essence the other players are no more than work-mates. I might hold a place in the team but there are always other players who want to take your place and who might take your livelihood as a consequence. Players move around to different clubs with little time to form worthwhile and lasting relationships, and, in any event, it's rare to find another player who you would spend time with outside football. In my whole career, amongst the hundreds of players with whom I have shared a dressing room, there are only 10-15 who I would call friends. Obviously I like my team-mates and we share common aims for the team but rarely do we have anything outside football in common.

I'd never really felt confident in relationships anyway up to now, and didn't socialise as much as others would. Drinking and gambling weren't my scenes really, although I had my moments with the former early in my career. With my Christian friends I felt a deepness, a bond and a unity, that was not manufactured, that I had never experienced before in my life. The one thing that unites us is Jesus and his unconditional love, whether we are from different backgrounds or lifestyles - no matter what - and it's unique and real.

One thing I did ask about very early on in all of this was whether my faith should affect my on-field performances and the will to win – i.e whether I could tackle and play as hard as before! The advice I received was: 'God gave you a gift. Use it with integrity and don't abuse it'. My lifestyle didn't have to change, and my attitude to football, not the way I played, didn't change until about a year later. I was still as nervous as ever before games, with all the niggling doubts as to how I would perform. It was still the same old me, with little or no confidence or self-assurance about my ability, despite being 'born again'. I still had to live with my old self which doesn't drop away instantly. 'The two Micks' would pray for me on Thursdays before a weekend game but that was not enough to fill me with confidence. If I was criticised for my play I would still take it to heart in a big way and find it difficult to handle, even if it came from a small minority.

'Be ready at all times to answer anyone who asks you
to explain the hope you have in you'
1 Peter 3.15

145

11

The 'Wow' factor 2002

Our introduction to the new manager came the morning after our night out with Graham when, after arriving for training still faintly reeking of drink, we found ourselves summoned to a meeting with Harry. He very quickly and forcibly made it clear that, for him, Pompey's days of being a 'sleeping giant' had to end and that he would be aiming to take the club into the top half of the table for a starter. There was some scepticism amongst the squad when he went on to say: 'It's not true to say that I had been lined up for the job. I never wanted the job, but the Chairman asked me to take it on, and here I am'. It was probably true, but the stories and rumours of his impending move into the job had been around for so long that they had almost become established fact.

Harry added: 'I am looking for hard work from you all. If any of you don't want to be here with me, then come and see me and I will be happy to let you go'. We began to wonder if he knew that we had been out on the town the night before when he made a point of saying: 'I won't tolerate drinking... I've got no time for that... I want only professionals at this club from now on'.

Harry was my fourth manager at Fratton Park in the space of two years but, despite the initial disappointment amongst the squad at Graham's departure, there was an undoubted 'wow' factor about his taking charge. Obviously Harry had seen me play often enough but I was missing with a hamstring injury so he went out and signed two central defenders - Scott Wilson, on loan from Rangers, and Eddie Howe from Bournemouth, who I immediately saw as a threat to my position.

Harry single-handedly took training, with some assistance from Mark O'Connor the youth team coach, and hard work was the order of the day, every day. He had not been directly involved with players for some time and we could tell that he relished and enjoyed being back out there on the training ground. By the same token we could sense that he wasn't impressed with the talent, or lack of it, that he had at his disposal. I returned to the defence for the 1-1 draw in the penultimate away game at Birmingham, after which Harry didn't mince his words about the team, despite the result: 'If we'd been in a relegation battle we'd have gone down'.

He was even more upset with our efforts when in the last home game of the season we lost to Watford, greeting us at the final whistle with the words: 'That's the worst performance I've ever seen... I'm going to have to ring the changes here... I'm not going to suffer that'.

It's normal for teams to do a so-called 'lap of honour' after the last home game of the season, not only to give the fans a chance to applaud the team for their efforts all season but for the team to acknowledge the support from the fans. So we were asked to go out again on to the pitch, and some of the players, as is also the habit, threw their shirts into the crowd. When we got back to the dressing room afterwards Harry was scathing about it all: 'There's no way you should have done a lap of honour after that performance... if I had been a fan I would have thrown the shirts back at you'.

In the early summer 2002 I was persuaded by Mick to go to Nigeria with a party of volunteers on a mission with him to a school in Ibadan, the biggest town in West Africa and about 90 kilometres north-east of Lagos. We had become aware of the work of the Soteria Trust, a Chichester based charity, who had funded the building of the Prospect Children's School and College there. Soteria, from the Greek for 'salvation', works closely with school staff to provide scholarships and sponsorships throughout their whole educational careers for the poor and most vulnerable children, many of whom are orphans caught up in child labour, prostitution, begging or are severely disabled. This also allows children who would not otherwise be able to afford to attend school to do so and takes them out of a life of poverty and deprivation into the dignity of employment. For the most vulnerable children this means they receive accommodation, education, school uniforms, books, food and water.

We wanted to support Soteria and the school in their work and provide some football coaching. It would be my first venture outside Europe, and, other than for short periods for football reasons, Trish and I had never been apart. Initially she was worried about safety and the conditions I would meet out there. I didn't want to go without her blessing but one morning she woke up to say that she was happy for me to go and was sure that no harm would come to me with God taking care of me. The Pompey players got to hear of my trip and were very supportive and approving of what I was doing.

Before leaving we met Andy Economides, the founder and director of Soteria Trust, and he explained how we could make a real difference to the lives of the 80 or so staff and almost 500 children at the school of nursery, primary and secondary age. On the day of departure it was with a sense of excitement and trepidation that we took off on our 8-hour flight, fully loaded with kits and footballs donated by both Pompey and West Bromwich Albion, and a large number of school books. When we landed at Lagos airport in the early hours of the morning we were immediately aware of what Europeans call 'the Nigerian Experience' – the very warm air filled with the strong and distinct smell of body odour.

Our reception at the airport was quite an experience – *'I'm really out of my comfort zone here'* was my immediate thought – and initially I was alarmed by the number of aggressive armed guards and the constant questioning about the contents of the various boxes we had as luggage. At one stage I was convinced I would be arrested, but eventually the security staff were satisfied that much of it was books for schools we were visiting. Outside the airport there was more concern when we found ourselves surrounded by a group of about 30 locals who we finally deduced wanted to load our luggage in return for tips. In the jeeps hired to take us to our hotel we had to take a policeman to get us past the various road blocks and avoid the bribes which were apparently normally demanded from European visitors. Then came the experience of drivers, roads and traffic that redefined every transport norm we had previously known.

Somehow, despite the heat and a noisy air-conditioning system that sounded like a helicopter about to take off, I managed to sleep in my room on the 10th floor of a hotel but wasn't too impressed when we had to get dressed in a shirt, tie and trousers for our first visit to the college to speak to the teenagers. With pupils from other schools also invited to attend, we spent three days there football coaching in 100 degree heat with a high humidity and finished up with a huge tournament on the Saturday attended by 10 local schools in which the competition was fierce but fair. We were able to give away all the equipment we had taken to Nigeria including the footballs and shirts as prizes and gifts, and they were all received with joy and gratitude.

Conditions for football aren't as they are here in England, and it's often played barefoot. There is little grass on the pitches that are covered with stones and rocks but that doesn't deter the youngsters from showing tremendous enthusiasm and application. It was obvious how African players develop into strong,

149

courageous and very skilful individuals when you see at first hand the environment in which their talents are nurtured.

In the afternoons we would go to the school and spend time in the classrooms with the nursery and primary school pupils from age three upwards. As a ritual we would eat in the same local Chinese restaurant each night in an attempt to avoid upset stomachs, but that didn't stop me suffering from a stomach bug in the last day or so and losing some weight as a consequence.

Darren Moore had been unable to make the trip but he donated his bonus for gaining promotion to the Premiership that season to provide up to two years of education for 16 children with the balance for the work at the college. It was a real highlight of our visit to meet the parents of the children that Darren had sponsored and to see their absolute joy and gratitude in response to his gesture of provision of their children's scholarship fees.

One area that moved us was the total lack of books in school and college; they had libraries but no books. To assist we distributed – very often at risk of being mauled in the stampede – a great many books. There was a hunger for reading matter, particularly amongst the older students, and, because of the shortage of books, when they receive any they become treasured possessions and are read again and again. We knew that the books and tracts we distributed were of immense value to the young people.

The staff were very gracious towards us and we were impressed with their Christian faith, their dedication to their students and desire for excellence within the very severe limitations of their resources. Knowing that most of their salaries were in the region of 5000 Nira per month, the equivalent of £25, we felt moved to make a gift and reinforce our support for them in a practical way. We came back from the mission determined to raise the money in the future to provide the funding for continued sponsorship of scholarships at the school and college.

What did surprise me was that everywhere we went people

were aware of Jesus. Businesses even had his name on their buildings as a sign of credibility so faith is a big part of people's lives in Nigeria. The children come from all sorts of religious backgrounds with lots of Muslims, but I gather there are more professing Christians than in England. There aren't any hang-ups about talking about Jesus and God, and they realised how far we had come to talk to them. By their responses, we knew that a lot of what we said to them clearly sank in. It certainly wasn't a case of them thinking: 'Yeah, they are only saying that because they want something from it'. In England a lot of material things take your mind off God's word. For them our going there was a very big thing and they showed that they felt this was something real to them. We got to experience church worship 'African-style' – it was supposed to last one-and-half hours but turned into three. Emotionally that was something you could never explain to anyone.

From the trip I now realise what beautiful and sincere people the Nigerians are. There had always been some rivalry and resentment between the West Indians and Africans in and around the area of London where I was brought up but my trip had given me a better understanding of the African culture and ways. I had always thought they exhibited a tough and often aggressive look on their faces, but I now realise that what looked like a scowl was in fact a permanent squint to keep the sun out of their eyes!

I had been humbled by the trip to the point that it changed my life. You think you're giving something, but in fact you are getting so much more back, because you are seeing what sort of lives these people are leading and how much joy and faith they have despite having so little. It was humbling just knowing that everything I had – my family, my health, my home, my everything - was a world apart from what those children have.

I had seen what I wanted to do with my life and it had completely opened up a new horizon for me. Football had been everything to me, all I knew, the be-all and end-all. Before the trip I had no idea what I would do with the rest of my life when I could no longer play football. But when I got back from Nigeria I felt that if my football career ended tomorrow I had found something that I would turn to immediately. The mission was so incredibly rewarding, seeing that the little we brought to them was the source of so much joy to the people and the children.

I came back with a strong resolve to enjoy every moment of my time in football, but, more than that, to go back to Africa one day, perhaps with my family, with another mission to meet the needs of those children as much as I could. The trip had shown me that Christianity didn't just centre on the church in England but there was work that needed to be done both here and overseas.

The summer of 2002 was also an amazing time for the Pompey fans as Harry got down to rebuilding the squad and it soon became apparent that he could attract players, and 'name' players at that. We knew he wanted success and knew the players he wanted to achieve it. I didn't know too much about Hayden Foxe, Matthew Taylor, Richard Hughes or Vincent Pericard but was impressed by the signing of Arjan De Zeeuw, who I knew from playing against Wigan, was a solid and reliable defender. That was nothing compared to the amazement I felt when a goalkeeper of the calibre of Shaka Hislop arrived from West Ham. It was clear that the Chairman was backing Harry in a way that the previous Pompey managers had not enjoyed. I knew what Jim Smith meant to the Pompey fans and when he arrived as Harry's No. 2 I got the feeling that something was developing at the club and that the Chairman was, at last, going flat out to achieve his ambitions.

Harry had a presence about him and a record at the top level, and there was an element of the 'fear factor' amongst the players toward him. When I returned from Nigeria with a severe stomach bug which caused me to suffer extreme diarrhoea it caused me to be three days late reporting for pre-season training. Before contacting Harry with my apologies, my thought was: *'This won't go down too well'*, but he was good as gold about it. 'No problem', he said.

By the time we moved to Woodbury Park Hotel for our customary West Country tour the writing was really on the wall as far as my first team prospects were concerned. I didn't start for the home friendly against Celtic, and I was also left out at both Newquay and Torquay. At that time I felt inferior to Arjan (De Zeeuw) and Hayden (Foxe) and could see little chance of displacing them in the centre of defence. It was becoming clear that the first choice four at the back were Howe, De Zeeuw, Foxe and Taylor. Most of the players from the Rix era, like Shaun Derry, Scott Hiley, Dave Waterman, Alessandro Zamperini, Courtney Pitt and Neil Barrett, had either left the club or were being completely left on the sidelines, and that looked like being my fate.

I was becoming desperate to play a full ninety minutes, having been restricted to the odd substitute appearance, as the season approached. So I was very disappointed when I found myself on the bench again, this time for a friendly at Farnborough in which Harry intended to field a team of players who had played under Graham from the previous season. We had a long tiring ninety-minute training session on the morning of the game that left every player 'leggy' and fatigued, which contributed to our 3-0 loss. After the game we discovered that a significant number of scouts from other clubs were at the game, so clearly we were put on show that night. In commenting on the embarrassing defeat, Harry was quoted in the Portsmouth newspaper 'The News' as saying: 'This is the team that we were supposed to get promotion with last season'.

Two weeks before the season started Harry took me aside and spelled out the situation to me: 'You will be in the squad, but you won't play as many games as you would like. I won't stand in your way if you want to find another club'. None of this

153

should really have come as any surprise to me, but I was still very disappointed, angry and frustrated and I knew it would unsettle the family and test us in a way we had never been tested before. Initially I took it personally but eventually came to accept that Harry was just looking to do what he thought was best for the club - not that I saw it like that at first. My agent John Mac spoke to Harry who repeated what he had told me, and I was left with a situation where I was in the last year of my contract with the manager making it clear that my long term future didn't lie with the club. So with my best interests in mind John circulated other clubs, although, if I was to move, it would have to be with some assurance of regular first team football. In the event there was no apparent interest from any other clubs so the question of a possible move never arose.

I had never found myself in this sort of situation before, and simply didn't know how to deal with it. Immediately I took up the attitude that if the club didn't want me then why should I make the effort in training. But after a lot of prayer, Bible study and discussions with Mick Mellows, I had a significant change of attitude to football knowing that God wouldn't want me to misuse the gift He had given me. I promised to do my very best for God, based on honouring Him in all I did, and serving Him with all my heart. So from then on I was playing for God first, then the manager and the supporters. Everything I achieved thereafter was not from my own ability or strength, but through God's grace and power at work in me.

It was a huge surprise when Paul Merson joined us just as the season was about to start. We had heard of the possibility from reports in the media but dismissed them as rumours, so to actually see him with us was nothing short of amazing. Merse had huge respect in the game and was immediately installed as captain replacing Nigel Quashie, Harry's original appointment. We were surprised at Nigel's happy acceptance of the change, given his usually boisterous attitude, but he obviously recognised that Merse had the experience of playing at the highest level and that he could help him as a player too.

No sooner had we seen Merse in action on the training ground than it became apparent that he could take us to a new level. With his inspiration came an increased expectation amongst the players as to how well we could perform, and much of that came from the high standards he set and expected to be matched by us. He was a winner, pure and simple, and that rubbed off on all of us. The quality of his passing was the main factor that inspired players to new levels of performance. Merse was a big voice in the dressing room, amongst a number of other big voices, and he in particular was never scared to make his feelings known for the good of the team.

Merse's level of performance was always so high that season that it never occurred to us that he might have personal problems off the pitch. We knew his problems from the past, but, out of respect, these were never mentioned in the dressing room. It was altogether a new thing for many of us to be around such a high profile player. The first we ever got to hear of any problems was through a newspaper story later in the season and then it came as a shock to us to think that he had been playing so well with such commitment despite carrying such burdens.

I was surprised to be on the substitute's bench for the opening league game at home to Nottingham Forest and came on for right back Eddie Howe who was unfortunate enough to injure his knee after just ten minutes. When Eddie first went down with the injury, Harry sent Jason Crowe and me down the touchline to warm up but knowing that Jason was a right back I expected him to get the call to go on if Eddie couldn't continue. When the whistle came from Harry to get back to the bench and get changed to go on it was me who got the call. I had never before played at right back so it was with mixed emotions that I went on – worried that I might let everybody down, but anxious to take my chance to impress. As it happened it went really well and I even played a part in creating our second goal scored by Vincent Pericard in our 2-0 win.

Three days later we travelled to Bramall Lane to play Sheffield United and I kept my place in the team with Eddie still missing with what turned out to be a very long-term knee injury. I was so very nervous in the twelve hours prior to the game. I felt as if I was all set up to fail – having to prove myself in a position on the right of a four in defence and expected to support the attack in an overlapping role - that was completely alien to me. My build doesn't allow me to gallop down the wing. Attacking is not my game – defending is what I do. But again I managed to adapt and it went well for me in our 1-1 draw.

On the following Saturday we were due to play at Crystal Palace but Trish was expecting our third child by now and, after two false alarms, was in hospital the Friday night before the game with the possibility of giving birth. I had to decide whether to travel up to London that night to be with the squad or stay at home and wait for the call from the hospital. I was very anxious not to sacrifice my place in the team and Harry agreed to allow me to drive up and join the team in the hotel later on the Friday night after it became clear that nothing was about to happen with Trish. In the end, our baby boy Cameron, our third child of course, was born a couple of weeks later.

I felt thoroughly jaded during the game, played on a very hot afternoon at Selhurst Park, after being up late the night before, and was not playing well. We were 2-0 down at half time and my old Barnet team-mate Dougie Freedman had come back to haunt me yet again with another great goal. In the dressing room at half time Harry came in and all he said was: 'It's not over yet... we can get back into this game... we haven't played badly... if we get a goal their crowd will turn on them'.

156

We scored three in something like four minutes midway through the second half – including two rare goals in a minute from Jason Crowe – and were heading for an amazing 3-2 win. In the very last minute however, I gave the ball away, when a long ball up field from me was intercepted, and in the Palace counter-attack they came close to an equalising goal. In those moments, as a helpless bystander, all I could think was: *'If this goes in, it could be all over for me'*, knowing that, with what had been said to me by Harry in pre-season, I couldn't afford to make any such mistakes. I was going into these games with no idea where my future lay.

As it happened, to my disappointment, I heard the very next day that Middlesbrough defender Gianluca Festa had been signed. We went to the top of the league after beating Watford on Gianluca's debut, but it's difficult to celebrate when you're not involved. Obviously you want your team-mates to do well but, at the same time, you really want to be out there playing. I knew it was all over for me and, when the following weekend I couldn't even get a place on the bench, I became resigned to my Pompey career coming to an end. That led to me questioning God in my prayers about his plans for my future and whether that included moving to another club.

There were rumours around about Brighton being interested in taking me, and I was attracted to the idea if it would give me a chance to play. There was mention of their manager Martin Hinshelwood wanting to talk to me but nothing happened, and I heard later that Brighton's move for me came to nothing after their defender Danny Cullip's proposed transfer to Leicester fell through.

Events took another turn just a week later when Hayden Foxe's injury opened the door again for me. Harry pulled me to one side to say he wanted to play three at the back – myself, Gianluca and Arjan – at Gillingham, saying: 'I've been pleased with your attitude in training… you're more than just a squad player for me'.

I had heard this sort of talk, by other managers to other players, so often, and, whilst I was glad to hear Harry's comments, I reminded myself that I still didn't know if I had a long-term future with Pompey – that conversation with him in pre-season was still ringing in my head.

I made up my mind to play as if every game was my last, and, by my performances from then on I was happy to be proving a lot of people wrong. I wanted to go on doing that game after game. Never again would anybody be able to say that I was not good enough to play in this company. Being one of three at the back really suited me, having got thoroughly familiar with the system under Tommy Burns at Reading, and it helped to become settled and a regular in the team.

I was playing well and soon was taking my game to a new level of performance. I was so impressed with the quality and sheer professionalism of the players around me – players who were all doing their jobs to the letter. Arjan was a top professional with an extraordinary desire and dedication – the like of which I had never comes across before. He would think nothing of working long and hard in the gym after training and as a defensive group we would do extra sessions together – perhaps sharpening up our passing between ourselves – and through that we built up good friendships. Gianluca came with a good pedigree and it was a pleasure to play with such a mentally and physically strong character who always did his job well. They were a really down to earth bunch, with 'no big-time Charlies' and no showing off.

Up front Toddy (Todorov) and Vincent (Pericard) were regularly opening up defences. Vincent would batter them with his physical strength and hard work, and Toddy would kill them off with his sharp finishing. We could see his eye for goal from close quarters in training and in games and I rated him highly as a goal scorer capable of taking difficult chances. Carl Robinson was do-

158

ing a good job in midfield at this stage and Matthew Taylor was getting lots of praise and looked a real bargain buy.

We were playing with a great deal of confidence and showing an ability to kill teams off rather than giving them any sort of chance. We were going into games knowing we were likely to win, and that was a new experience for me that felt good, very good. What did surprise me was how quickly what was a new team gelled, and the ease by which we picked up points steadily from the word go. It was no strain and, for once, I was at a club with nothing going on in the background and no undercurrents. The only topic of conversation was the football on the pitch and how well we were playing. We were riding high and pulling away in what was a strong league with the likes of Wolves, Sheffield United, Norwich and Leicester in pursuit. No-one was thinking of promotion, literally taking one game at a time. We had really clicked and were a team people feared, not only at home but away as well.

Harry's style is to let players play and give them a free rein to do what comes naturally to them. He had signed players that season for what they could do, and allowed them to be free spirits, never one to want to change or influence their styles in any way. He's certainly never been one to complicate things too much in training. You don't need to do much when you are winning games the way we were in the League, and there was little need to spend time worrying about the opposition. Harry did training sessions with the defenders when we would work on various patterns of play and on rehearsing certain scenarios. He never criticises players in public, but is ready with his praise when it is warranted. Equally he will tell you quietly when you've gone wrong in some way.

Jim Smith worked so well with Harry, although they were two different characters, and they would bounce things off each other behind the scenes to good effect. Jim complemented Harry's approach with his direct, sometimes abrasive, style. If we were not doing well in some respect then Jim would tell us in no uncertain manner. Occasionally he would go too far and get close to the mark in his criticism such that, if you didn't know him better, it could be taken personally. But he never did it for any reason other than to get you to react, and it was always for the sake of the team and the club. In doing so Jim wasn't scared to use the f-word in five out of six words to very great effect. We used to find it quite funny at times, and his mouth would race on ahead of his brain once he had launched into a tirade. To everyone's amusement he once called me 'Rufus', after the QPR player Rufus Brevitt who had the same hairstyle as me, and didn't realise his mistake until someone interrupted and corrected him.

In contrast Harry is not given to outbursts and will tell you in a calm way where you have gone wrong or what is expected of you, always treating players like adults and having respect for your independence. A simple matter of give and take, you will get back from him as much as you give him in return. As a squad he set targets for us at the beginning of the season – 16 clean sheets, 75 points for the play-offs, etc, etc – and it was soon becoming clear that we were well on our way to easily achieving them.

Despite not being a huge influence or a big voice in the dressing room, coach Kevin Bond played a full part in our success that season, quietly working hard in the background and putting on the training sessions that suited our needs. Bondie was clearly someone whom Harry trusted and confided in a great deal.

Our 3-2 away win at Rotherham stuck out in my mind as one of our biggest tests, in a very challenging environment at a small ground with the noisy crowd close to the pitch. Harry got into an argument with the referee in the tunnel as we were going out over the colour of Shaka's cycling shorts that he was wearing under his shorts. The referee insisted that they should be the same colour as the shorts but no other cycling shorts could be found. So it was finally settled with Shaka having to roll up the cycling shorts to a level higher than the line of his shorts.

In an astute move Harry changed our tactics that day, putting Vincent out wide on the right, with a view to outjumping their left back. It worked a treat with Vincent scoring one goal, and setting up another. But it was a close run win after we had been pegged back to 3-2 and in stoppage time Shaka produced the save of the season, for me, to earn us another two points. Their forward shot from the edge of the penalty area and the ball was heading for the top corner of the net before Shaka tipped it onto the bar. I had already seen enough to rate Shaka highly; up there, for me, in the top three in the country.

When Coventry came to Fratton Park in mid October, under manager Gary McAllister, they were the first team to give us problems at home. They were a good passing team and Gary had done his homework on us. By working hard to stop Quashie and Merse playing we struggled to get a point from a 1-1 draw. But the following week we were absolutely brilliant in annihilating Burnley at Turf Moor in one of our best away performances of the season. Our preparations had been all but ruined the day before by a nine-hour coach journey caused by horrendous traffic delays that prevented us from training and working out our set plays. Despite some light training on the morning of the match, we were unstoppable. We scored just three but it could have been 6-0 and this against a team who were previously unbeaten in twelve games. We could tell that their players were clearly intimidated and scared of us.

Steve Stone made his debut in midfield that day, and he was a really big capture in our eyes with his great pedigree. Here was another big name and we were again amazed that Harry had been able to attract such a player to Pompey and persuade him to step down to our level. Our position at the top of the league helped but it was more evidence that players were convinced of our ambitions as to where the club wanted to be. Our performance that day at Burnley was a great way to introduce ourselves to Steve, and afterwards in the dressing room he was sufficiently impressed to say: 'There's nobody we should fear in this league, if we play like that week in and week out'.

Steve had so much to offer in addition to his great experience, with his work-rate, excellent dribbling, accurate passing and all-round consistency. He gave so much in midfield in games and, at 31 years of age, you need a lot of rest between games to maintain that level of commitment in the Premiership. Harry was astute enough to manage the situation carefully by allowing Steve to limit his training to just two or three days per week. If anybody is struggling for fitness for whatever reason Harry prefers that you miss training and concentrate on recovering for the weekend. Once out there on the training ground everything has to be done properly with every game, big or small, played as if it is for real – with the maxim: *'how you train is how you play'*. When the training ground pitches were wet and boggy that season and passing practice became difficult during the week it was noticeable that we immediately lacked fluency in our play on a Saturday.

By now I had picked up my first Supporters Player of the Month award and eventually went on to pick up six awards out of eight that season, to beat the club record, I believe. I knew I wasn't blessed with great ability, but always gave 100% and that was largely what the supporters were looking for and relate to. They saw something of themselves in me – someone who might not be the best in the world but who was working hard to make the most of his ability. They could recognise in me what was instilled into them – a desire not to give up or go down without a fight.

I even had the chance to play international football, being eligible for Jamaica on my mother's side. I was approached by the Jamaica High Commission in London again, after I had turned down an earlier approach whilst I was at Reading. It was an honour to be asked but the timing was not ideal and I was anxious not to compromise my career at Pompey by putting any extra toll on my body or risking injury by playing in high intensity games abroad. I was also anxious to spend as much time as I could with my young family and doing God's work with our newly-formed 'Faith and Football' charity. Not being one of the 'Reggae Boys' anyway, I never regretted my decision to decline the invitation.

In response to what God was doing for me I wanted to use the gifts He had given me for others. For some time Mick Mellows, Darren Moore and I had felt that we ought to be out there serving the community, and showing something of God's love for young people, but we were finding it difficult to find a suitable way to give help where it was needed. Our first venture, which also prompted the formation of our charity, came in the autumn of 2002. It was Robbie Porter, who was to become one of the volunteers at the Paulsgrove community league, who came up with the name for our charity, based simply on the fact that we comprised men of faith who liked football.

I had been going to Gosport every week for some time to help out at a mini football league being run by a lady called Tracey Jackson, who was a steward at Fratton Park, with help from the local police. The non-Christian league seemed to fill a real need to provide something for the children to do in the evenings. Aaron Flahavan was their original patron and, when he passed away, I agreed to go over, act as a patron and work with one of the teams. Mick came over to see what it was all about and immediately was convinced that such leagues could be our point of contact with local communities and fulfil real needs in areas of Portsmouth and surrounding districts. Mick already had skills in this direction having organised and run the Royal Mail Cup tournament in Portsmouth for teams from all over the world.

I felt that God had used my involvement in the league at

Gosport to lead us to extend the concept to areas in Portsmouth where young people were especially in need of opportunities to be encouraged and valued. In Gosport the teams formed themselves, thereby collecting the best players, but we were anxious to bring children together with a mix of abilities so as to ensure they had the opportunity to play football. So with the help of volunteers from the local churches, community wardens and the police, we launched our first community football league in Paulsgrove and Wymering serving nearly 90 youngsters – boys and girls between 7-13 years of age – who registered for the fortnightly competition at Wymering Community Centre. Before football came along the children had nothing to do in the evenings. A lot of them would hang around, and that's when some of them would get themselves into trouble.

Many of the youngsters had never played organised football before – they didn't have to be good players, all they needed was to be keen to join in and play. What we were looking to do was to enable them to enjoy their favourite sport whatever their ability in a safe environment with positive encouragement from role models. All shapes and sizes are totally immersed in their games – running and chasing all evening to earn points for their team, with no dissent to be seen. The overly competitive element prevalent in many local leagues is avoided and there are always parents and friends watching the children in their new-found means of enjoyment and building confidence and self-worth. A little girl who was disabled with cerebral palsy was one of the 'stars' who were welcomed into one of the original competing teams. There is plenty of rough and tumble but the youngsters quickly pick themselves up off the all-weather surfaces and get on with the games.

I like going along and chatting to the youngsters and I tell them that they don't have to be great footballers – they just have to try. You have to be there to see the pleasure on their faces when something they try comes off. The parents tell us that their children

164

tear their hair out in the week we're not there. But instead of getting into trouble they're out practising and training for when the games restart. We also found that youngsters want to help us out and not only play – they want to help us organise the tournaments and assist on the night. That's particularly true of the youngsters who are unable to play when they get too old for the league. The football isn't all about us trying to force the church on anyone. Obviously we're Christian people and we care. The spiritual side is important to us, but that's not all there is to it. We've built relationships and seen more and more lives change because of someone showing an interest in what they're doing.

A year later we opened another league in the Somers Town district of inner-city Portsmouth with similar support and interest. Since then further leagues have been opened in the districts of Buckland and Crookhorn in Portsmouth and Rowner in Gosport. Following his move to Derby County, Darren Moore has overseen the launch of a similar league in Handsworth in inner city Birmingham and the 100 places were snapped up in less than 45 minutes. These leagues are still thriving as I write, with us using football as a platform for serving the community, for developing relationships, placing the church at the centre of communities, and providing role models for young people.

Each league has its own end-of-season presentation evening every year at Fratton Park with the youngsters, their friends and families packing out the Milan Mandaric Suite to receive the medals and trophies, with every participant receiving a goody bag and a medal. We have also been able to take up to 60 teenagers, who don't get the opportunity to go on holiday, for a long activity weekend in the Hampshire countryside at YMCA's Fairthorne Manor, and organised Fun Days with barbecues for the families in various areas. Much of the money for these is raised from Charity Dinners/Auctions at Fratton Park each year supported by local businesses together with Pompey players and supporters.

Even some of the mums wanted to join the action and those who come to watch their youngsters in the Somers Town league in Portsmouth have challenged the organisers to a sponsored football match. We also launched 'Dads and Kids Kickabouts' where the Dads can spend quality time with their children.

It was great when our work in the community football leagues was the subject of features on both local and national television. BBC TV's Songs of Praise presenter Diane Louise Jordan interviewed me and filmed football action from the league based at Wymering Community Centre.

As I made rapid progress in my Christian journey Mick O'Brien sounded a note of caution for me not to run too far ahead of Trish and even warned that this might lead to frustration on both our parts which could bring moments of unhappiness. Being a novice I thought that all Christians went through the experiences and emotions I had, but Mick was in no doubt, telling me: 'God will push you forward in the fast lane – what you will experience in your first two years some Christians won't experience in forty years'.

I had a similar indication of what might lay ahead for me when we went to a meeting held by an American evangelist Tom Hall. When several people, including me, went up for him to pray over us he said to me, without in any way knowing who I was: 'You will go into areas where Christians have not been before, and there you will defeat giants'.

I had become convinced of Mick O'Brien's gifts too when, early on in one of our first meetings, he had told me, without having met her or known anything of her past, that he was aware of what Trish had gone through and of the hurts and experiences that had shaped her life and led her to become depressed. A month or so later the two of them met up and Mick spoke to her about her life in more detail.

Understandably Trish felt and resented that 'the two Micks', and God, were taking me away from her and the family as my association with them and my commitments to God grew stronger. So there was an increased strain on our relationship, and it was a difficult time.

Trish had always been there for me through everything I had come up against in football, but now I was running away from her, on my own on this great adventure, leaving her behind. At first I didn't feel or see what she was going through. I had got caught up in this whirlwind and I was working on the basis that the more I chased after God and got close to Him the more He would take care of everything else for me.

As much as we still loved each other, it made for a difficult year or so in our marriage. Trish had made little progress in her faith, and was clearly frustrated at what was happening to me. Spiritually I was being fed and nurtured 24/7 – as easy as being a Christian was for me, it was hard for Trish. Our friends Keith and Sam could see what was happening at an early stage and warned me, but I didn't share it with 'the two Micks' and just felt that if I was doing the right thing by God, then He would make it right. 'After all', I told myself, 'I could be out drinking, gambling and womanising!'

Trish put on a brave face, but her frustration at what was happening to me, at how I had changed, and more particularly how she was being left behind, came to the fore eventually, accumulated, erupted and was brought home to me. It all came to a head when she broke down in tears during a meeting with our church pastor at our home, and he made it clear that it was time for us to resolve our relationship problems and time for me to face a few truths. I saw how selfish I had been in my new life and how I had to get the balance right. For the first time I realised that I had never been taught how to be married and that, although we had our feelings for each other, I had to learn from the Bible how to be a husband and a father, and to apply the changes for myself. For no longer could I run on and expect God to sort out my marriage and my family.

Its not easy being the wife of a footballer with its insecurity and uncertainty, whether that's around the highs and lows of results and performances or the worries and doubts of contracts. It's never 'nine to five', with your husband at the beck and call of the football club at weekends, festive occasions, and for training camps. Often Trish has to share me with any number of people who want a piece of me whether it's out shopping or in a restaurant. Our family environment is very important to Trish and she ensures that we do everything as a family, with one meal a day together when we each get to talk about our day.

I still make mistakes to this day – sometimes I forget and run off to do my own thing, but I have changed into a more Trish-conscious person. With time there has been a slow healing and softening of her heart as Trish has let God renew her mind and into her life more and more. God let us know that for Him to work his power in our lives we had to be obedient. Now lots of things have changed in Trish's life as a result and she has found a peace, a growing self-confidence and positive outlook for her life as well as being a wife and a mother.

On the football front, despite my now regular appearances in the first team, I wasn't taking anything for granted and still didn't feel entirely established as a first choice in defence. There was still a hint of resentment in me towards Harry over what he had said in pre-season, and I still got a good deal of my motivation from a desire to prove Harry and Jim wrong. People were saying that Harry had made me a better player, but I was by now firmly playing for God to whom I wanted to give the glory for my performances.

At the end of October 2002, after that Burnley win, I was left out for the Preston home game, with another defender Paul Ritchie having arrived by now on loan from Manchester City, and Gianluca taking over from me. I remember Harry was ill that night and not at the game, and I was really shocked when, for no reason and with no explanation, my name didn't appear on the team sheet. From a man-management standpoint it left a lot to be desired. We scraped a 3-2 win but it was no consolation when the supporters told me: 'We struggled in defence without you – there wasn't the same understanding'.

I have always thought that if you're not playing well then you don't deserve to play. This time however, I felt: *'It doesn't matter how well I am doing, they will drop me if they get the chance'*, as if to prove to myself that I couldn't really trust them. That feeling was reinforced when one or two of the players confided in me: 'I can't believe you have been left out'.

On the following Saturday, with Harry's return, I was back in the side against a very direct and physical Leicester City team in a game that was a complete nightmare for the whole 90 minutes with the torrential rain turning the pitch into a lake. When we went out for the warm-up we were fully expecting the game to be called off. The referee said it was playable but the ball wouldn't move more than a couple of inches and when you kicked the ball it would often stop. If you went in for a sliding tackle you would find yourself sliding 10-15 metres away from your target. In our heads as we played we were all coming to one conclusion: *'We should not be playing in this'*. The conditions suited Leicester but, for us, as a passing team, it was a great disadvantage. At half time Merse told us that the referee had said to him that he would call it off if we equalised, but he obviously was reluctant to do so whilst Leicester were winning. The conditions caused Leicester's first goal when I slipped in blocking a shot, and was unable to recover my footing in time to stop their forward skipping past me and scoring from a yard out. I immediately thought: *'I bet I'll get the blame for the goal... I've got an eerie feeling that the finger will be pointed at me'*. In the event nothing was said, and when I

169

later watched a replay of the goal on TV, I was relieved to see that there was nothing that I could have done to prevent the goal.

At Wolverhampton the following Tuesday we had Arjan, Foxie, and Gianluca missing and I had to form a new central partnership with Paul Ritchie, with Steve Stone filling in at right back in our emergency. Our coach broke down as it was about to leave the hotel and we had to be ferried to the ground in a fleet of cars, not arriving until 7 pm for a 7.45 kick off. Shaka was in director Terry Brady's car with the team sheet, which had to be handed in one hour before kick off to avoid a hefty fine, and they had to jump red lights and drive down the wrong side of a road to get to the stadium in time.

It wasn't the best preparation for such an important game at a packed Molineux ground but it was a massive performance and result to get the 1-1 draw with a scratch side. It was real backs to the wall stuff and I was pleased with my own good solid game, which not only earned praise from Harry, but also from my good friend Darren Moore who was watching from the stand. I've always like playing at Wolves – it might have something to do with the fact that I once was linked with a move there under manager Colin Lee and felt the need to prove to them that I was good enough to be at their club.

Three days later the 2-1 win at Derby, one of the favourites to go up, was one of the many great away performances of that memorable season. We knew it was a big game for Jim Smith, returning to Pride Park where he had been manager, and he spent far more time than usual in our dressing room geeing up everybody beforehand. We went behind early on to a penalty but had the confidence to come from behind and win, despite being under a lot of pressure in the second half. It was a big victory, keeping up the momentum and, firmly at the top of the table, taking us further away from the chasing pack. The winner came from Mark Burchill, one of the handful of us survivors from the Rix

170

era. Burch was a good finisher, but, after his serious knee injury, we could detect an understandable fear factor in his game when the tackles were coming in. You could see the worry he had about full-blooded tackles and that obviously affected his game.

Our performances were giving us a solid belief and a feeling of invincibility, knowing that we could cause teams problems. Even if we didn't start too well in games, we were convinced of our ability to come through to win, and so it proved, time and time again. The thousands of our supporters who travelled away from home that season were simply tremendous and very vocal – we often felt as if we were playing at home. We took so much satisfaction from being able to reward them so often, and it was just great to see their joy at some of our performances. After all that many of them had suffered over the years it must have been simply amazing to watch, week after week. On a personal level I had come from not being wanted or part of Harry's rebuilding plans to being at the heart of the club's seemingly relentless march to the Premiership. I knew only too well that it was all down to God's power being demonstrated in my life.

'Serve wholeheartedly, as if you were serving the Lord, not men'
Ephesians 6.7

12
Amazing transformations
2002-2003

As each weekend passed there we were still, almost permanently it seemed, sitting at the top of the league and everybody's favourites for promotion to the Premiership. As we approached the vital Christmas/New Year period I was looking forward to going back to the Madejski Stadium but on the day I was surprised to be greeted by some booing from the Reading fans. It only served to increase my determination to put on a performance that would prove to people there that I was good enough to play at that level. Reading manager Alan Pardew couldn't resist getting in a dig in my direction just ten minutes into the game - I'm sure it was just to wind me up. Recalling that under him I would sometimes tire in the last quarter of games, he shouted in my direction: 'You're getting tired already!' My reaction to that attempt to psyche me out was to look Pards in the eye, and point up to heaven. He smiled back, knowing of my faith and that I was referring to my faith in God and the strength I was obtaining from Him. I was well satisfied with my performance in our goalless draw, but, for good measure, Pards couldn't resist one further dig afterwards, this time via our fitness coach Jon Dalzell, by saying: 'Linvoy never seemed to be that quick when I knew him'.

Matthew Taylor was making a name for himself that season and he came up with brilliant, priceless goals at Nottingham Forest and Leicester. Mattie is a confident lad with a great left foot, and we had often seen him shoot with such accuracy from a distance in training. Since then of course he has produced astonishing long range goals in the Premiership.

When we were drawn to meet Manchester United in the FA Cup third round we knew it would be our biggest test of the season and that it would be seen as a measure of our Premiership credentials against one of the top teams in the country. I had never played at Old Trafford before and it was an exciting and new experience, even if I was more anxious and racked with nerves than usual. As we walked out I was struck and, just for a few moments, overcome and intimidated by the sheer enormity of the stadium. The welcome and ticker-tape from our supporters, numbering 9000 and massed at the top of the stand behind the goal at the far end, was one of the highlights of the season.

Immediately United put us under enormous pressure with their tremendous pace, passing, and, more than anything else, their dazzling movement. I was completely undone after just four minutes, giving away a penalty after bringing down Ryan Giggs. When he ran across me with the ball his pace was such that, in attempting a tackle, I was too late and ended up taking him and not the ball. It was two soon after when David Beckham bent in an unbelievable, trademark free kick from 25 yards, when we thought we had all the angles covered. I was hugely impressed with that effort in particular, ruefully thinking, as we prepared to kick off after the goal, that I could now see what all the fuss surrounding Beckham was about.

It was amazing to be on the same pitch as the likes of Beckham, Van Nistelrooy and Keane but we did ourselves proud. After pulling it back to 1-2 we might have equalised if Nigel Quashie had not missed a great chance in the second half. Nigel was not

173

renowned for his goal scoring, but you do wonder how much difference it might have made if he had not squandered that golden opportunity. Two late goals gave the 4-1 scoreline an unflattering look but we were not too disappointed afterwards. The cup was not any sort of priority and in truth there was some relief that going out of the competition would mean a weekend off to recharge our batteries in readiness for our final promotion push.

Two new signings in the January transfer window – the Nigerian striker Yakubu and the former England midfielder Tim Sherwood from Spurs – impressed everybody on arrival and gave us a huge lift. The Yak was very quick with a real eye for goal, and great body strength into the bargain. It was soon apparent that he wasn't match fit, not having played for a while, but he looked capable of doing plenty of damage to opposing defences, as it soon proved. We knew that Harry had been chasing Tim since the summer and it was a sign of the respect we all had for him when, at his first training session, our usual practice match was played at a particularly high tempo with all the lads at pains to impress him. Inevitably when a big name player comes in someone has to drop out and it's a tribute to the professionalism of people like Vincent Pericard up front and Lassina Diabate in midfield that there was no obvious resentment on their parts.

We went into a bit of a stutter through December and to the new year with a number of draws and only one win in seven in the league, but we were still at the top and there was really no panic amongst the players. The experienced players like Merse, Shaka and Stonie, who had done it all and seen it all before, would tell us it would come right again, and we had no reason to disbelieve them. The squad took a lot from the confidence they exuded and our promotion drive duly took off again in February and March kick-started by a 6-2 home win over Derby in which we looked so much sharper and quicker than we had done in the preceding few weeks.

My contract was due to expire in the summer and, after meeting Harry during January, I was offered just a one-year extension with a small increase in wages and better appearance money. It was nowhere near Premiership money but I felt I had no choice other than to accept, with the chance of playing Premiership football hopefully coming up on the horizon.

The recruitment of Jon Dalzell, a specialist fitness coach, introduced a different formula and approach to our fitness training – in particular higher intensity work over shorter periods - that bore real fruit after just a couple of weeks. For me the speed work, in particular, often with a bungee cord around my waist for resistance purposes, was really beneficial and made me fully realise, what I had always suspected, that I was built for speed and that I could be really quick over short distances. Our work with Jon took me and the squad to another level fitness-wise and added another dimension to our game at just the right time.

Physio Gary Sadler is not only very knowledgeable, very thorough and a key member of the medical staff but popular for his dry wit and positive nature. Gary is meticulous with his treatment of injured players and will err on the side of caution rather than risk a player going back into training too soon. I always joke with him that I am 'high maintenance' in that I often need some therapy from Gary, or his fellow physio Ian Catchpole, to help my body prepare for the rigours of training, perhaps in the form of some back manipulation to loosen up.

Chris Neville, our masseur, is another key member of staff who has also been the England masseur for some years now. Most players have a massage daily on their legs and back to help warm up the muscles and remove any stiffness after training or a game, so Chris and his assistant Colin Clement are kept very busy. It's more about prevention than anything else in that, after a hard work-out, muscles can tighten up which leads to pulls and tears. Relaxing the muscles in this way enables them to heal and aid recovery, particularly after a game, which is something that Gianluca Vialli first introduced to the English game at Chelsea.

Whilst I am handing out plaudits to the backroom staff I must mention Kevin McCormack ('Big Kev') our Kit Manager who works more hours than anybody else at the club, and without whom the club would fall apart. Kev says he is *'the masking tape that holds everything together'* and no-one would dispute that. He will help anyone in any way he can and is truly an unsung hero at Fratton Park.

I had now reached a consistently high level of performance week in and week out that had previously eluded me in my career. I was playing for God and my prayers, before each game and during the game at times, were being answered in the form of these performances. I had found a peace on the pitch and a stillness of mind that meant that my head was not filled with the sort of tension and pressure to perform that had previously constrained me. No longer did I feel anxious to please everybody and that stress that I put myself under had gone. God had changed me and that allowed me to play with a freedom to express myself and reach my full potential. I felt detached, with my head no longer full of the game and its pressures. No longer was I striving or trying any harder to play well, now it was effortless. I was doing the same things in my game as I did five years ago but now I had confidence in my ability. I found myself timing my tackles and headers better, feeling physically stronger and, stamina-wise, lasting games better. When the praise, the plaudits and the awards came my way my faith kept me humble, just knowing it wasn't out of my own strength but God's power at work in me.

Kevin Harper was an unsung and underrated hero of our promotion that season with some vital contributions, none more so than his performance at Leicester – a crunch first v. second game – in which Matthew Taylor scored a spectacular equaliser. Both teams were on top of their game, not wanting to lose, and we were chuffed to get the draw against a team who always seemed to get a result against us. Harps gave everything that night, as always, with his usual high work rate. He never gave defenders an easy time with his strong running and pace on the ball, and they would know they had been in a game when he was around. With his fiery character Harps was an aggressive tackler for a winger and most Pompey managers during his time at the club wanted him in their team. Unfortunately he regularly picked up niggling injuries, probably down to that high work rate, that meant he never got a lengthy run in the team.

By now the media were rating us as certain for promotion but no-one in the camp thought it was done and dusted. I had never been in such an exalted position before, but I was never one to count my chickens and it was always at the back of everyone's mind that we might suffer from some sort of 'blip'. It was not unknown for teams in such a position as ours to blow up, miss out on automatic promotion and have to settle for the play-offs. We knew we had to retain our consistency, keep our concentration and drive, and focus on getting to that finishing line. The experienced voices in the dressing room, like Merson, Hislop, Sherwood, Stone and De Zeeuw, provided all the reassurance and calm we needed, after Harry and Jim had had their say and left us to ourselves.

I always felt that Shaka brought success with him to the club when you consider his talismanic record in the game right from his time in college football in the USA. His college went to a final for the first time ever when he was there and then Reading got promoted on his arrival. Newcastle went into the top six during his time and then Pompey were promoted in his first season at Fratton Park. After moving to West Ham from Pompey the Hammers promptly reached the FA Cup Final and then to cap it all Trinidad qualified for the 2006 World Cup finals with Shaka in goal.

Shaka is a big man who commands his area well without ever being too vocal, and he gave us defenders great confidence. He's a great shot stopper and can be relied upon to make key saves at vital times, and stop penalties regularly. It was reassuring, as a defender, to know that if a striker went past you then it was very unlikely that he would be able to take on and beat Shaka in a one-on-one. He is a happy-go-lucky model professional, very intelligent and a real family man who never lets things get him down. With his degree in mechanical engineering Shaka worked at the NASA space agency in the States before moving into professional football and I would pull his leg about it and say: 'All you can manage is a game of Space Invaders on the computer'. I roomed with 'tall man', as I would call him, and he would fall asleep within two minutes of getting into bed – a habit that had earned him the nickname 'Dropsy' in his native Trinidad.

All away fans were barred at Millwall that season so it was a pity that our fans missed our outstanding performance at the New Den early in March. It was strange walking out to be greeted by silence with our usual terrific support conspicuous by its absence. For some reason this unreal situation seemed to give us a lift and we proceeded to overrun Millwall in every single area of the pitch scoring five without reply. We were in such total control, and scored some brilliant goals, not least a fantastic individual effort from Toddy in which he skipped past several defenders like a ballet dancer before hammering the ball past the keeper. Steve Claridge was in the Millwall side that afternoon, and, typically, came into our dressing room afterwards to say: 'Well done, all the best for when you go up, as I just know you will'.

Three days after thrashing Millwall 10,000 of our supporters travelled up to south-east London on a blustery evening in party mood fully expecting us to dish out more of the same to Wimbledon at Selhurst Park. We too were all geared up to take the three points but we couldn't find the same magic touch and, although we looked OK, we just weren't firing on all cylinders that night. So Wimbledon duly spoiled the party with a late winner to inflict a surprise 2-1 defeat on us. We were more upset and disappointed at letting down so many of our supporters who had come so far after work in midweek, than we were at dropping the points. Harry had been linked with some of Wimbledon's players – McAnuff and Reo-Coker in particular – and the fact that they were out to impress him on the night didn't help our cause.

We were soon back in the groove however with successive wins over Norwich, Wolves and Coventry, and in beating the latter 4-0 away from home we were back to the irresistible form we showed at Millwall three weeks earlier. With six games left we had the chance to clinch promotion against struggling Sheffield Wednesday at home. There was a high level of expectation amongst our supporters, and, on the car radio on my way to the game I was listening to them 'phoning in with details of their celebration party plans for later that night. But we knew that the Wednesday players would be fighting for their lives given their bad situation at the other end of the league table. Ironically Lee had been recalled from a loan spell at Wednesday ten days earlier and scored our opener against them, only for two late goals, including a farcical winner in the last minute, to put an end to all those party plans temporarily. We were left to deal with a huge anti-climax in the dressing room after the game and an inquest into Wednesday's winning goal. One of their players had intercepted a free kick from Gianluca Festa who maintained that he hadn't actually taken the kick but was moving the ball to the right spot. There was confusion over the referee's instructions for the kick and some real misunderstandings over his decision to award the goal. It proved once again that you can take nothing for granted in football, but it really wasn't a case of if we were going to get promoted, rather a case of when.

We had another chance three days later in a re-arranged game

179

at home to Burnley – in fact we only needed a draw - and this time the tension level was even higher. That was increased when word reached us in the dressing room beforehand that their manager Stan Ternent had told his players: 'Let's be party-poopers, and make sure they don't get the result they need'. When we were awarded a penalty at the Milton end in the first half I really thought, as Merse stepped up to take it, that we were on our way, so it was a real shock when he missed with a shot that hit the bar. That racked up the tension even more and, just before Toddy scored the winner a quarter of an hour or so before the end, Burnley had what looked to me like a justifiable claim for a penalty turned down.

We and all our fans knew that we had done it once Toddy had scored and it was an absolutely brilliant moment - as if someone had just released a valve from a pressure cooker. An explosion of relief engulfed the stadium and from then on, as the whole ground rocked with all the singing and chanting, there was absolutely no way in which we were going to let go of that lead and it was just a question of counting down those fifteen or so minutes until the celebrations could begin. When the final whistle went I fell on my knees, with a huge exclaimed 'Yes-s-s-s'. It was an incredible moment and every emotion of happiness – joy, satisfaction and no little relief - was there. The fans were quickly on to the pitch and we were soon engulfed and struggling to get to the dressing room. Down there was champagne everywhere and we spent what seemed like hours taking congratulations and finally getting changed. Everyone in my family was there and we just couldn't get away from the ground until about 11.30 pm. Then we had to fight our way through the traffic to get to the local Marriott hotel for an impromptu party until about 3 am.

I had said to Trish about two years earlier: 'I've never won anything with a team in my career, you know', and that remark came back to me that night as I savoured the feeling. It was a proud moment for my Mum and Dad and they knew, having always shared things with them, what I had overcome in my career to reach this point of achievement. I remember thinking that God can do anything with the confidence He has given me, and that, as important as the achievement was as a team and for me individually, the reality was that, in changing my life, God had done it for me.

We had the next day Wednesday off before travelling to Ipswich on the Thursday for our Good Friday game at Portman Road. Merse was insisting that we had to go up as champions but, after all the celebrations, we looked and felt really jaded. The supporters knew only too well why we were not at our best in the 3-0 defeat. The following Sunday evening came our last home game against Rotherham and a chance to secure the title. In many ways there was more emotion and excitement than the Burnley game 12 days earlier when we had clinched promotion. I can never remember hearing such applause as we took the field and there were flags everywhere. Before the kick off there were the various Player of the Year awards to be handed out and I was fortunate enough to take four of the six. When the ceremonies were over my name was chanted by the fans as never before, in acknowledgement of my achievement, and the sound of it echoing around the stadium made the hairs stand up on the back of my neck and took me close to tears. I still feel so thankful to our fans for giving me those awards and for the reception I received that night.

After the 3-2 win there was another pitch invasion and the fans were grabbing players and lifting them into the air – Merse was lifted highest like some sort of king. Words can't describe the feeling of exhilaration we all felt as Merse was presented with the trophy on the pitch. After we had individually received our medals, everybody erupted with joy and it was simply the biggest moment of my career up to that point. I remember thanking God so much for blessing me, the team, the club, the fans and the city with this achievement. I was pleased for the Chairman Milan Mandaric whose dream had come true and who had made the decision to appoint Harry as manager, and for Merse who had driven us on and turned us all into winners. I thought of all the dozens of people who had contributed in so many ways, but particularly of the medical staff who had largely been responsible for introducing Jon Dalzell the new fitness coach who had taken us ahead of the game.

Our final game at Bradford was the perfect ending to a perfect season. Gianluca Festa had started a football boot company and we all decided to wear his company's white boots to mark his last game before returning home to Italy, although there weren't enough for Lassina Diabate to wear a pair when he came on as a substitute. When Harry saw us all putting on these boots in the dressing room he was a bit concerned that it might be seen by the Bradford players as 'taking the mickey' and provoke an angry reaction from them, but nothing would dissuade us from going ahead and honouring Gianluca in this way.

Gianluca was one of the very few outfield players not to have scored that season and we had been ribbing him about his failure to score. Bradford put us under some pressure early on, but amazingly Gianluca scored our opening goal after 20 minutes, after getting surprisingly far forward in support of a breakaway attack. Our 5-0 win turned the game into one big party, and Shaka was happy for Yoshi to take over in goal for the second half to enable him to share in our success.

We ended the season with 97 goals for and 98 points to our credit, but even that drew a tongue-in-cheek comment from Jim - always demanding more: 'You could have made it 100 goals with 100 points with a little more effort'.

Pards 'phoned me with his congratulations at the end of the season and I was touched by his call – our friendship, despite the damage done, went deeper than was usual between a manager and player. He put our performance into perspective: 'You've achieved something 92 teams set out to do - to try and be champions in their respective leagues. But only four teams achieve that'.

After the years of hurt and torment Pompey fans had suffered in supporting their team it made us so happy to reward such really special people, who had finally come out of the shadow of Southampton at last. It was amazing to be part of it and, when we took our bus tour of the city and then on to Southsea, it was simply astonishing, even though it was a rainy afternoon, to see so many thousands of fans cheering and clapping.

Harry gave a speech when we stopped for the main event in Southsea, and pledged: 'We are not going to be in the Premiership for just one season'. Those words brought home to me the challenge that was ahead of us next season and how, even now, people were looking for us to go down. On the personal front, through my performances that promotion season at the end of which I was voted the Professional Footballer's Association Divisional Player of the Year, I felt I had earned the chance to prove myself in the Premiership but I could not have imagined what challenges lay ahead for me.

13

Premiership challenges 2003-2004

Obviously I was anxious to play in the Premiership and felt, by my performances and the part I had played as 'Player of the Year' in the promotion season, that I had earned the chance to prove whether I could cut it at the top level. I had been given no assurances in that respect however and I sensed that, yet again, I was under-valued and faced another battle to get into the team. That foreboding increased when Harry's summer signings included not one but two international defenders with European experience, first Dejan Stefanovic and then Boris Zivkovic, both of whom could play in the centre of defence and at full back, to supplement Arjan De Zeeuw and Hayden Foxe.

I was disappointed when Merse left and felt that there should have been an element of loyalty to him from the club after all he had achieved. Originally I was confident that he would stay and saw no reason to think that he couldn't make it in the Premiership given that he had played for Aston Villa at the top level in the season before moving to Pompey. It seemed to me that he wanted to stay but it all hung on the possibility of an extension to his contract, to which the club seemed reluctant to agree.

In order to correct a small problem I had a groin operation during the summer and on our return to pre-season training, I appeared to be struggling and not in my full stride during a running session one of the coaching staff commented to me that: 'You don't look right'. When I had to remind him that: 'I have just had an operation', it began to dawn on me that perhaps I didn't figure too prominently in their thoughts and plans for the new season. Even my chances of competing for the right back spot were scuppered by the signing of Sebastian Schemmel.

During the pre-season tour of Scotland we suffered a few injuries and I was included at Dunfermline, but at left back where, being distinctly right footed, I felt so uncomfortable and out of place. For our final friendly at home against Feyenoord a week later I didn't make the squad thanks to a back spasm, but a week later, despite being fit, my worst fears were realised when I wasn't included for the Premiership opener at home to Aston Villa.

Just a few days before that season's opener Toddy (Todorov) suffered a very serious injury in training that eventually, as we know now, caused him to be out for a year and miss out on our first year in the Premiership. It came about as, with training almost finished for the day and Harry saying: 'Just play until the winning goal', Toddy chased back to retrieve the ball. He went to turn with the ball but, after planting his foot down, his studs got caught in the turf causing his weight to be twisted through his knee. His scream of agony and immediate collapse to the ground left us in no doubt of the seriousness of the injury. We all felt for him and since then, of course, Toddy has had more than one operation and months of rehab. Even now he is fit he has suffered from other niggling injuries – something to be expected as the body tries to adapt to the demands of training after so little activity for so long.

Toddy's injury, and similarly serious knee injuries suffered by my close friends Lee Bradbury and Darren Moore, are a reminder of how fragile and tenuous our football careers are and on a knife-edge virtually from tackle to tackle. I consider myself so blessed not to have suffered a serious injury of any description. If

I do, I just hope I can find the depth of character that people like Lee, Darren and Mark Burchill have shown in fighting back to resume their careers.

With the addition of signings like Teddy Sheringham, Patrik Berger, Amdy Faye, Jason Roberts, Alexei Smertin, Harald Wapenaar, not to mention early arrivals Dejan, Boris and Sebastian, it was like being part of a new squad and for me yet another challenge, with the urge as strong as ever to prove everybody wrong. As the season unfolded, with no place in the starting eleven, I felt somewhat hard done by, not even to be given the chance to fail, if nothing else.

Teddy's signing was a real coup – yet another 'wow' – and we were almost getting used to welcoming big star names. We knew all about his quality of course, but he too brought huge experience and technical ability, and that unique 'presence' to the club – the sort of 'presence' that Merse had brought to such devastating effect a year earlier. Teddy was portrayed by some in the game as arrogant and somewhat aloof, but I didn't see that in him at all. He was just someone who simply enjoyed playing football and even after all those years in the game was still like a big kid in training.

By the time Patrik Berger arrived I had stopped pinching myself at the prospect of training every day alongside people who I had only ever watched on TV in big games. But it was still slightly surreal to have people like Teddy and Patrik as team mates. To have such quality around makes training so special and gives everybody a lift. Such quality rubs off on you day after day – you just know that you are with gold medallists who will perform at a high level every week. It really challenges you to consistently match that every week if you want to be in the team with them. Initially it's intimidating but then it's enormously encouraging, as the days pass, when you get to realise that you can compete and match these guys in training.

I found being on the bench week after week as an unused substitute very discouraging – with the names of Zivkovic, Schemmel, De Zeeuw, Stefanovic, and Foxe ahead of me in the defensive pecking order - and it became difficult to deal with as the situation dragged on towards Christmas. Knowing that I was out of contract at the end of the season didn't make the situation any easier to cope with. I did finally make my Premiership debut when I came on for Sebastian, albeit for the last few minutes of the 4-1 home win against Bolton that took us temporarily to the very top of the table. Gary Sadler, our physiotherapist, adequately summed up my feelings when he said afterwards: 'At least you can say you have appeared in the Premiership now'. In fact it meant that I had appeared in all four leagues with Pompey and my previous three clubs.

Not playing has a real effect on your home life with an unfulfilled and unhappy husband, with no way of letting out his frustration, around a wife who increasingly feels helpless in that there is nothing she can do or say that will help. The football world is all-consuming and the whole family's life revolves around that game on a Saturday.

As time went on and I continued to warm the bench, I developed a real fear, as a central defender, of coming on as a substitute in the Premiership. The games are played at such a high tempo that, having come on, it takes a while to get used to the pace. If it's a tight game with the defence under pressure then, if you're not ready, there is a good chance of making a costly mistake. The longer I went without coming on the worse it got. Every time someone was injured my heart would jump and I would be praying that they would recover. When Dejan took a knock at Wolverhampton, stayed on but struggled to carry on, I was warming up constantly, up and down the touchline, really dreading having to come on as his replacement. Being left on the sidelines for so long had made me unsure of my ability at that level and severely knocked my confidence such that I began to doubt whether I could handle the responsibility.

By early November 2003 I had completely lost my focus and, with the team sitting comfortably in mid-table at this stage, there seemed little chance of getting picked to start. That realisation brought a build-up of real frustration and it didn't help that my usual preparations through the week for the Saturday first team game were disturbed by having to play for the reserves on a Wednesday and having to train on Thursday and Friday when I really needed that time to recover.

I had been going through the motions for the reserves but when we played against Arsenal's second string at Fratton Park I found myself up against one of their hot young prospects up front and I simply couldn't cope with him. My pace and my timing had all gone, in fact all my strengths were to no avail that night. All I could think of was: *'I want to get off this pitch - I know this isn't me'*.

Andy Awford, the reserve team manager, could see that something was wrong and soon after half time I was substituted. He must have thought I had a physical problem, little did he know that for the first time I had a real mental problem. I was a very angry and frustrated figure in the dressing room – frustrated with my performance, frustrated with Harry and more particularly with myself for not being able to express to him how I felt. Gary Sadler joined me and asked: 'Is everything OK with you, Linvoy?'

I explained the whole situation to Gary – how I was not being challenged in the reserves, how I was struggling to get motivated for the games, how I was in the last season of my contract and whether I should leave the club to get a better future. Knowing my character and honesty, Gary sympathised with me and encouraged me to see Harry and tell him how I felt, adding: 'I'm sure Harry will listen to you and understand your situation'.

After the game, when I knew he was alone in his office in the club's admin block, I went up to see Harry: 'Gaffer, I need to have a word'. It was the first time for nine months or so, since we had talked about a one-year extension to my contract after the game at Brighton the previous season, that I had spoken to Harry on a one-to-one basis.

I started off: 'I just can't do this anymore - play reserve team football and play well. I can't do the things I usually do. I'm struggling. Perhaps I could go out on loan or have a move so I can play first team football?'

Harry said: 'I've watched you in training and your attitude has been poor. I can't pick you on those showings.'

In reply I just said: 'Well, if possible I would like to go out on loan so I can get to play'.

We parted with Harry promising that he would think about my situation, but I was no more certain of my future after the meeting then I was before going up to his office. I knew deep down that he was right about my attitude and that in displaying a 'can't be bothered' approach to training I had been trying to attract his attention to demonstrate to him how unhappy I was. In my mistaken way of thinking I had thought that the only way to show him how it was affecting me was to perform badly – that he might be moved to ask me the reason. With hindsight it would have been healthier if I had confronted him earlier with my feelings.

But I couldn't escape the feeling deep down that even if my attitude had been right it wouldn't have made any difference and I still wouldn't have been preferred to the new signings. I knew that one of the unwritten rules in football was that the manager's signings are always selected first, and particularly those on higher wages. I knew that it cost the club less to leave me out than those international players.

Looking back on that whole episode I can see that my anger, resentment and frustration with the situation were clouding my mind, and know now that those strong emotions that had taken me over didn't come from God. I was relying on my human instincts rather than trusting God as I had done before. But I had gone through five months of not playing and sitting on the sidelines. I had prayed about it but nothing had happened to change the situation and I had begun to mistrust God. When I had faced rejection at the start of Harry's first season in charge God had immediately brought about a change in me that had transformed my situation at the club.

Now I began to wonder whether God was telling me to wait, testing my patience and faithfulness; whether He was preparing me for a new adventure at another club; whether my time at Pompey was coming to an end. All I knew was that I was finding no peace in the situation. Every player will tell you that if you are fit and not playing then being a footballer is a very difficult life.

A week later I had a phone call from an agent representing Crystal Palace to enquire whether I would consider going on loan there, but, despite my earlier desperation to get away to play, when it came to it I wasn't too keen on spending all week in London away from the family and decided to sit tight at Pompey to see how things would develop.

Then I found myself having a real set-to with John Mac over the situation, but it was just what I needed to shake me out of the pit of self-pity I was sinking into. John had a right go at me on the 'phone, saying: 'I've spoken to Harry and you've got to listen to me carefully. I'm speaking to you as my son on this – if your attitude is not right then you've got a problem at the club'.

That made me cross and I interrupted John, saying: 'If that's what Harry is saying then he's challenging my honesty and integrity because I always give 100%'.

John came back at me: 'So why is he saying your attitude isn't right then? Look here Linvoy... what's the time now?... 1.30 in the afternoon... you shouldn't be talking to me... you should be doing extra training'.

Afterwards I was angry inside particularly over John appearing to side with Harry. I had raised my voice to John – something I had never done before. I sat in the car for five minutes and soon, not only was God urging me to apologise to John but insisting that I take his advice and get down to extra training. I was urged to get back on the manager's side and do things right otherwise I could find myself without a club and out of the Premiership. So I had to swallow my pride and hurt that I had felt at two major figures in my life telling me my attitude was wrong.

I called John back to apologise for the way I had spoken to him and agreed that I would take on board all that he had said. My second call was to John Dalzell to tell him that I wanted to focus on getting fitter and to arrange extra work with him to which he agreed with immediate effect.

My focus had completely changed, much of my frustration had dissipated and I felt that I had got my head right. John was working with me on my preparation for games as a sub – based on the premise that I was going to start each time. However the extra fitness work had no immediate effect on my prospects and I was still watching games from the bench with my chance of a start appearing just as slim.

When we walloped Leeds 6-1 in early November I was ignored when the chance to make some late substitutions came up. But poor results at Fulham and then at home to Leicester left me sensing that the team were struggling and I did manage to get a two-minute none-too-confident appearance as a sub at Middlesbrough.

Harry was careful, and even canny, with the players he signed in that he was at pains not to bring in any 'bad eggs' who would give him problems. It was at this time that his relationships with both Boris Zivkovic and Sebastien Schemmel went sour, and it quickly became clear, for different reasons, that both didn't want to work with him, or even be around him for that matter. Sebastien's position deteriorated when first he was upset at, as he saw it, being made a scapegoat for our defeat at Fulham, and then when he asked for a week or two off to go home to France for family reasons to which Harry objected.

Boris felt strongly that he was not being played in his strongest position as a central defender where he played for his national team, but Harry saw him as a full back. When Boris then went public with his complaint and also criticised Harry's coaching methods, it hastened his exit from the team and eventually the club. His performance in our 2-1 home defeat by Everton, when he made a monumental error to let in Carsley for the vital equaliser, was clearly the last straw for Harry, who blew his top in the dressing room – one of the rare times I saw him let rip in such a way.

I was on my way home from the match listening to the post-match interview with Harry on the local radio station – 107.4 The Quay – when, after hearing the manager complain about his team's defensive performance, the interviewer Sam Matterface asked him outright: 'Why don't you play Linvoy Primus?'

Harry immediately responded by saying: 'OK, I'll play him. He's playing next week at Southampton'.

I just couldn't tell if Harry was being serious or merely flippant with Sam – perhaps reacting on the basis of: 'You pick the team then, you know best'. But when Steve Rolls, part of our 'Faith and Football' charity, called me to say: 'Did you hear it, Lin? You've only been picked to play next week', I began to wonder whether this was the break I had been waiting for.

When it came to training on the following Monday everybody seemed convinced that I was playing. That feeling in me was reinforced when significantly I was switched to right back in a rearranged midweek reserve team game at Fratton Park against Crystal Palace in front of the watching Harry. Strangely enough I made the exact same error that Boris had made against Everton, in allowing the winger to get in behind him, that had cost him so dearly, but no goal resulted for me. Before the game Andy Awford, the reserve team manager, said to us: 'There are places up for grabs in the first team – so the chance is there for you all this afternoon', to which one player replied: 'Someone's already grabbed his place!'

As the big local derby against Southampton, five days before Christmas with a Sunday lunchtime kick off, drew closer I was included in the Friday and Saturday team play preparation as Harry changed the formation, but it wasn't until the morning of the game at the hotel that I finally had the confirmation that I was playing. As a result I didn't have too much time to get nervous. I hadn't played in the 2-0 defeat in the Carling Cup game at St Mary's three weeks earlier and surprisingly I didn't find the atmosphere as intimidating as I expected. I was chuffed with the massive cheer I got from the Pompey fans when my name was read out over the PA. I was determined to enjoy the day whatever happened in the game. I prayed to God: 'This game is for you'.

We started well enough before conceding the decisive first goal on the half-hour through an own-goal from an in-swinging corner which deceived Harald Wapenaar in our goal. We didn't finish too well in the 3-0 defeat which gave the Saints fans the bragging rights, but I was pleased at how it went for me personally. Hundreds of their fans signalled the score to us on their fingers as we left the ground in the coach and it was hard for me to take as I knew how the defeat would hurt our fans. I am not sure that some of our team, as outsiders who didn't come from the city of Portsmouth and had little interaction with the fans, really knew how deep the rivalry went. Portsmouth and Southampton are not considered as big cities in the UK in football terms and not having played each other too often this derby didn't seem to mean too much to outsiders. Our build up was as professional and thor-

193

ough as usual but I didn't sense the sort of extra nervous tension in the squad you would expect for a big derby match.

Harry never ever said whether my change in attitude had influenced his decision to give me the run in the team which followed. Our next game, at home to Spurs on Boxing Day, was special for me against the team I had supported as a kid. As I was warming up out on the pitch before the game I could see their team in those famous shirts and I was hit with a powerful realisation that I had made it to the top league playing against the top teams and the top names in the country.

The pace of the game in the Premiership was quicker than anything I had previously experienced but I was hugely encouraged that day to find that, in runs and sprints, I could match anything and anybody I came up against. But you have to be on your toes every second and there's not a moment when you can switch off. Your concentration levels have got to be a lot higher than in any of the other divisions. For me the secret has always been to keep it simple and not try anything complicated.

As much as it was a challenge that I positively relished, I found myself excited by coming up against big-name players, particularly when we went to Stamford Bridge the following week. The profile of the game is so much higher in the Premiership and I had to rapidly get used to the extent of the coverage and how everything was highlighted throughout the media. I used to worry about being shown up on live TV games at Barnet and Reading, and even Pompey initially, but you are being watched all the time in the Premiership and I have got used to the same level of intensity and interest each week. Darren Moore had told me, from his experience at that level, not to be worried by the close media analysis, whether it's TV, radio or the newspapers, to which the action and performances in the games were subject, and not to let any adverse comments from the pundits affect your confidence.

There's no hiding place in football with so many platforms

now on which the fans can express their opinions about you or the club, whether it's phone-ins, internet message boards, fanzines or letters columns in the local newspaper. They can give you a distorted view of what the fans are thinking. You're always likely to hear or read something that you don't like or agree with, whether it's on a personal level or about another player, so I tend not to watch, listen or read what people or the so-called experts are saying. It can take only one critical letter of comment to start you questioning yourself which is emotionally draining. I used to worry about what people thought of me, always wanting to be the one who did well and pleased people. But I realised that you just can't listen to everybody's opinions, or change them for that matter, and they are usually so varied and contradictory anyway.

Within a few games I was feeling part of the team and comfortable in the Premiership, even though we were teetering close to the relegation zone just outside the bottom three. Some fans even kindly said that I should have been in from the start of the season. When Petri Pasanen, another defender, arrived on loan from Ajax I felt I had done enough by now to hold on to my place. I needed about four games to get into the rhythm of it and it's so important to have such a run to help you get settled.

Harry pulled off another coup in recruiting Eyal Berkovic to replace Tim Sherwood who we had lost to injury. In his first few training sessions we marvelled at his skill and unique passing ability. Here was a really positive signing who could find a pass to open up a game and steal a goal in a way that few players could match. Again Eyal was a player who fitted in with the way Harry wanted the game played.

Eyal made his debut against Manchester City which was a big game for us, given the position we were in, in which we defenders found ourselves up against two top strikers in Nicolas Anelka and Robbie Fowler who gave us big reality checks that afternoon, despite our 4-2 win in a brilliant match. First Anelka scored with

195

an instinctive first-time volley that was simply world-class and then Fowler gave me a real 'Premiership moment', one that made me realise that I had arrived at the very top level and that I was witnessing pure Premiership quality. The ball was loose and I was confident that I could get there in time and make a challenge on him before he had time to get in a shot. I didn't think he had the time to peel off a shot, but with no back-lift whatsoever he smacked a shot from 30 yards out against the crossbar.

The two FA Cup ties in February 2004 against Liverpool will live long in my memory. At Anfield the hairs on the back of my neck stood up, as we walked out, at the sight of this famous ground and the sound of their 'You'll Never Walk Alone' anthem. To play against and match Emile Heskey and Michael Owen gave us defenders such confidence and Mattie Taylor's great equaliser gave us the replay at Fratton Park we deserved for all our hard work. To compete with Michael Owen was unbelievable and I wanted to ask him for his shirt afterwards but thought it might be disrespectful as if it was some trophy involved.

At Fratton Park in the replay a week later the referee Matt Messias awarded Liverpool a penalty for a handball against me. In fact it was Liverpool's Milan Baros who had handled and, after we had protested with Eyal leading the strong vocals, the referee changed his mind after consulting a linesman, which was a very rare occurrence. Then amazingly Mr Messias awarded another penalty after a legitimate challenge from Mattie, but Shaka pulled off the sort of save that we knew he was capable of from the spot kick by Owen. It was a very rare goal from Richard Hughes – his only one for the club as I write – that took us through in a famous victory. One key tackle of mine on Michael Owen has stayed in my mind from that game. The ball was played to him and with a touch he flicked the ball on with the outside of his right foot. Then he sharply turned and went after it with a turn of pace, but I was able to read it, turn, go with him and then get half a yard on him that enabled me to make a heavy tackle and take the ball.

Both Arjan and I were out of contract at the end of the season and by now we were both free agents and able to speak to other clubs, not having signed a new contract before the end of the previous year. Then, out of the blue, in the week between the two Liverpool cup ties, the club approached us with the offer of new contracts and at the same time told the local newspaper of their offers to us. My agent John Mac was unhappy that the club had not contacted him in the first instance, but I couldn't help thinking that a club approaching me about a new contract was something of a first for me, having always, seemingly, had to chase after clubs with a begging bowl.

Arjan and I felt in a strong position negotiation-wise because of the form we were both in, the extra effort we had put in and having proved ourselves in the Premiership. We reasoned that, even if we were relegated, the club would need the pair of us as an investment for the future. Arjan is financially astute and I took advice from him on the length of contract and the relative clauses. The negotiations dragged on for about a month and, whilst I was happy with the two year deal on offer, I found myself at the lower end of the Premiership wage levels, and subject to a substantial reduction on relegation that was worrying, despite some lengthy haggling.

When I moved to the centre of defence, where I most enjoyed playing, I found myself, in partnership with Arjan, unbelievably almost, up against Alan Shearer for Newcastle at Fratton Park. It was another huge challenge for me against someone who I had watched so many times for club and country. I knew that it was my job to mark him out of the game and that it would require a great deal of concentration and discipline to ensure that I didn't give him a second to play. You knew that you had to be ready for a physical game against him, but funnily enough he didn't look too confident that afternoon. But he still gave me no peace

197

at all, always getting in a challenge when I was trying to clear the ball whether in the air or on the ground. In no way unfairly, he cleverly used his body, when jumping with you, to put you off balance. The more I took on and triumphed in challenges against players like Shearer the more confident I became.

I make no apologies for talking about Arjan again. It's just because I felt so confident alongside Arjan because of his total reliability. He would win nine out of ten of his headers and tackles, and his commitment was second to none. Everything he did was to the limit, to its ultimate end. What a top professional and such a strong character with a real never-say-die attitude. We had a togetherness and a bond borne out of a strong desire to do well, borne out of all the work we had done together after training on our fitness and on different ways of passing the ball out of defence. We built such a good understanding and would drive each other so hard to go on getting that little bit of extra out.

We lost 5-1 at home to Arsenal in the sixth round of the FA Cup in a quite remarkable game, for lots of different reasons, but it was possibly my best performance in a Pompey shirt. The build up to that game was huge with so much national press attention after we had knocked out Liverpool in the previous round. I had never been that far in the Cup before and we were genuinely confident of causing an upset. But we found ourselves up against an extremely good Arsenal side who were simply superb on the night, with Thierry Henry on another planet with his skill, touch and movement.

By now we had become used to being featured live on TV and I was told afterwards that the studio pundits Alan Hansen and Peter Schmeichel had said that I had a chance of playing for England on the form I showed that night. I was certainly pleased with some vital tackles of mine, and in particular one piece of skill I showed in beating Henry before clearing the ball. Henry gave me his shirt at half time, without being asked, as if to say that I deserved to have it. I had great respect for him after that gesture to me.

Our fans were simply amazing that night with their unbelievable support – chanting: 'We're going to win 4-3', when we were 3-0 down, and singing not only for us but in appreciation of Arsenal's performance and Thierry Henry's in particular. I know from what the Arsenal players said to us afterwards that they had never come across anything like it. The fact that Henry put on a Pompey shirt before leaving the field at the end of the league match at Fratton Park a couple of months later was a mark of his appreciation for the reception he had received from our fans in both games.

Other than the great technical skill in the Arsenal team, I was struck that night by their athleticism and high level of fitness. Patrick Vieira in particular impressed me hugely in that respect. I recall that we had a corner and, when it was cleared, I ran stride for stride with him as Arsenal counter-attacked. When this attack broke down I was struggling for air after the chase, but was astonished to see Vieira running back at pace in an attempt to retrieve the ball. I remember thinking: *This guy is so, so fit!'*

Before that Arsenal game I was interviewed by The Sun's chief football writer, who happened to be a friend of Harry's. He opened the interview by saying: 'When Harry first saw you play he thought you were no good and wouldn't have a future at Pompey. His view on you has really changed to the point where he doesn't know what's happened but something in you has changed'.

My reply to The Sun reporter, which rather took him aback, was largely summed up as follows: 'It was my faith that had got me through my difficult times in football'. On the Saturday morning before the match that night The Sun had my interview on their back page under the headline: 'God is on my side'.

In fact I remembered that some weeks before John Mac had told me: 'You're one of the few players that Harry has ever

199

changed his mind about, and now you're one of the first names on his team sheet'.

By now early matchday arrivals at Fratton Park, just after one o'clock, had grown accustomed to seeing me wandering up and down the touchline in deep conversation on my mobile 'phone. They probably thought I was 'phoning Harry's bookmaker placing a bet for the 1.30 at Wincanton, but I was praying with Mick Mellows who was by now part of the Pompey chaplaincy team. We usually speak for about ten minutes; not praying for the outcome of the game, of course, but that I can glorify God by what I do on the pitch that afternoon. As I am speaking there's always the same group of fans who keep shouting: 'Linvoy, get off the phone. You've got to get in that dressing room for the team talk'.

For our return to Liverpool in the league we were full of confidence following our cup exploits against them, and we worked for two days beforehand on our game plan. But we found Liverpool to be a completely different kettle of fish this time around – very sharp and quick, with a much higher level of aggression than we had encountered in our three previous unbeaten encounters with them that season. Steven Gerrard was unbelievable and Hamann scored with a thunderbolt after six minutes to really put us under the cosh. I remember turning to Arjan after that goal and saying: 'That wasn't in the script!' We escaped with a 3-0 defeat and afterwards Jim Smith said to us (omitting his usual colourful language!): 'If you think performances like that will keep you in the Premiership then you had better think again. More performances like that and we'll get relegated'.

So we had ten games left to pull ourselves out of the bottom three and the first of those against Southampton at home was, for us, more about the three points and starting off a run of results than any local bragging rights or avenging our two defeats at St Mary's that season - although the fans would probably have seen things differently. It really was, as people are in the habit of saying, a 'massive' game and there was an FA Cup tie-like atmosphere with every side of the ground singing and masses of blue and white ticker-tape. Certainly the atmosphere was much more intimidating and intense than that at our two previous meetings at St Mary's and there is no doubt in my mind that even some of Southampton's big players, like Niemi, Lundekvam and Beattie, were affected and daunted by it and didn't play. Those sorts of occasions and atmospheres positively lift me.

For some reason we felt invincible that afternoon and full of confidence. I never felt that we were going to lose, that feeling reinforced when Yakubu scored with 20 minutes left, even when Kevin Phillips hit the post in the last minute. Having experienced players that you could rely on in the side, like Steve Stone and Teddy Sheringham, was a key factor that day and in the games to come. We felt so happy for the fans that we had restored the bragging rights for them, but more importantly we knew how vital it was to our chances of retaining our Premiership status. A common theme heard around the city was that Southampton had helped us to stay up and, as it transpired, that win set us off on a run of good results that propelled us to safety.

Our win at Blackburn the following week was a huge result, given our away record that season, and it was largely down to Lualua, on loan from Newcastle, who came on and proceeded to terrorise their defence in a way that only he can. Harry had recognised that he was a free spirit who could win you games. With his potential Lua was showing why Newcastle paid over £2 million for him from Colchester.

By now, where possible, we were flying to games from Southampton or Bournemouth airports but on our return journey from this Blackburn game we arrived at Manchester airport to find that the aeroplane had broken down and was unavailable for the flight back. I remember that we had a very long, but happy, journey home by coach that would have been unbearable if we had lost the game.

We took a point from our next game at Charlton to take us ever closer to our target of 40 points. I returned to The Valley as a Premiership player for the first time since my release, and I took a lot of satisfaction from my display that afternoon. It had been ten years since I left Charlton, but, no matter how many times I return, I always feel the need to show them what they are missing.

Our subsequent 3-1 home win over Birmingham took us very close to safety but it was the sending-off of my old friend Maik Taylor, close to half time, which was crucial. Ironically it was my punt upfield that led Maik to handle outside the penalty area which led to his dismissal and the free kick from which Dejan Stefanovic scored for our opening goal.

Moving to right back for the visit of Manchester United next I found myself marking Ryan Giggs and, knowing his history and ability, it was another challenging pressure moment for me at the highest level. Just before kick off, as we lined up, I made eye contact with Ryan and stared him out. He looked away with a somewhat sheepish expression, and from that moment I knew I had won the battle before we had started. I had psyched him out. It came naturally to me, being something I had done before at Barnet and Reading, usually in the centre half versus centre forward situation. By now I was relishing the challenge of taking on famous names and was full of confidence. As a team we were playing well, having won three of our last four, and with our home record, knowing by now how intimidating Fratton Park could be for visitors on such a big occasion, there was a strong belief in the squad that we could turn over United.

Very early in the game Nigel Quashie made a big tackle on Scholes that seemed to set the tone for the afternoon. Every time Giggs got anywhere near the ball I was up close to him, rarely letting him run at me. I was coming in quick on him, forcing him to lay the ball off quickly for fear of being dispossessed. When Stoney gave us the lead in the first half it felt as if we had already done something amazing but the job was only half done. We came under enormous pressure in the second half and I have rarely headed so many balls clear as I did in those frantic last 15 minutes or so. At that time the win was one of my greatest moments in football for what we had achieved against one of the giants of world football, and, on a personal level, I must confess to enjoying the accolades, such as Man of the Match, that came my way from the press afterwards. I even looked in the Sunday papers, to check on my high performance ratings, which I was not in the habit of doing I hasten to add.

A win at Leeds in front of a big intimidating Elland Road crowd the following Sunday lunchtime made us virtually safe, but, by now, I was struggling with a hamstring injury that had seriously curtailed my training for some weeks beforehand. I managed to get through the game despite being gripped by pain from the hamstring every time I chased James Milner as he started to sprint past me. Funnily enough that injury caused me to feel valued and recognised by Harry. He was happy to continue to keep me in the team despite missing training all week and receiving constant treatment instead. I saw another side to Harry in that he demonstrated to me how loyal he was to players who worked hard and did the business for him.

I only lasted 22 minutes against Fulham before the hamstring injury became too much to bear and Richard Duffy had a chance at right back. My season was over with three games left, but there was still time for some drama to unfold before the summer when there were strong rumours that the Chairman and Harry had fallen out over Jim Smith's future at the club. Initially it was all just whispers and murmurings but it wasn't long before it all went public with Harry strongly resisting any changes to his management team. Soon we were glued to the TV where it was embarrassing to watch and listen to all the counter-accusations and wrangling being aired via Sky Sports News.

After all our good work in staying up and the positive vibes from the season it all seemed most unfortunate and unnecessary and was making the club a laughing stock by the way it was handled. Much of it appeared to centre on the Chairman's wish to modernise the coaching network – something that harked back to Boris Zivkovic's comments earlier in the season. There was an uneasy truce eventually and, as we headed off for our summer break, we finally put it down to the usual sparring between Chairman and manager that was often played out at clubs up and down the country. Little did we know that it would re-surface to devastating effect a few months later.

By now Faith and Football were continually being invited to visit schools and colleges with the teachers encouraging me to share my faith wherever I went so hundreds of youngsters across the city of Portsmouth and beyond came to hear my testimony. I hope it's been a powerful message for the youngsters who hold professional footballers as role models. Since 2003 I have addressed dozens of school assemblies and academic achievement and award presentations, attended Christian Union meetings and RE, Citizenship and Personal Development/Life Skills lessons, as well as promoting literacy and other educational schemes. Wherever I go the youngsters' faces light up at the sight of a Pompey player – they all know about the football club even if, for many, they don't get to go to the games.

I am also a real fan of 'Alpha' – the course that aims to introduce people who don't go to church to the Christian faith and to explore the meaning of life – and I remember going on one in the spring of 2002, soon after becoming a Christian. The course was great and there were about 15 of us, including a Pompey team-mate Stefani Miglioranzi, meeting at Keith and Sam's home.

It covered a lot of things – the whole range of Christian truths – and I found it very instructive. We were all at different stages but we all grew together and built friendships in a totally different environment. It definitely worked for us and we wanted to go on meeting so we have continued as a house group ever since.

Pompey were the first football club to host an 'Alpha' course in the autumn of 2003 and since then up to 250 guests have been coming to the Milan Mandaric Suite at Fratton Park for invitation suppers to launch the courses twice a year. Faith & Football'have undertaken to co-ordinate and facilitate the running of free city-wide 'Alpha' courses in Portsmouth in both the spring and autumn each year and it provides a great means for Christians to invite friends and help them discover what Christianity is all about. I am usually invited to speak about my faith and experiences in football. Many people who have come, whether to seek God or just out of curiosity, have found God and had their lives transformed.

More recently we have arranged 'Youth Alpha' courses and our vision is to bring them to all the Portsmouth city and surrounding area schools for all those students who may be interested in what the Christian faith has to say about God. The courses are available on a purely voluntary basis, with parental consent organised and run by Christian teachers and Faith & Football team members. Our first schools 'Youth Alpha' course has just been successfully conducted in conjunction with Milton Cross School with the enthusiastic support of the head teacher together with the committed Christians on the staff and local church members, and more are planned in other senior schools in the coming months.

'Your light must shine before people so that they will see the good things you do and praise your father in heaven'
Matthew 5.16

14

From India to Pompey upheaval 2004-2005

Faith and Football's next mission to India in the summer of 2004 came about through an introduction from the Elim Oasis Church in Portsmouth, who were supporting the work of the Mustard Seed ministries at an orphanage on the island of Goa. The pastor at the Elim Church had invited us to visit the home that accommodates, feeds and educates children who are abandoned and orphaned in Goa and see what we could do to help them at that time and in the future. It was one of a number of invitations we had received in the preceding months from overseas but we felt that God was drawing us to visit Goa after two separate people, with no connection with each other or the Elim Church, had mentioned the orphanage concerned, Shalom House, to us as worthy of a visit.

It was exciting for us to take our mission to another continent and, after visiting Nigeria two years earlier, I felt like a veteran of such trips with none of my previous trepidation. However hard it might be, I knew that it would be worthwhile and rewarding, but little did I know how much fun we would have amongst the group - eleven guys and one lady, Naomi - who flew out of Heathrow bound for Mumbai. It was such a bonus to have Darren Moore on the trip and very soon he was making me laugh at his fear of insects, flies, germs and infections and the variety of tablets and sprays he was taking to combat and repel every known contingency.

With the stop in Kuwait, it was a long and exhausting flight to Mumbai and, by the time we finally landed, I was suffering from tiredness, jet-lag and a serious bout of heartburn brought on by the two very hot curries served on board by the Kuwaiti airline. Luckily I had packed two boxes of dry oatmeal bars and was happy to consume several of those as my first meal in the YMCA hostel, where we were based, rather than face another curry. In fact I came to rely rather heavily on those bars in the coming days, rather than risk an early attack of a 'bad belly'. On our third day I foolishly let Darren have one and he got really excited at this unexpected treat.

Our guide for the trip took us to an underground Christian house group, based in an area where native Indians who are Christians are under threat of persecution, and it was good to join them in praying and praising. There were lots of tears from the Mumbai group when they allowed us to pray for and with them. For me, as a relatively new Christian, it was both humbling and encouraging to come across such faith in such circumstances and witness how real God was to them.

Whilst in the city we organised some football coaching for a private school and shared our testimonies, through an interpreter, with the parents and children, that led to several being converted and joining the underground Christian house group.

After three days we took the nearly nine-hour train journey to Goa accompanied by our 33 items of luggage that not only included our suitcases but several carrier bags stuffed with footballs and football kit. The station was absolutely packed and our first priority was to negotiate a price with a porter for loading our luggage amongst the cows, goats and chickens on board.

The intense heat, the lack of air coming through barred windows, and the hard upright seats – not to mention the absence of any fluid - made it a long and uncomfortable journey. In fact Mick O'Brien became somewhat dehydrated and, in desperation, we did manage to discover an abandoned, half-consumed bottle of 7-Up drink on a chair in the carriage that Mick was only too happy to swig, to the disdain of Darren and I. But we had not got to that level of desperation for a drink.

Our journey took us through some tea and rice plantations before encountering some remote countryside, with the train gradually emptying at every stop and the heat becoming even more intense as we neared midday. We were worried about unloading our entire luggage in the time allowed for a stop at each station but, as it transpired, we were joined in our carriage by an Asian football team with whom we made friends. They were only too happy to make a long line through the train so that the luggage could be quickly passed down the carriages and on to the platform at great speed.

An old bus transported us to a guest house, with very basic facilities, close to Bagga beach but we were advised not to bathe due to the dangerous currents. Shalom House was built on high ground to prevent flooding from the nearby fields and was situated close to a shanty town in which cows wandered around at will. By the time we got to visit the children I really felt that 'this is the place where we are needed'. All the children came out excitedly to meet us, calling us 'Uncle', and calling me 'Booker T'(an American wrestling star with dreadlocks). Very soon we were hearing the heart-rending stories of the circumstances surrounding the entries of some of the children to the orphanage. We were amazed at the way in which the lives of these orphaned and abandoned children had been transformed through their devoted Christian house parents. They were lovingly restoring hope in lives, which were formerly in situations where there was no hope, through a vibrant home life and education opportunities.

Many of the children had previously faced danger every day living on the streets, deserted and abandoned, trapped in homelessness, begging or their disablement. The streets were not safe, not least from rats roaming around at night scavenging, even attracted by human flesh. To avoid them we noticed that the taxi-drivers, whilst waiting for fares, would sleep on the bonnets of their cars or on the walls rather than sit or lie on the ground. Now the lives of the children at Shalom House had been rescued from the dangers of the night and the streets.

We met Kumar who had been spotted in the garbage dump area of Panjim in Goa. He was a severely undernourished child, who was totally abandoned by his parents as he was mentally retarded. He was being looked after by an old lady who had no shelter herself and they were living in a paper house. He suffered acutely, both mentally and physically, and was dirty and filthy when he was found, his stomach bloated and in need of urgent medical attention. He also had hearing problems, but, with support from a generous donor, the doctors at the local hospital operated on him and we heard that he is now able to hear much better than before. He is learning to speak and is now attending a school for children with special needs. We found Kumar to be a delightful young man but, at 19, he has the mental age of a much younger boy. He will always need support but he now has the security and loving home he needs at Shalom House.

Gabrielle came to Shalom House after being found at the railway station living like an animal with long hair, torn clothes, dirty, smelly and heavily infested with scabies. As soon as he was found he begged and cried for food, as he had not eaten for days. His parents used to send their children out on the streets to rob every day, and if they did not bring anything back they were severely beaten. When he was only four, following another beating, he left the house and jumped on a train. For the next few years he travelled all over India moving from compartment to compartment begging for food. The police often beat him after detaining him on the trains. After four years at the orphanage Gabrielle is a lively, happy and healthy boy who is always chatting. His emotional scars have healed considerably through the love, security and support of his house parents.

One of the children had previously lived on a garbage dump for 13 years. He couldn't speak and was barking because he had only ever communicated with dogs. He had been pulled off the tip and, after three years in the orphanage, was just beginning to speak a few words and then to form sentences. When you see that you just think: *'What else can we do to help these children and enable others to be rescued?'* In India you can see children looking after little babies on the street and washing themselves with the rainwater from the gutter. People say that it's only one life, but I could see that one life can change another life and so on. It is possible to change lives and I know that brings such happiness inside. I find it really, really humbling.

The accommodation for the fifteen children in the house was surprisingly basic with none of the comforts we take for granted, and with access to old and worn, but scrupulously clean, clothing only. During our five-day stay we saw loads of love showered on them however and the level of discipline was amazing – with 'No' meaning 'No' to them – and immediate responses to every request without question. It was a real eye-opener for us and we couldn't help comparing it to some of the indiscipline in the UK. They enjoyed the football coaching and impromptu matches we organised for them and the children from other neighbouring schools in a nearby field. When we were challenged to a game by a local adult team I got the chance to show off and score two goals as a striker.

When we visited a local church with the children on the Sunday the pastor told us that he had often prayed that God would send somebody to help him in his work with the poor and needy in the area. He took us to a piece of land in the village of Brittona where he dreamed of building a new medical centre, school and orphanage to help both the young and the elderly who are without any medical facilities. The plan was for the building project to house young people from the streets who would be provided with accommodation, education, food and water, health care and schooling. Mick O'Brien spoke for everybody in our party when he told the pastor: 'We want to help you and we will raise the funds from England so you can realise your vision'. From that day our Faith & Football fund-raising mission was established and drove our challenges in subsequent years to walk the Great Wall of China and trek through the desert to Mount Sinai.

My time in India was another experience that shaped my life, and even more so now, as I reflect on the freedom, opportunities and advantages we have in this country. It comes home to me when I meet and speak to youngsters here and try to emphasise to them, during my visits to schools in particular, what great opportunities they have and help them to recognise how important it is to realise their full potential. I think of all the youngsters out in India and Africa who have so little opportunity to do more with their lives. I know that for every one child who is rescued from a life of begging and homelessness there are fifteen others who are not, and you just feel compelled to help them to obtain a passport out of poverty and deprivation into the dignity of employment and accommodation.

The trip had reinforced my belief that I wanted to go to different countries and make a difference to people's lives. It's a calling in my life and it feels like the most natural thing for me to do.

It was after my return from India, whilst I was away with the family on holiday in the summer of 2004, just before we were due to return for pre-season training, that I received a surprise 'phone call from John Mac, my agent, to say that Norwich, newly

211

promoted to the Premiership, were going to put in a bid for me, and would I be prepared to consider moving to East Anglia. After I had got over my initial shock at the approach, my first reaction was: 'Obviously I've got to do what's best for my family.'

I was conscious that a year ago I had not been part of Harry's plans and I could not be completely sure that my place in the team or even the squad was assured for next season. On the other hand I had just signed a new two year contract three months earlier and the family was really settled and happy in the area. For the first time since we had moved out of London we had found a place we could call home. But in football, of necessity, you are always looking for more security, but would trying to secure this prejudice our happiness in the future?

In the space of two seasons I had gone from not being wanted by Pompey at the start of the first, to being wanted by another club at the start of the next. So there were a number of uncertainties and issues to be considered and we returned from holiday to find that Norwich's interest was being reported extensively in the press. Initially Norwich and their manager Nigel Worthington didn't make a formal approach, and Harry didn't mention the matter on our return to training, so I was not put under any pressure to make a decision.

Obviously I prayed about the situation with Mick Mellows who told me that we must follow God's will: *'If He wants it to happen it will, if not He will shut the door on it'*.

Norwich finally tabled a formal bid and then it was a question of whether Pompey were prepared to accept it. The newspapers reported that they had turned down a bid of £500,000 but that Norwich had come back and increased their bid to £600,000. Through John Mac I was allowed to obtain details of the actual terms on offer, and the wages were substantially more than I was earning currently, with a year longer on the contract. So it was clear I had the opportunity to set myself and my family up and have a year longer in football. There was a big decision to be made.

Whilst we were away on our usual pre-season West Country tour, word did reach me from home that Harry had been talking about me in the local newspaper saying: 'He's been brilliant and he's got a big part to play next season. I like Linvoy. He's been fantastic and I want to keep him'. The key to all this for me was finding out what the club's thoughts were as far as letting me go was concerned. So, with the squad and management having travelled to Woodbury Hotel for the tour, it gave me the chance to tackle the Chairman and Harry there and then on the issue. So I asked to see them and met with the Chairman Milan Mandaric, the Chief Executive Peter Storrie, and Harry on the hotel patio. I was very nervous and uncomfortable as I walked over to them, whispering under my breath a quiet prayer: 'Lord, speak for me'.

I sat down with them and first they invited me to have my say: 'Obviously I know that Norwich have made a bid, and I know that the terms they are offering me include another year over and above my present contract. It's a fantastic offer but what attracts me more than anything is the security of another year on my contract. I believe that that this club is on the verge of great things and I want to be a part of that, but I've got to think of my family and the opportunity this offer gives me to be financially secure and in a better position than I've ever been'.

I think they realised that it wasn't a question of greed on my part but the Chairman stressed that: 'As easy as it is for us to give you the contract you want, it's hard, given that you've just agreed and signed a new contract'. After some small talk, that included some appreciation from them of my efforts for the club over the past two seasons, the 'meeting' was over after no more than ten minutes, with Mr Mandaric closing it by saying: 'I'll let you know what our decision is after talking it over with Peter and Harry'.

Two days later I had a phone call from Mr Storrie to say that the Chairman was prepared to extend my contract and give me a pay rise. John Mac went to see him and discovered that the pay rise didn't match the Norwich offer, and the one year contract extension was subject to a certain number of games being played by me in the two years left on my existing contract. I told John that, despite all that, I was happy to stay at Pompey and I duly signed a new contract in August, just four months after signing the last one. It would have been a really hard decision if I had to go and I just couldn't see myself playing anywhere else other than at Pompey. With the relationship I had built up with the fans and the city it seemed like a part of me.

Throughout that whole period of uncertainty, from that day on holiday when I first learnt of Norwich's interest, I felt at peace with the whole situation with none of the frustration or anxiety that I'd felt before in such matters affecting my future. That was through putting it all into God's hands and I felt that I was blessed by my final decision.

Once again, as we worked through pre-season, I had no indications from Harry as to whether or not I was in his plans, but the fact that I started all the friendly matches and was playing well gave me no reason to think that I wouldn't be included from the off. It was still a great feeling to find myself starting the season in the team for the first time under Harry, and we welcomed a couple of new full backs in Andy Griffin and David Unsworth. David got straight on the score sheet with a penalty in our opening home 1-1 draw with Birmingham, but our first away trip to Charlton was marked by a rare mistake by Shaka that cost us a point.

With his Premiership experience, David was another big signing and he made a big impression on me immediately as a good, confident and often boisterous character who was a natural, enthusiastic leader with a strong voice in the dressing room. He

214

liked to enjoy life but was in no way a 'big time Charlie'. I always felt David had all the ingredients to become a successful coach and it will be interesting to see how his career develops.

We had a pretty decent start, sitting in 8th position by the time Manchester United came to Fratton Park in late October 2004. We were confident that we could pull off another win against United and this time we had to take the game to them rather than coming under a lot of pressure from their attacking flair. Our 2-0 win was a good deal more comfortable than the previous season's narrow and nail-biting triumph. It gave the defence, with myself and Dejan in the centre and Arjan at right back for once, a great deal of confidence to match the likes of Wayne Rooney and Alan Smith all the way.

By the time we went to Villa Park the following week, and were woeful in a 3-0 defeat, there were strong murmurings around the club that there had been a 'falling out' between the Chairman and Harry. At that stage however there was no hint that Harry would resign. Their dispute, which appeared to, once again, centre around Mr Mandaric's insistence on dispensing with the services of Jim Smith – for what reason I never ever did get to find out – had resurfaced, and probably had never quite gone away. The word was that the Chairman wanted to freshen up the coaching side of things and was concerned that the club was not making sufficient progress on youth development. With this in mind it seemed that Mr Mandaric was keen to bring in a Director of Football, and that apparently was something that Harry would simply not tolerate.

It took me back to the season in which Graham Rix found himself with Harry as Director of Football looking over his shoulder, and it seemed really ironic that it was Harry who was involved with the situation reversed. With years of management experience behind him, Harry was tactically astute and knew the game inside out. From an attacking perspective, as far as the first team is concerned it was just a question for him of getting the ball to the sort of players who can unlock teams through their special abilities. For Harry it was quality players who won games, not tactics or coaching.

In the week before we travelled across to St Mary's to meet Southampton in the big, local derby match, there were press reports appearing with the news that the former Panathinaikos Sporting Director Velimir Zajec was set to join Pompey from Greece in a Director of Football role and Harry was expressing his surprise at the possible appointment.

When, as predicted, Zajec did arrive he was introduced to us by the Chairman as 'someone to oversee and help Harry'. It seemed just like any other addition to the management team, in this case perhaps someone to act as a go-between for the Chairman and Harry. Clearly for Harry it was an ominous development. Other than Dejan, who knew of him as a former player and manager at Panathinaikos, none of us had heard of him, but we were told he had a great deal of knowledge of European football and it's players. It struck me how uncomfortable it would be for Harry to have someone overseeing your every move, and how inevitably it must end up as a battle of wills. Certainly there was strong evidence that in England, unlike Greece, the Director of Football role was untenable, and it didn't help when it soon became clear that Zajec had no defined role. He could not have guessed what sort of situation he had walked into or what turmoil his appointment would bring.

Zajec would say 'hello' to us, but otherwise he had no contact or input with the players. There was a noticeable change in the atmosphere at the training ground, merely caused by his presence alone and Harry's obvious discomfort. We knew full well that Harry was far from happy, not from anything he said to us, but from his reaction to Zajec's arrival, heavily reported in the press. Again I was reminded that this all mirrored the Graham Rix scenario, and we all began to wonder whether Zajec too would become the next manager just as Harry had replaced Graham in the same context. As if to reassert his authority Harry was at pains to confirm to all and sundry: 'I make the decisions and pick the team', but it was clear that something had to give. It was all very unsettling for the team, knowing that there was so much more on Harry's mind than team matters.

We followed up the defeat at Southampton by losing at home to Manchester City – three defeats on the bounce – but then, as seemed almost inevitable in the end, the storm broke. First Jim Smith resigned and the next day it was Harry's turn to go, claiming that he needed a break from the game. The players were in a state of shock; somehow we knew it would happen, but then again thought it would never happen. One or two of the players openly expressed their personal disappointment, but the overall feeling was that, despite two or three bad results, it was such a shame in the light of our good start to the season, and the chance we had to push on and establish the club in the Premiership. As a player, when a manager goes, selfishly you always wonder about your future under a new manager, but on this occasion I wasn't over-concerned – after all I had just signed a new contract and was established in the team.

After he left Harry made straight for the training ground to say goodbye to the players. Very often managers leave clubs without seeing the players – the last time I bid farewell in person to a manager it was Terry Bullivant at Reading. Clearly it was harder for Harry to walk out on the team than it was to leave the senior management behind. He shook hands with each player individually and addressed us collectively, saying: 'You've been a great bunch of lads – it's been great to achieve what we did together. Unfortunately it's time for me to move on'.

There was no doubt that a subsequent interview the Chairman gave to the Daily Mail, and which took up the whole of the back page, increased the animosity between the Chairman and Harry. In the interview Mr Mandaric was bemoaning the £3.4 million in agents' fees the club had paid during Harry's time. It was something that was best left unsaid and, to my mind, tarnished our promotion season by its inferences. It caused such great offence to Harry, clearly inflamed the situation and sparked his move to Southampton. Despite what had been paid out to agents for the necessary transfers, it was surely a price that was worth paying given where we were in the Premiership as a result. It all seemed so unnecessary and could have been done differently.

Like everybody else we were shocked when Harry moved to Southampton. I'm not sure that he fully realised exactly what he had done. It was almost a knee jerk reaction and perhaps not gauging the extent of the hatred and resentment felt by the Pompey fans towards their neighbours or the level of betrayal they would feel.

Looking back now on the whole affair it's obvious that strong emotions were allowed to rule the heads of the parties concerned and, not only did that break the friendship between the Chairman and Harry, but could have caused lasting damage to the football club. Happily that friendship has been rebuilt and restored, and the damage to the club was repaired in the nick of time.

Having clearly been coaxed by the Chairman into taking the job, Zajec was at pains to make it clear to us that his managership was only a temporary measure, saying: 'I'm only taking over for a short time', adding: 'I don't know enough about English football'. Speaking little English, it was soon obvious that he would rely on Joe Jordan to a large extent to give the team talks, pass on instructions and deal with the media. Joe is a deep thinker and can seem a bit dour and withdrawn but he was always clear and straight in getting his point across to us.

In fairness to Zajec it must have been tough for him to be thrust into the first team limelight. He came in thinking he was going to be working with Harry, only to be thrown in at the deep end a few weeks later taking the teams, the training and the games. But he didn't make himself too popular with the players by immediately switching our training from the morning to the afternoon, presumably to match the Greek custom. It was a move that was totally alien in the English game, with the players' lives and families organised around a morning training schedule e.g picking up children from school etc. The players made their feelings about the consequent disruption to their lives known to Arjan who approached Zajec on our behalf, but his appeal fell on deaf ears.

His first game in charge was at Bolton and Zajec's 4-5-1 formation came up trumps with a 1-0 win. On the pitch during the warm-up before the game Arjan and Stoney went round amongst the squad and gave us all a real lift with the sort of talking-to that epitomised the leadership qualities and overall unity in the squad. In essence they said to us: 'We have to show that all this off-the-pitch stuff is not affecting us and that we're still united. After all it's all about us and what we do, not about all the other rubbish going on. Let's get the press talking about us and what we're doing on the pitch'.

That game was marred by the spit in the face directed at Arjan by El Hadji Diouf. I didn't see the incident at the time but, after seeing it in slow motion on a TV replay later, it was clearly the most disgusting thing I've ever seen on a football pitch. I remember Arjan chasing after Diouf to remonstrate with him, but his restraint and dignified response to the 'assault' was amazing and rightly attracted much favourable comment in the press. Most players, including myself, would have reacted violently to such a vile attack, and there was a lot of anger and disbelief around in our dressing room afterwards. It certainly built up a lot of resentment in our squad towards Diouf, even though one or two of the Bolton players attempted to defend him by saying what a nice, gentle guy he was off the pitch.

I was dropped to the bench for Zajec's first home game in charge against West Brom which was somewhat mystifying for me, but a warning nevertheless. It left me suddenly wondering whether I had a long-term future at the club after all. The problem for me was that I had been playing at right back and finding myself in competition with Andy Griffin whose natural position it was. Knowing that I had to start 50 games over two seasons, of which this was the first, to seal a further one-year extension left me increasingly anxious not to be left out for any length of time.

As we prepared in training for a stern test at Newcastle, Zajec made it clear that he wanted me to play on the left side of three defenders and man-mark their star striker, Ameobi. As it happened, knowing my unease at the prospect, Dejan, as one of the few players who could converse with Zajec in Greek, managed to persuade him to use Arjan in the role instead. We took a point each from both Newcastle and then Liverpool in successive away trips, and if you add in the win at Bolton, this most unlikely of 'caretaker' managers had taken five points from three games in which we had very much been the underdogs.

You couldn't deny that Zajec's tactics were spot-on, mainly based on one up front, but inevitably his man management and motivational qualities left a lot to be desired. He was a very quiet, introverted character who, as I said, spoke little English and was still assessing a lot of things about the English game. He was obviously embarrassed that he couldn't communicate with us and had to rely on Joe Jordan to get his points across. English players seem to thrive on, and almost need, plenty of inspiration and gee-ups in the dressing room – even if it amounted to no more than a kick up the backside.

Changes were afoot at the club as players who were considered as 'close' to Harry, like Shaka, Arjan, Nigel Quashie, David Unsworth and Patrick Berger, were increasingly being marginalised. The signs were that the team was being dismantled and the heart was being taken out of the squad. I felt sorry for Shaka, who was sidelined after being perceived as showing some loyalty to Harry. One of his press interviews was unfortunately interpreted as meaning that he was angling for a move to Southampton, when he meant nothing of the sort. In effect he was asked: 'Would you go and play for Harry if you had the chance?' To which Shaka answered blandly: 'I just want to play football and I would be prepared to play anywhere'.

Jamie Ashdown was playing regularly as a consequence, and Shaka's reaction to his fellow goalkeeper getting a chance was typical of him. I remember him telling me: 'I'm disappointed at not playing but not unhappy that Jamie has a chance now. What I am concerned about is being frozen out because I am supposed to want to play for Harry again, and that means that the decision to play Jamie is more personal than professional. In fact Jamie needs competition from me and, as well as Jamie is doing, he needs to be pushed. If he has a dip in form, as young players are liable to have, then he needs someone there ready to step in'.

On Boxing Day at Crystal Palace I scored the goal in our 1-0 win – my only goal of the season. I'm aware that I really should score more goals from set-pieces but for some reason the ball never seems to reach my head. It's all about the delivery and, despite all our practice on the training ground, it's difficult to carry off. It was to be exactly two years – amazingly Boxing Day again – before I scored again and then I managed two from set pieces at West Ham.

A goalkeeper, Kostas Chalkias, and a midfielder, Giannis Skopelitis, arrived from Greece, presumably on Zajec's recommendation, and both immediately struggled to cope with the move to England. As an international keeper Chalky came 'highly rated', but I had heard foreign players described in such terms before and then watched as they struggled to come to terms with the different type of game they found in this country. We didn't get

221

to see too much of Chalky in training before he went straight into the side for the derby match in the FA Cup at Southampton. It was clearly a game too early for him, giving him no chance of settling into the English game or establishing a relationship with his defence, but we knew it was a political decision to include him. Chalky never looked like a natural keeper to me, and his judgement and handling immediately looked faulty. A mistake that cost a goal, in his home debut against Middlesbrough, seemed to set the tone for the rest of his short time at Fratton Park. Giannis Skopelitis was a hard-working lad and he too was thrown in at the deep end when he was obviously not ready for it and needed time to settle in English football.

When Jamie Ashdown was left out, for no apparent good reason, to give Chalky that immediate debut in goal at Southampton in the cup game it left him very frustrated and angry. In fact, when the team was read out at our meeting at the hotel before the game, Jamie just couldn't contain himself, shouting out: 'What a joke'.

The last minute penalty decision against Mattie Taylor in that game at St Mary's in the last minute, that cost us the game, was no joke. It was harsh to say the least, with Mattie having his arm alongside his body and finding it impossible to get that arm out of the way of the ball that was hit towards him.

We had of course come up against Harry, as the Southampton manager in that cup tie, and it was significant that, before the game, he came to our dressing room to shake all our hands and wish us 'good luck'. Again it seemed to me that he was at pains to demonstrate that he had no problem with us as players and that it was important to him that he remained on good terms with us.

It was apparent by now that Zajec preferred Arjan and Dejan as his central defensive partnership and I had to compete with Andy Griffin and Aliou Cisse for the right back spot. Aliou was being converted to a right back by Zajec, somewhere he didn't really enjoy playing, but not having really featured in midfield under Harry, he was happy just to be playing. Defensively I was OK in the position, but, as I have previously said, I just didn't find it easy to get forward and support the attack. I began to wonder whether Zajec was not totally convinced by me as a centre-back – if that was the case then my future at the club was in some jeopardy.

You may remember how much I dislike coming off the bench into the defence, and even more so in a game in which we are being totally overrun. When Griff came off injured at Arsenal it certainly didn't do me any favours coming on at right back with Henry rampant and on his way to a hat-trick. It would be fair to say that Chalky was having a tough time in goal and let in a soft goal from a free kick. It meant that Jamie didn't have to wait too long – just six games – before Zajec realised that he had to be recalled at Chalky's expense.

I kept my place at right back, in Griff's absence, and against Newcastle at home, found myself marking Laurent Robert. Griff was an old team-mate of Robert from his days at St James's Park and told me that he didn't like 'close attention'. I knew what he was capable of so, from the off, I was more confrontational than usual and tried to intimidate him by being more aggressive with some early tough tackling. The Pompey fans were egging me on and, after one particularly late challenge, Robert was left writhing on the ground. When he finally recovered after treatment he came up to me, in the referee's hearing, and said: 'I'm going to kill you' (in football terms meaning 'I'm going to give you a roasting!'). Whereupon the referee, Matt Messias, a fellow Christian, came up to me and said: 'Linvoy, stop it... don't get yourself sent off ... you know who's behind all this... take it easy'. I knew immediately that he was referring to the Devil and that he was trying to get me to let myself down. That brought some clarity to my mind and I started to play my normal game, such that Robert posed no danger and was eventually substituted. The following season it was all forgotten when Laurent signed for Pompey and, as soon as he arrived, we recalled our set-to, laughed it off, and shook hands.

Things were beginning to get tense as we slipped closer to the relegation zone, but we could have made ourselves virtually safe with a win at Fulham in early April. We were a goal up at half time but two uncharacteristic mistakes, late in the game, from first Arjan then myself, handed Fulham a 3-1 win that left us teetering four points from safety with seven games to go. The players were becoming increasingly disenchanted with Zajec and, in particular, his motivational qualities. The team talks were leaving us distinctly uninspired and we were even losing faith in his tactical qualities. Even worse he was looking increasingly out of his depth and more and more uncomfortable with the situation in which he found himself. In fairness to him it was not the sort of job that he was brought in to tackle, or even one that he was keen to take on. You could fully understand that his motivation to succeed in the job would not be as high as it would have been if he had been striving to keep the job.

The players were worried at the way the situation was developing, given that we had won only once since Boxing Day, and desperately needed some points to avoid slipping into real trouble. So the senior players – Dejan as spokesman, Stoney, Arjan, Patrik and myself – asked to see the Chairman to express our concerns and enquire what he was planning, particularly in regard to the managership. The meeting lasted for an hour or so and was very positive and amicable, with the Chairman acknowledging and respecting our concerns. He made it clear that he appointed Zajec with a view to trying to get the club through to the end of the season before making a permanent appointment in the summer. The meeting closed with the Chairman giving us an assurance: 'Leave it with me, I will do something about it'. What that 'something' was going to be, we had no idea at the time.

Within 48 hours we were told to come into training early to a meeting and on arrival we were introduced to a new manager in the form of Alain Perrin, the former manager of Troyes and Marseille (soon to be nicknamed 'Reggie'). On first impression he appeared very smart, organised and calculated and, when he spoke to us, he told us that he was looking for us to work hard together, and how much value he placed on a good team spirit and discipline. He spoke in broken English, but we could understand what he was saying. Most of the lads hadn't heard of him before, but the French boys in our squad told us that he was known in France as a taskmaster who was very thorough and organised. Obviously I couldn't come to any immediate conclusions about this new manager, but was well aware that I would have to prove myself all over again.

Two days later, without any explanation, I was dropped in favour of Aliou Cisse at right back for the vital home game against my old club Charlton, which made it even more disappointing. At 2-2 Perrin put on two extra forwards as subs in a move that had everybody hailing his tactical skills and sense of adventure when two late goals brought a really valuable 4-2 victory.

At Birmingham a week later Perrin changed the tactics and brought me into the centre of defence to man-mark Emile Heskey. My pleasure at being recalled, and in my performance as we secured a valuable goal less draw, was heightened by another factor. With the renewal of my contract in just over 12 months time in mind, I knew that every game I played now was counting towards the magic total I needed, reducing the number of appearances I would need to clock up next season. Despite my strong contribution that afternoon at St Andrews, I couldn't help but notice that Perrin showed me no respect afterwards by ignoring me with no eye contact or a 'well played' coming my way. His almost complete lack of communication with me led me to wonder if it was not in some way personal.

I wasn't surprised, although disappointed, to be left on the bench in midweek at home to Liverpool, but I did come on – this time at left back where everybody knew I was totally unsuited. When Andy Awford called me off the bench to get changed ready to go on and told me where Perrin wanted me to play, I said to him: 'You're having a laugh, aren't you? You know I'm not left-footed!' By the way I was being treated and selected, it seemed to me that Perrin was making some sort of statement about me. It occurred to me that, knowing my relationship with the supporters, he might almost be trying to lay the ground and soften the impact for the fans of my departure in the summer.

Perrin was unhappy about the players being with their families pre-match when we were at home, and we had to meet up on a Saturday morning at the ground before being taken by coach to a Southsea hotel for a meal and team talk. At the hotel before the massive home derby match with Southampton (and Harry's return to Fratton Park) I was expecting to hear that I was either playing or, at least, on the bench. I was upset when I realised I had been left out of the squad all together, and, to add insult to injury, it was too late for me to get any tickets for myself or the family to see the game. Trish and the children were left at home, and I couldn't get a seat in the stadium. So I was left to watch the game on TV downstairs in the Chimes Bar, with only one or two bar staff for company, feeling completely dejected and out of it.

It was disappointing not to be part of such a famous win and brilliant occasion that made us almost safe and Southampton's position perilous. Lua came up with two brilliant individual goals during that first 30 minutes or so when we completely overwhelmed the Saints, and from then on it was game over. In the euphoria following the 4-1 win most supporters were saying that Harry would do us a favour and take Southampton down. Perrin had done his job, steadied the ship, and put it back on course but up to now he had not imposed himself and his ways upon us. For now any questions about his methods and ability could safely wait until next season.

With Griff injured, I played in the last three games of the season and, in doing so, reached the 40-game mark leaving me with just ten games to play in the season to secure that one-year extension. In the first of the three, at Manchester City we were 2-0 down and playing so badly that some rare plaudits from Joe Jordan came my way during his half time lashing of the team: 'The only one of you who has turned up to play is Linvoy'. Curiously I was assigned to man-mark Sibierski and spent most of the game in midfield following him around. Results went our way that afternoon and we were finally mathematically safe and could relax.

Yakubu scored in our draw with Bolton in the last home game of the season but, by now, everybody knew he had secured a big money move to Middlesbrough and the fans had become unhappy with his apparently lazy attitude. The Yak was certainly a different sort of player and there could be no doubt that his head had been turned by the offer to treble his wages. Despite his experience playing Champions League football as a 19-year old in Israel, he was still a very young guy who was being propelled into the big time, and you couldn't really blame him for being somewhat distracted.

There was a weird atmosphere at West Bromwich in the last game, where we were already safe, and they had to win and hope that three other teams in the mix, including Southampton, all slipped up. We knew that, amongst our fans, a West Brom win over us would give them a great deal of satisfaction if it ensured that Southampton were relegated instead. I spoke to some of our fans in the week before the game and all the talk was about how 'we can send Saints down' by conspiring in a West Brom win. I was having none of it, of course, but the fans had vengeance on our local rivals in mind and that was obvious on the day when many Pompey fans bought and were wearing West Brom colours.

Even Trish and the three children were sitting amongst the West Brom fans with Darren and his family. The strange unity of purpose between the two sets of fans in party mood soon became apparent with our fans cheering both teams onto the field and both sets of fans singing: 'There's only one Harry Redknapp'.

However there was no way we were going to 'roll over' and in the dressing room beforehand, after Perrin had gone through the tactics, Joe Jordan gave us a strong talking-to, saying: 'No one in football does you favours. We must go out there to win because, ask yourself, if we're in this position next year would they do the same for you?' We had two good chances in the first half that we didn't take, and in the second half our performance levels dropped. Once Horsfield had scored for West Brom there was only going to be one winner. All our fans saluted their goal, joined in all the cheering, and later the celebrations, as the scores from the other grounds were coming in and it became clear that Southampton were going down. It was all completely surreal to see our fans so happy in defeat but we were disappointed to lose.

I departed for the summer break with some slight anxiety for my future with my place in the side appearing insecure. But of more immediate concern was the challenge I faced in taking on the walk of the Wall of China with Faith and Football.

'Defend the rights of the poor and orphans, be fair to the needy and helpless, rescue them from the power of evil men'
Psalm 82.3

15

From China to Harry's return 2005

For our 2005 Faith and Football mission we set ourselves the seven-day challenge of walking the Wall of China to raise funds for the two overseas projects closest to our hearts – the Prospect Children's School in Ibadan, Nigeria that we had visited in 2002 and the planned building of a new medical centre, school and orphanage in the village of Brittona in the Goa region on the west coast of India that was our vision after our visit in 2004.

With myself, Darren Moore and Wayne Jacobs from Bradford City were 13 other members of Faith and Football – including one lady Naomi Hargreaves – taking on the physical and mental challenges presented by trekking the mountains to reach the Wall, and then up and down several steep sections of the 15th century hardrock wall. When it was all over it was calculated that the party had taken 1.2 million steps, 80,000 steps each (as measured by a pedometer).

It was harder and more physically challenging than any of us could ever have imagined. Many of the group had prepared thoroughly with gym work and long training walks but nothing could have prepared us for walking on that dangerous and rugged terrain. It was the most amazing thing that anyone of us had ever done, but it was great to think that all those steps and climbs were taking us nearer to helping give some of the most desperate and vulnerable children in Africa and India a chance in life.

On our 10-hour flight to Beijing we were, as usual, loaded up with footballs and football kit to give away to the Chinese locals, not to mention pens, pads, balloons, toys and sweets for the children we met en route. Beijing was our first shock, having expected a typically dour Communist city, the economic revolution in China in recent years meant we were greeted with modern new buildings and skyscrapers as they prepared for the 2008 Olympics. But an afternoon tour of old Beijing provided a massive contrast to that with a real taste of the culture and traditions.

The next day we left Beijing for a four-hour drive into the country with our support staff – the guide, a state appointed doctor and a 'sherpa'. We got our first glimpse of the Si Ma Tai mountain we were going to climb, and then the Wall itself, and a silence descended on the party as the enormity of the challenge we were facing began to dawn on us. To reach the Wall we had to get to the top of a hill, in the midst of a mountain range, and the ascent was as difficult as negotiating the Wall itself. Any fear of heights had to quickly be overcome, and, after a long climb of over 11,000 steps (measured by pedometer) and negotiating an Indiana Jones-style rope bridge, we took our first steps on the Wall itself.

We expected stunning views but nothing could have prepared us for our first sightings. At evening-time we ascended into a valley to find our small two-man tents up and ready as sleeping quarters. No en-suite facilities, just a detached toilet tent with a hole in the ground. After a candlelit Chinese meal, it was a sleepless night for us all, despite our exhausted state, with the ground hard to sleep on, and the temperatures falling below zero. No one found it harder than Darren Moore who had never camped before.

Our second day was the longest and hardest. Our guide pointed to a tower on the Wall up in the distance, sited on the top of a mountain 7000 feet up, and announced 'We're aiming for that today'. When we had got over the shock of that challenge, it took almost six hours to reach with very steep ascents along rugged pathways littered with rubble and overgrowth. The fact that the worst blisters were on our hands proved what it was like. For some, every step they took was a real challenge and inevitably the pace was set by the slowest in the party. Often there was a need to carry each other's bags to provide some relief.

At one point, with most of the Wall having crumbled away, we were left to negotiate a 40 cm wide rock ledge, with 3000 feet drops either side, to reach the next section. The wind was strong and gusty at times on the Wall and one false step would have spelt disaster. I can't imagine what Harry's reaction would have been if he could have seen me perched precariously on that ledge. It didn't cross my mind at the time how dangerous it was – I just got on with it – but looking back I realise how risky it was. As a reward came the most amazing views any of us had ever seen.

In the afternoon the descent provided an even greater challenge as we zigzagged through the rough loose rock and we often gave up all dignity to backslide down the pathways. After several hours we were down to the valley and into a small basic farming community in Hebei Province who relied on breeding and selling pigs to survive.

For the first time we met a local family there and gave them some money – we later found it amounted to two months income – with gifts for the kids who came out to greet us. A local farmer came up with some emergency facilities for me, in the form of a hole in the middle of his pig sty, after the different diet and complete change of routine on the trek had severely affected my toilet habits causing me major discomfort. One old lady was crippled with arthritis and we took time out to pray with and for her. After a campfire and a football trivia quiz that proved that professional footballers know nothing about the game, with 23,500 steps be-hind us that day, the exhausted group had no trouble sleeping. In fact one nameless member snored so loudly his companion had to take refuge in the dining tent for the night.

The next day brought nearly eight hours of walking with plenty of difficult ascents and descents and at last we met two other par-ties on the Wall, both English – the first contained a West Brom fan who couldn't believe he had met his hero Darren Moore, and the second with a lady from Chichester who recognised and intro-duced herself to Mick Mellows!

By the fourth day we were all feeling really tired, with stiff legs and aching limbs, but we had to tackle our steepest climb so far. Mercifully by early afternoon our guide had taken us down into another valley surrounded by beautiful mountains with the camp-site alongside a river. A village full of goats and pigs was nearby and that gave us a chance to meet the locals and hear of their cul-tural traditions. An 84-year old matriarch took us to their burial mound where we learnt of their worship of ancestral spirits.

We felt we couldn't come to China without playing a game of football. So we found a field, with long grass and rocks unfortu-nately, and with Darren Moore and I as the managers, two teams of eight in Pompey and West Brom shirts, including our Chinese support team, played out a 4-4 draw, with a shepherd and his flock of sheep as the bemused spectators. It was amazing how we produced the energy to play after all that walking and the nearly 15,000 steps that day alone.

When we got back to Beijing, after another two days on the Wall, there was an enormous sense of achievement amongst the group, despite our painful aching legs. One guy had a real fear of heights beforehand but his overcoming of that challenge was one of the greatest things to come out of the trip. There was a genuine feeling that everybody who had sponsored us had got value for their money!

We had amazing support from many local organisations, schools and clubs in and around Portsmouth who took on their own sponsored mini-challenges to raise money for our cause. There were car washes, school non-uniform days, leisure club physical challenges, marathon runs, and an extraordinary, record -breaking '2000 Minutes of Praise' at Drayton's Springfield School with continuous Christian music for over 33 hours over a weekend in a local church organised by John Morley. In total we were delighted when the challenge raised nearly £50,000, giving us strong reason to feel our efforts on the wall were worthwhile.

Back with Pompey for pre-season, Biarritz, the tourist resort on the south-west coast of France, was the location for our training camp. However, in the week or so before we left, my future at Fratton Park, mirroring the situation of almost exactly one year earlier, was once again up in the air, and, as before, it was Norwich City – now newly relegated from the Premiership – and their manager Nigel Worthington who were bidding for my services.

It all came to light after a particularly tough training session culminated with a running session in which I had been placed with the fittest group, including youngsters like Gary O'Neil and Mattie Taylor, and had really struggled. As I have said before, such long power-running is not my strong point. I was way be-hind and drawing little looks of disapproval from Perrin and his assistant Christophe Galtier when, a few minutes later, I noticed that the manager had gone back early into the dressing room which was most unusual for him. After we had finished our running and subsequent warming-down, I went to have a shower and get changed but was met by Perrin who said: 'The Chairman has 'phoned me to say that he has had a call from Norwich. They have made a bid for you that we are prepared to accept, so if you can agree personal terms you can go'.

To which I simply replied: 'I seem to have heard that one before', as if to say: *'It's not the first time you've tried to get rid of me'.*

It was actually a different situation this time – the previous year Harry had not been prepared to let me go and Norwich had their bids rebuffed. I told my agent John Mac of the conversation and his immediate response, having got an insight into what Norwich were offering me, was: 'Don't worry; you're not going anywhere if it's not right for you. At the moment it's not worth you leaving on what they are offering'.

I felt a little unsettled by it all, not helped by Perrin's signing of central defender Andy O'Brien from Newcastle and full back Gregory Vignal from Liverpool, and, once again, it was difficult to envisage a long term future for me at Fratton Park. Mick Mellows was convinced that my future lay at Pompey and I was generally at peace with the situation, being reminded again: *'If He wants it to happen it will, if not He will shut the door on it'.*

We were left in no doubt from Perrin that hard work would be at the root of everything from now on and, in the warm heat of Biarritz, we were put through a hard intensive fitness programme that left us extremely tired at the end of each day. If it's going to be beneficial and get results in the long run then no player minds this sort of preparation. Unfortunately I hurt my knee during a practice match whilst we were out there. I went to pass the ball and my knee simply gave way. It was completely new to me to have my knee so unstable and a day later it locked completely. That put an end to my training in the sun and on my return a scan showed some damage to the knee cap, caused by wear and tear, which required an operation to put right. So a week before the season was due to start I came under the surgeon's knife and faced being out for two to three months. The move to Norwich, who needed a defender immediately, died a death as a consequence.

Arjan, the previous season's Player of the Year and a huge figure at the club, was in a similar position to me, with his future far from clear, with Wigan interested in taking him up north. He went to see the manager to ask if he would be first choice and was told by Perrin: 'I can't guarantee that'. To which Arjan replied: 'My career may not have too long left to run, and I want to be playing'.

Arjan discussed it with me and it looked like another of the moves to clear out players from the old regime. He went up to speak to Wigan, he trained with them and returned south without signing. For some reason the move was delayed and Arjan did unexpectedly report back for training with us one day which shocked Perrin who was clearly not expecting to see him again. When the move was finally completed the players were very disappointed that he was allowed to leave, and I had lost a soul-mate. After Arjan's huge contribution to our promotion it was such a shame and the way it ended for him was undeserved.

Perrin lost an enormous amount of respect from the players as a result of an incident at the training ground three days before the opening match of the season at home to Tottenham. I was injured and recovering from my knee operation, but, for the squad, there had been the usual session in the morning, only to find that Perrin had ordered a hard running session to follow in the afternoon. At first two of the players objected saying that they were too tired and then the other players took the same line, going to Dejan with their grievance. On hearing this Perrin promptly came into the dressing room and confronted the players: 'How can you be tired?

To which one of them replied: 'Because we've worked hard'. Perrin's response was directed at the whole team: 'You are mentally weak'.

It was a defining moment in some ways in that we had discovered his true nature. When I heard of his comment I thought how little he knew of his players. He had been with them for six weeks and they had worked hard with no hint of trouble. When, with the best of intentions, they had been honest with him, he had shown a lack of trust in them and made an unfair judgement of them. There was even punishment to follow when he increased the running area that afternoon to make things even harder. As a result there were considerable murmurings amongst the players against the manager. The team did not go into the opener against Spurs fresh, and, from my perspective as a spectator, looked one-paced in the 2-0 defeat.

One win in eleven games, including a Carling Cup defeat by Gillingham, signalled that it would be a very hard season. The performances were OK but we couldn't score goals and new striker Dario Silva was making little impact. In defence, I thought Brian Priske from Denmark was a good signing who was doing well and it was good to see Jamie Ashdown, who is a good stopper and a big presence in goal, getting a good run in the side and taking his chance.

Colombian midfielder John Viafara struggled at first to adapt to English football, which was a different tempo to what he was used to in South America. I felt sorry for him because his real problem was that, although he understood a little English, he was completely unable to understand it with a French accent. Perrin would shout at him but it was clear to everyone that John simply didn't understand what he was saying. So it made it extremely difficult for him to follow any instructions whatsoever.

For other reasons, communication was still a problem. Players will always have opinions on what should be done when things are not going well, but, when these were taken to Perrin by Dejan, as captain, he simply wouldn't listen and the squad still carried on training in the same way. The squad was firmly of the opinion that they were being overtrained, as far as the intensity and length of training time were concerned. The training was going on into the afternoon and that meant a long time out on the pitch. Perrin was trying to get the team fitter than everybody else and whilst that was a worthy aim you do need to achieve a balance of work and rest otherwise the body becomes tired. That's counter-productive and realises the opposite of what you are trying to achieve. I was still working on my rehab in the gym so it didn't affect me but it reminded of a similar problem that had arisen under Tommy Burns at Reading.

In both the French and Scottish leagues the pace differs from that in the English leagues. In England, no matter how hard you have trained, you need players with a good turn of pace. If however you have trained at a certain pace that's all you will be able to manage in a game, and if you try and step it up then inevitably you will discover that the muscles and the body are not ready for it.

I found Perrin very stiff, rigid and precise in his approach to everything. Every training drill had to be to the exact number and time ordered, for instance, and always it was a case of 'his way or no way' with no room for compromise. His organisation and tactics were spot-on and thorough but he was not hugely inspirational. He was a disciplinarian and Lua had a couple of run-ins with him over his time-keeping at the training ground. Physically we trained at a low level of pace and that was reflected in the way we played. That was down to fatigue – there was little energy left amongst the players to spark and explode.

Perrin took the squad away, a few games into the season, on a team bonding exercise at Hindhead, that was relatively successful and quite a laugh. Whilst the players were taking part in the human table football, the human sheep herding, archery etc, the national press were homing in on the manager with stories of unrest and unhappiness amongst the squad. Obviously there was some truth in all this, but the source of the stories was unknown to us.

By October I was back to fitness after a few reserve team games, but with Dejan and Andy O'Brien doing well in the centre of defence I had resigned myself to not featuring in the first team unless there was an injury. Midfielder Salif Diao had arrived on loan from Liverpool and, with his pedigree, was a comparatively big signing. He was clearly not match fit, having rarely featured at Anfield, and struggled in midfield in his two or three outings prior to our visit to Roker Park for a pretty vital game against bottom of the table Sunderland. When Andy O'Brien cried off with a hamstring problem Perrin tried to convince Salif to play out of position in the centre of defence, but he successfully protested that he wasn't fit enough. So Perrin had to fall back on me to solve his defensive problem – after me there was only the kit man, physio or coach driver left to ask.

So I found myself one of the five defenders in a 5-4-1 formation at Roker Park, where we were 0-1 down at half time after Sunderland scored when the referee and linesman had let the game go on after the ball had clearly gone out of play. Our poor first half performance brought a rollicking from Joe at half time: 'This lot are down there below us and have a chance of catching us. We must give it more second half'.

Before we went out for the second half Perrin astounded me by announcing that, if things hadn't improved, he proposed to change things around after ten minutes and take me off. I can tell you that managers are just not in the habit of saying, in advance, who they will take off, if and when they make a change. As it was we equalised three minutes into the second half through Zvonimir Vukic and went on to a rare win by 4-1 with two goals from Mattie Taylor including an outrageous long-distance volley. So Perrin never made his change but it was a further reminder, if I needed one, that I would never be one of his first choice players.

After a home defeat by Wigan we only escaped a drop into the bottom three through goal difference and the players sensed that Perrin was under extreme pressure and facing the sack. Most of the players were unhappy with his training methods but all the complaints and dissent had fallen on deaf ears. There was still a good atmosphere in the dressing room – that hadn't changed – but our confidence in our abilities and in the manager had been severely dented by our run of poor results.

The press were even speculating about his successor and I remember Neil Warnock's name cropping up when there was talk about the Chairman turning to an English manager to bring the motivational skills that Perrin plainly lacked. By the time we travelled to meet Liverpool there was a strong feeling around the club that the manager would be sacked if we failed to get a result at Anfield. I watched from the bench as we were simply blown away and fortunate to escape with just a 3-0 defeat.

That prompted the Chairman to invite a group of senior players to a meeting at a Portsmouth hotel, in Perrin's absence, to get their viewpoint and they had the chance to give full vent to their feelings about the manager, his methods and their relationship with him. Obviously the results and our league position spoke volumes and probably forced the Chairman's hand as much as anything else.

I was unaware of the meeting, but the next morning I heard on the sports news that Perrin had been sacked, and we were called in for an early morning meeting with the Chairman at the training ground. By this time I had lost count of the number of times this sort of situation had arisen in my career, and I had become used to hearing the sorts of things that Mr Mandaric said that morning: 'There is no way I am going to allow this club to get relegated... I've listened to what the players had to say... clearly something needed to be done... I will do what's right for the club and the supporters... I will bring in someone who will do the job for us'.

Immediately the rumours centred on Redknapp and Warnock. There was a strong suggestion that Harry wasn't popular with one or two board members at Southampton and that Sir Clive

Woodward's appointment as Director of Football had unsettled him, but I completely discounted any suggestion that he would return to Fratton Park. After all the acrimony that had gone before, the way he had left and his seemingly irreparable relationship with the Chairman, I just couldn't see it happening.

With Joe Jordan in temporary charge I watched from the stands as we were beaten at home by Chelsea, and afterwards a supporter approached me and said: 'Harry will resign from Southampton, and come back here, mark my words', to which I replied; 'No chance, mate'. Sometimes the players get early notice of things, but I had heard nothing of the sort and put it down to the rumour mill being in full swing. A week later Harry did resign at St Mary's but his return still seemed an impossibility, although I had come to think that only Harry, or perhaps someone like Martin O'Neill, could get us out of the desperate position we were in.

When I heard from one of the local press that Harry was coming back it really did take some believing. But listening to both the Chairman and Harry speak publicly at the subsequent press conference it soon became clear that the previous problems between them had been resolved and that the reconciliation was for real. Both had made brave and courageous decisions to make it happen. Harry had realised that he had made a mistake in going to Southampton and wanted to right the wrong he had done. I was so pleased and, for the first time for over a year, I felt as if the club was back together, united and equipped to take on the challenge of fighting relegation.

On the personal front, with Harry knowing what I was capable of doing, it was good to think that it gave me a chance of getting back in the team. Certainly it was better than having to prove myself all over again to a new manager. I was confident that Harry would be able to use his influence to get two or three quality players to come and sign for us in the January transfer window. I knew that he would get us playing in the right way and, with his way with players, would bring and gel us together.

We could rely on Harry keeping everything very simple and uncomplicated. We could go into games with our heads clear, rather than crammed with instructions. We went out to play knowing exactly what our roles were in certain match situations and Harry would trust you to deliver what you were good at. His simple instruction to us defenders was often no more than a simple: 'Defend with your lives'.

The key to all this for Harry lay in finding players who were capable of doing what he needed them to do. It was never a question of trying to get players to do things they couldn't do, more of getting them to do what they were good at. In my case it was simply asking no more of me than winning balls in the air and tackles on the ground.

On his first day back Harry pulled us all together out on the training ground and said simply: 'Some of you I know, and some of you I don't. I won't let this club get relegated and I want everything you've got to make sure this club stays in the Premier League. I want you to know that I'm going to strengthen what we've got here as it's plainly not good enough. But it's up to you to keep your place in the team'.

The training routine changed immediately and, although we spent much less time out there, it was with a higher intensity and tempo. I felt for some of the newer players who had arrived during the Perrin regime as they coped with the worry and uncertainty that the arrival of a new manager brings – *'Is he going to stick with me or bring someone else in to replace me?'* – but for myself it was reassuring that Harry knew all about me.

I was restored to the side for Harry's first game back at Tottenham and it was noticeable how much more in the way of effort and commitment were on show. We deserved something from the game and a contentious decision from Uriah Rennie five minutes from time at 1-1 cost us dearly. Minutes earlier John

Viafara had been brought down in the Spurs penalty area but, after turning that claim down, Rennie had no hesitation in giving Spurs a penalty at the other end, after he had judged Gary O'Neil, in the defensive wall for a free kick, to have handled when a free kick was hit firmly straight at him. It left us firmly in the bottom three six points adrift of safety.

Harry's first home match in charge, a week before Christmas, against West Brom was a nervy must-win affair – a real 'six point-er' - settled by a typical classy finish from Toddy, showing great composure in coolly 'dinking' the ball into the net from a couple of yards out. The Pompey fans were clearly going to need some time to warm to Harry on the basis of his muted reception that afternoon. That was disappointing for the players as we desperately needed everybody to be pulling in the same direction if we were going to get ourselves out of the mess we were in. We could understand how the fans were feeling after, in their eyes, Harry had committed one of the worst 'crimes' imaginable, but it was now a case of moving on even if that had to be a gradual healing process.

I had to come off with a groin injury during the 1-1 draw with West Ham on Boxing Day, forcing me to miss five league games, including a 4-0 battering at Arsenal and the horrific 5-0 hammering at fellow strugglers Birmingham that left us staring down the barrel of relegation. After that defeat, on our return to training on the following Monday, Harry came down hard, forcing us all to watch the whole 90 minutes on video in the canteen. Everybody was very vocal that morning and, as you would expect, Harry was very animated. It's hard for anybody in any walk of life when you're criticised in your job. As players you don't go out to perform badly but many of the players, particularly Andy O'Brien, had to feel and bear much of the wrath that was around amongst the fans and the management. It demonstrated to Harry how bad we could be, and he made it obvious that he wouldn't tolerate a repeat performance.

By now new co-owner Alexandre Gaydamak had arrived with a significant investment, raising the possibility of a future takeover. In our situation we knew that we needed some quality players and Sean Davis, Pedro Mendes, Noe Pamarot and Benjani Mwaruwari had been signed in the January transfer window. The first three had good pedigrees but, although we knew nothing of Benjani, we figured that for a record fee of £4.5 million he had to be a quality player. We did notice that, not having played first team football for some time, all the new signings, including Andres D'Alessandro a couple of weeks later, displayed low fitness levels. Initially that affected our performances until, on getting match fit through playing regularly, they all began to play to their full potentials and we began to reap the benefits.

We could see immediately, with his great touch, vision and passing, what a very good player Andres was. In fact, after a few games, looking at his ability, two or three of us – myself, Gary O'Neil and Richard Hughes – were saying: 'He's too good to be playing for us... what's he doing getting involved in a relegation dog-fight?... he's should be playing for a top-four team'.

After the Birmingham defeat, looking for more experience, Harry brought in keeper Dean Kiely, from Charlton, and he was a great character with a strong, positive personality. I was well aware what a good keeper Dean was and it was no surprise to me when he made such a great impact on our season. But it was a surprise to me that he was allowed to leave Charlton in the first place.

Amidst all these arrivals Laurent Robert had moved to Benfica and it was a big opportunity for him after his problems with Pompey. The crowd had turned on him and, never having played in a struggling team or been involved in a relegation dogfight before, he just didn't have the characteristics or qualities needed. Everybody knew how good he could be going forward but defending wasn't his strong point and not an aspect of the game he relished.

Our performances were improving but scoring goals was our biggest problem, having only once scored more than one – four at Sunderland – all season. By the end of February defeats at Newcastle, at home to Manchester United and inevitably at Chelsea left us eight points adrift of safety and I was starting to get worried. There was no talk of relegation from the players or the manager, but the media and all the pundits firmly felt we were doomed and in an impossible position.

I remember that our financial adviser came to see us at home and seemed to reflect the prevailing mood when he said: 'You've got no chance of staying up!' Whereupon Trish promptly said to him: 'I have been praying that Linvoy will continue playing Premiership football, and I believe he will'. To which our adviser replied: 'If Linvoy plays Premiership football next season I will come to church with you!' which was a big commitment for him to make at the time! Regrettably I have to say that he has still not kept his side of the bargain.

Whenever I got the chance in interviews or just in conversation I would say: 'I firmly believe we will stay up', on the basis that, having prayed to stay in the Premiership, whatever you ask for in prayer you should believe that it will happen, according to the Bible.

We had seriously targeted our game at Aston Villa for some much needed points to kick-start a late push to survive but we were simply terrible that day – again looking short of goals and confidence. We didn't start the game at the sort of high tempo that suited us and we needed everyone to be on their game from the very start. It might have been goalless but we gave away a very sloppy goal in the first half, from a corner, scored by Milan Baros who was supposed to be picked up by Andy Griffin. To Andy's credit, before an inquest into the goal could get started, he immediately put his hands up in the dressing room at half time and confessed: 'I didn't see him there'. It was the only goal of the game and the defeat left us eight points adrift of safety. The pundits were unanimous that our chances of catching both Birmingham and West Brom above us were faint. But in just a week's time the course of the season was to be changed in the most dramatic fashion.

'I have the strength to face all conditions by the power that Christ gives me'
Phill. 4.13

16

'The Great Escape' 2006

With ten games left relegation from the Premiership was clearly staring us in the face. On the Friday before the absolutely vital home game with Manchester City we had a team meeting in which it was put to us that, after Villa, we desperately needed a good performance and that only hard work would bring us a win. So the coaches set us all goals to increase our work rate for the game, and those individual rates could be measured from the ProZone football analysis system that uses cameras to provide valuable information via PC on player performance and fitness levels. The stats include reports on performance such as distance covered, headers won, successful tackles, successful passes etc etc. Some players like to set their own individual targets, others are not so keen. The coaches pass the reports to the manager and he may pull a player aside if there are any areas that need improvement.

Our fans will never forget the two fabulous volleys from Pedro Mendes that brought the goals in our dramatic 2-1 win over Manchester City, with the second coming in the very last seconds of the game. Those long shots had to be special to beat David James in the City goal, but Pedro had shown in training that he was capable of producing such volleys from a distance. Apart from showing his great technique with long range volleys from either foot, Pedro was a real playmaker who could dictate the flow of the game, spread the ball from wing to wing, and split defences with his passing. Add to that his high work rate and his experience in the game and you have a very valuable player who is sorely missed when he is out of the side.

I had been involved in last minute victories before but none as significant and season-changing as that, and that was clear at the reaction of supporters and players alike afterwards. As Harry said afterwards: 'If we didn't win today we were dead and buried'. The importance of that victory – our first in the league in 2006 – was immense from a psychological standpoint and the all-round belief it suddenly instilled was amazing.

A couple of weeks before that crucial win Mick Mellows, my regular prayer partner, had suggested that we start praying as a team before games and I had agreed to ask the players if they wanted to join in. As it happened I asked around at the team meeting before the Manchester City game – some said 'Yes' and some said 'No'. So an hour or so before that game we got together in the laundry room – about seven or eight of us including two or three staff – and linked arms to say a simple prayer committing ourselves to playing for and bringing glory to God through our performances. We never pray to win but that we can glorify God in everything we do on the pitch; in essence that means asking God to help us to realise the full potential of the talent we have been given so as not to abuse that gift. We want to win as much as anybody else and I know that God wouldn't want it any other way.

In the week after that win the frequently expressed view was that we would look back at the end of the season and say that it had turned our season around. I couldn't help but wonder if it was our prayers that had changed everything.

We went through the ProZone stats the following Monday to highlight what we had done well in the game and the increase in the levels of our individual work rates was a big feature. We had seen a formula that could work and knew that if we could regularly take that into games it would pay dividends. In that knowledge we went to Upton Park the following Saturday to meet an under-strength West Ham side who had one eye on an FA Cup replay 48 hours later. As the saying goes, you can only beat what's put in front of you, and sometimes it's not always easy to play against second-choice players who have something to prove.

I always enjoy going back to London with my friends and relatives in the crowd, and there was also a huge away following from Portsmouth. For the first time we could sense that they believed that we could stay up, much of it borne out of that dramatic win against Man City, and those positive vibes just poured down from the away end. We got off to a brilliant start and were three up by half time, including another 'Mendes special', and eventually ran out 4-2 winners to leave us just three points off safety. With two successive wins we were pulling other teams into the mix, and, when the Birmingham manager Steve Bruce complained at West Ham fielding a weakened team against us, it became clear to us that the other clubs were getting rattled by the threat to their safety that we were now posing.

By now I was back in my favourite position at centre half, this time partnering Andy O'Brien, for whom I had a lot of respect. After helping Bradford into the Premiership in partnership with Darren Moore, Andy had clocked up over 200 appearances at the top level and I looked up to him as he had done well at Newcastle, not to mention his extensive international experience with the Republic of Ireland. Andy is a Christian and a good, honest character who would do anything for you, and, after a couple of games, we struck up a good understanding. Our life was made easier by the increased level of defensive work, as shown by ProZone, coming from the midfielders and forwards.

As a striker, Benjani, in particular, brought a high work ethic, working the channels, closing down defenders and tracking back, and that allowed other players to score. At a fee of over £4 million, Benjie came under pressure when he didn't score the goals that were expected of him but he made a huge contribution to our eventual 'Great Escape' and it was great to hear our supporters regularly chant their appreciation of him. He's a quiet and very modest guy and I know that their backing means an awful lot to him.

As a break from training Harry organised a day out at Cheltenham races and after travelling up by coach we joined a long queue to park along with all the other corporate hospitality guests. It was a great day out but we had a reminder of how the other half lives on hearing that the Chelsea players there were flown in by helicopter from London!

After our great win away at West Ham, we were anxious to follow that up with another good result at Fulham where we were due to play next. Peter Storrie, the club's Chief Executive, suggested to Harry that we vary our routine and, after dinner in a hotel, take in a London show on the night before the game – all with a view to relieving the pre-match tension. After some indecision the players voted to go and, rather unsuitably dressed in track suits, we went to the Apollo Victoria theatre to see a musical - 'Movin' Out' (based on the songs and music of Billy Joel) – with a Pompey fan James Fox in the lead. It wasn't quite what we expected or to some players' tastes with non-stop music and virtually no dialogue. When finally there was a lull in the music Wayne Routledge was heard to spurt out: 'At last someone is going to speak!'

Whether it was the effect of that theatre trip or not, our new irresistible form continued at Craven Cottage against a Fulham side who boasted one of the Premiership's best home records. Sean Davis, a former Fulham player, had promised to treat the whole squad to a meal out if we won. We grabbed a vital 3-1 win, after going ahead a minute into the game through Gary O'Neil.

Lomana LuaLua came into his own during this vital spell with his blistering pace and ability to upset even the best defenders in the world. He had been unfortunate with injuries, not to mention picking up malaria during Perrin's time, picking up all sorts of little troublesome knocks. Lua finds it all very frustrating and doesn't miss training lightly - like all of us he doesn't like to have to sit around and be out of action.

Our new-found resilience came to the fore when two fantastic strikes by Craig Bellamy for Blackburn meant we had to twice come back to force a draw at Fratton Park. Then four days later we took another priceless point from a 1-1 draw in the rearranged home fixture against Arsenal, whose weakened team prompted another complaint from Birmingham manager Steve Bruce.

Our prayer group in the laundry room was now a regular part of the pre-match build-up 45 minutes or so before kick off, and, with some of the new players joining in, had grown to 12 or 13 of us pressed against the huge washing machines and dryers. I'm happy to say that the group is still going strong to this day and continues to add to its members. It's something that we could never have imagined happening two or three years earlier.

My personal prayer was that I would stay in the Premiership for the rest of my career no matter how, whether it was a struggle for survival along the way or not. I had come by now to recognise that I should be a light for God in the world, as are all Christians, and by the way I play, conduct myself and even give interviews I can bring glory to God, i.e. lift Him up and show His power. I can demonstrate that there is nothing that can't be achieved by faith in His power. Although I don't try to force my faith, the Premiership has the highest profile and is the most televised league in the world and that enables my story to be shared on a much bigger scale.

I wasn't feeling any pressure whatsoever now before or during these vital games. I was playing well in my own position and finding real enjoyment and peace, with a real trust in God. Everything I was achieving was not through my own ability or strength, but through God's grace and power at work in me.

On Easter Saturday we finally moved out of the bottom three with a single goal win over Middlesbrough. Beforehand all the talk was about my crucial battle with Yakubu, making a return to Fratton Park with the visitors, and I was up for the challenge. The Yak is a strong and instinctive player, with a powerful right foot, but it helped that I had played with him in training and was well aware of his strengths and tricks. I had to be on top of my game against him and knew how important it was to get close and tight to him, restricting his movement and giving him little chance to turn and run with the ball, to stand any chance of stopping him.

By now the groin injury that had caused me to miss a series of games in January had flared up again and, after a couple of unsuccessful injections, our medical team had discovered a hernia problem that meant I needed painkillers, to reduce the inflammation, to get through games. Harry had reservations about playing me at Charlton on Easter Monday - our fourth game in ten days – and told me: 'I didn't think you would be able to last this many games with that bothering you'. We were ahead at half time through a fantastic goal from Andres D'Allessandro and I managed to keep Charlton's star striker Darren Bent quiet for most of the game but he popped up near the end to make one goal and then score the winner in our 2-1 defeat. For me it felt like we had lost a cup final and at the end of the game I fell to the ground with my head pressed to the ground, saying to myself: *'We've done so much work, don't let it go now'*.

After being underdogs for so long, suddenly we found ourselves expected to beat already-relegated Sunderland at Fratton

Park. That pressure to claim what was expected to be an easy and absolutely essential three points lay heavily on the team that afternoon and for the first time for some weeks we were lethargic. Clearly the mental and physical effort expended during the Easter period had caught up with us. We were drawing 1-1 with two minutes left when, under no pressure and with nobody near him, Sunderland's Kevin Kyle inexplicably put his hand up and pushed the ball away as it came across from our corner. It was quite extraordinary and I had never seen a penalty conceded in such a bizarre way before. Funnily enough, a few minutes earlier, my friend Mick O'Brien, up in the stand sitting with my son Nathan, had said to him: 'We're going to get a penalty any minute now'.

I had complete faith in Mattie Taylor to convert what was our first penalty of the season and he duly slotted it home with ease to bring us a massive win. He regularly practises taking penalties in training and strikes the ball so well. I just don't fancy taking penalties but I know you have to develop a technique and have the right temperament for the job. Mattie, like David Unsworth and Yakubu before him for Pompey, has the rare quality of being able to withdraw from this high pressure situation to remain calm and collected. For all that it has always seemed to me that taking penalties is something of a lottery, largely based on hoping that the goalkeeper doesn't dive the right way.

Now with two games left we had to play Wigan away and then Liverpool at home in the final game. Like our supporters, we worked our way through all the scenarios and one thing stood out above all else – with Liverpool still needing points to claim a Champions League spot we simply did not want to go into that last game needing a result to ensure our safety. We were desperate to win at Wigan with the hope that at the same time Birmingham would fail to beat Newcastle at home. As I describe in the first chapter of this book, it really was a case of 'mission accomplished' with the 2-1 win on that momentous afternoon going firmly into

Pompey folklore. The game and its aftermath will live long in the memories of all those Pompey fans and players who were there at the JJB Stadium, not to mention the untold numbers following events from afar via the media.

Afterwards in the dressing room at the JJB Stadium it was just pure happiness, laughter and further embraces all round with the champagne flowing. There were congratulations from the Wigan Chairman Dave Whelan and manager Paul Jewell, together with their skipper Arjan, who had missed the game with a shoulder injury, and was so obviously pleased for us. The squad were a bit subdued during the flight home, drained by the effort, tension and celebrations and that put an end to any thoughts of a night out to celebrate further. The idea was to get everybody at the club together at a later date for a suitable celebration so Trish and I settled for going back to Gary O'Neil's house where we had a few quiet drinks with Dean Kiely and his wife whilst reliving the afternoon's events.

Harry deserves a great deal of credit and it must have been a huge relief for him to lead us to safety after making the brave decision to return to the club, given the perilous situation that we were in at the time. It must have taken some courage to not only come into such a difficult situation, but to face the animosity and resentfulness he found on his return amongst many people who couldn't accept having him back. If it had all gone wrong for Harry, as seemed likely at one time, then he would have been in an even worse position.

On a personal level I again owed a great deal to Jon Dalzell, our physiologist, for all his time and effort on those one-to-one sessions with me when he put his expertise on the way muscles function to good use by helping me to strengthen those areas where I was both weak and strong. He would, for instance, work with me on new drills and exercises for my legs that would enable me to become even more powerful and effective in those areas where

I was already strong – e.g. my pace on the run and my spring for headers. Exercises and drills to improve my core stability, particularly in relation to strengthening the stomach muscles, enabled me to become less liable to groin, thigh and hamstring strains and pulls.

Jon has also been instrumental in increasing the influence of sports science, particularly with diet and nutrition, and we regularly receive talks and advice on our intake of vegetables, meat and carbohydrates. A chef is employed in the training ground canteen to serve specially balanced meals each day, with particular care and attention on the Thursdays and Fridays before a game.

As we prepared to wind up the season with a match of really no significance against Liverpool, that great sense of relief amongst the squad heightened when a number of 'what-ifs' started to dominate our conversations: *'What if Birmingham had beaten Newcastle?'*, *'What if we hadn't got the win at Wigan and had to beat Liverpool?'* and *'What if Liverpool had needed a win against us to qualify for the Champions League?'*.

There was a slightly subdued feeling of anti-climax around amongst the squad for that Liverpool game – for us it was a matter of 'Job done', we are staying up' and the fans' carnival atmosphere was to celebrate that more than anything else. We had given so much and just to rest on the knowledge that we were still in the Premiership – win or lose on the day – was enough for everybody. Harry wasn't happy with our performance in losing 1-3 but, like our supporters, was pretty forgiving afterwards when he reflected on the 'mission impossible' we had achieved the previous week.

The Chairman, with joint owner Alexandre Gaydamak and the board, invited all the club staff and their partners to an end of season meal at his favourite restaurant – Pizza House at Hilsea – with free champagne flowing, in appreciation of what we had achieved. During the latter part of the evening the Chief Executive

254

Peter Storrie called me over to say that he had spoken to the Chairman and Harry who had agreed to give me a new two-year contract as a reward for my efforts. I was, of course, due to have a further one-year contract extension kicking in on the basis of my appearances in the previous two seasons, so this new offer was a welcome surprise and very pleasing. The terms were of no real concern to me, but the security of a further year over and above what I was expecting would enable us to move house as we had been planning.

I suppose it was confirmation, if I needed it, that, at long last, I had established myself in the Premiership. I now felt that I knew what was needed and that I could cope with whatever was thrown at me. In fact I had loved and relished the challenges that came my way week by week.

It was during that difficult season that Faith and Football launched the annual Linvoy Primus Enterprise Challenge, joining forces with the South East Hants Education Business Partnership (EBP) and the South East of England Development Agency (SEEDA) to promote an enterprise challenge to pupils at Key Stage 4 in south east Hampshire secondary schools. I must admit that I didn't have a clue what it was all about until it was fully explained to me. I certainly didn't realise what an impact it would have with so many schools and pupils entering.

The challenge is for pupils to form businesses that actually trade, making it as real a business environment as possible, with up to six pupils in a team. The pupils have to register their business with EBP, raise the capital, and then trade the business with all profits from their trading going towards the work of Faith and Football supporting orphans and the needy in Goa, India and Ibadan, Nigeria. I try to visit as many of the teams working on their businesses as possible to see how they're doing and give them some encouragement.

The pupils are not only judged on the amount of funds raised, but on their business plan and their demonstration of team work, sales and marketing initiatives. The prize for the winning team each year is an all-expenses paid trip to Goa, with their teacher, in November to view the work at the orphanage we are supporting. In May 2006 the winning team of girls – 'Pashion UK' – from the City of Portsmouth Girls School took the prize and made the trip a few months later. They set a high standard in making their business work and practising skills – creativity, leadership, teamwork, decision making, accounting – that would stand them in good stead in their future employment.

Our 2006 – 2007 Challenge was launched by me in November 2006 as part of National Enterprise week in the Milan Mandaric Suite at Fratton Park. The popularity of the challenge and a measure of its success and impact on young people resulted in more schools and pupils entering this second annual competition. In fact the entry increased from 67 to 101 teams providing a genuine enterprise challenge and opportunity for young people in the Portsmouth and South East Hampshire area. Portchester School's team of boys, 'Save Our Neighbours', were announced as the winners at a presentation evening in May 2007 attended by 200 members of the participating teams together with teachers and parents, and they later travelled to Goa to see how the funds they raised were being used for the needy children there.

'When you pray and ask for something, believe that you have received it, and you will be given whatever you ask for'
Mark 11.24

17

Top ten security 2006-2007

Before the 2006/07 campaign got underway, I was working with Jon Dalzell on some loosening-up exercises before training and we got talking about our prospects for the season. I remember saying to him: 'Next season is going to be the best in Pompey's history, and I'm going to have my best-ever season so far'. Jon turned to me with a wry smile and a look on his face that said: 'I'll believe it when I see it'. In a prophetic sort of way I believed that these things would happen, just as during the low points of last season I had told everybody that I firmly believed that we would stay in the Premiership.

There was a feel-good factor at the club and amongst our supporters as we approached the new season and Glen Johnson on loan from Chelsea and David Thompson from Wigan moved to Fratton Park. There were rumours about various centre halves coming in, with the names like Senegalese star Souleymane Diawara, Manchester City's Sylvain Distin, and, more unlikely, England star Sol Campbell being mentioned. I was quite relaxed about the strong possibility of a challenge to my place figuring that I might have to bide my time and leave the matter in God's hands again.

It was a real surprise when Sol signed for Pompey when there were obviously bigger clubs in for him, but Harry reportedly met him in a pub and sold the club and its dreams to him. On Sol's first day in training there was a huge press presence to greet him with their cameras at the ready. As it happened Gary and I drove in together and, knowing that we were arriving before Sol, decided to have a laugh with the press. I pretended to be Sol by covering my face with a bag as we drove in and went to park. The cameramen rushed over, surrounded the car and began filming and snapping away before I exposed my face to them with a big grin.

Sol was so big physically that it was funny to see him out training in kit that didn't fit him, with Kev the Kit Man unable to find anything in his size. Sol didn't know anybody other than me and that was only on a casual basis from our days playing together for the Newham district schools Under-11's team. My first words to him were: 'What are you doing here?' to which he replied: 'I'm here ready for a new challenge'. His arrival gave everybody a huge lift and showed plainly that the club really meant business.

We had heard rumours about the likes of Andy Cole, David James and Kanu coming and thought they would go elsewhere, but, to our surprise, here they were at Fratton Park. The sense of optimism increased and there was a strong feeling amongst the squad that we could realistically, although unofficially, aim for a top half finish. As for my own prospects, I figured it was two from five for the central defensive spots, with me a clear fifth in the pecking order behind Sol, Dejan, Noe, and Andy. Two days before the season started everybody reckoned that, on the basis of the team-play in training, the back four would read (from the right): Glen Johnson, Sol Campbell, Dejan Stefanovic, and Mattie Taylor, with Noe Pamarot and myself making the bench as we could play both at right back and centre half. Then surprisingly, during an attack versus defence session, Harry moved Dejan to left back with Mattie going into midfield and Noe came into the centre. Then I was swapped for Noe during the play and it became apparent that I communicated better with Glen and Sol, with Noe's command of English proving a problem. That's how, I heard later, I got the nod to start against Blackburn in Saturday's opener at Fratton Park.

With all the anticipation it's important to start well in any season and to be able to get to measure your performances and fitness levels against the other teams. There was a buzz in the dressing room and at 1.30 pm a large group of us slipped into the laundry room for a few minutes for our usual prayers. Then Harry walked into the dressing room at 1.50 pm with the team sheet. Once you've heard your own name you don't hear the rest. That's the signal to get into game mode with your senses heightened and I focused on the battles ahead with my key opponents Benni McCarthy and Jason Roberts. As usual I resolved to win the first header and the first tackle, and not let them settle and get into any flow. At 2.55 pm Harry was back again with some last motivational bits and then it was time for us all to go round the dressing room and wish each other well. After a series of little individual reminders from the coaches, there was a silence as we waited on the benches for the bell to go out.

For an agonising 30 seconds there was a pause. Suddenly I felt a nervous energy rising within me and I thought: 'I can't do this... I'm nothing without you, Lord'. A quick silent prayer followed: 'Take me Lord for your glory today'. As the bell went and we walked down the tunnel, side by side with the Blackburn team, the hairs on the back of my neck were standing on end. I felt very peaceful and relaxed and just knew that I would play well.

I did speak quietly to God during games; often just two or three words of thanks if I found the ability or strength to deal with a certain situation, or if I got tired I might ask for more strength.

I started that Blackburn game in an amazing way, tackling and

259

running strongly and afterwards I was told that I had won my first eight headers. I felt as if I was jumping out of the sky that afternoon. My timing, anticipation, positioning – whatever you care to mention – came right and Bennie and Jason up front for Blackburn just didn't get a kick. Just to look along our defensive line that afternoon with Sol, absolutely awesome in marshalling us, and Glen, out on the right with all his athleticism and ability, was so inspiring. I thought it would be hard for us to replace Brian Priske at right back but Glen was showing why Chelsea paid so much money for him. David James had little to do as we totally controlled the game and made the start we wanted. Kanu came on for Toddy and quickly scored twice, even affording to miss a penalty, as we cruised to a 3-0 win. It set the pattern for our season at home and what struck me that day was that we could vary the tempo of our game – looking strong at a slow pace but then able to up the tempo and look very quick. Such a contrast for me from the one-paced tempo we could only manage under Perrin.

Our game at Manchester City on the following Tuesday evening will be long remembered for Ben Thatcher's sickening challenge on Pedro rather than the goalless draw. It wasn't an ill-tempered game and, to this day, no one knows what prompted Thatcher to attack Pedro and leave him unconscious by the side of the pitch. We were getting the upper hand and it happened soon after City manager Stuart Pearce had been geeing up his players from the touchline to greater efforts. Initially from my angle, and that goes for most of our players too, it didn't look too bad, but from Glen's reaction as the nearest player, it was clearly a very serious situation. I just saw Thatcher run into Pedro and didn't see the contact from his elbow. There was just no need for it and the ball was going out of play. After we had seen the challenge on ProZone via a PC at the airport, we became very concerned about his condition, knowing that he had been left unconscious in the dressing room. There's no doubt that if we had realised how bad it was at the time then more would have been done and said both toThatcher and the referee.

In retrospect it was the worst challenge I have ever seen and it was fortunate that Pedro was not seriously injured and made a quick recovery. To inflict such an injury on another player is unheard of in football. The modern game has come down to the players' skill and ability and no-one wants to see another player hurt in either team. It's a short career and, if there had been any long term damage, who can say what effect it might have had on Pedro's career and life. Football is just football, life is life.

Five days later we hit top form in a 4-0 thrashing of Middlesbrough, with that high work rate that had epitomised our 'Great Escape' last season as the key. At 3-0 Yakubu, now with Middlesbrough of course, said to me: 'We're going to come back from this', but such was our confidence that I replied: 'Not today you're not!'

There were two more goals from 'King' Kanu who had brought a skill level to the team that was world class. He was a good finisher who later proved that he was good in the air with a number of goals with his head. With his great touch he can unlock defences, create chances for others and had a great ability to link up and draw people into the game. For me it was also a bonus that his arrival meant another Christian at the club. David James made two great saves proving why Harry had signed him, and put such faith in him, and Noe, at right back as a deputy for Glen, had a great game against England winger Stewart Downing to show his worth.

Playing in a team so full of confidence and belief reminded me of the 2003 promotion days and soon we were sitting in the top three after beating Wigan at home and Charlton away with no goals conceded in the first five games. We were much less concerned than the media and the punters about a possible record

261

number of successive clean sheets and a 1-0 home defeat to Bolton burst our bubble. By now Mr Gaydamak had taken full control of the club and it was a shame that we couldn't mark Mr Mandaric's departure that afternoon with a win. With their long-ball game based on percentages, Bolton are always difficult to play against but their unique style does suit their players who have the ability to create goals out of nothing. Maximising their set pieces is key for Bolton and even if you clear the first they will put you under pressure again by putting the ball straight back into the penalty area.

Once in a while players, who have played and trained at a high intensity, have a little dip and that came at Tottenham where our work rate fell and we lacked composure on the ball. Five or six of our players just didn't perform, when you need all eleven to be playing and working hard. Despite that only a blatant dive by Zekora, that brought a Spurs penalty, prevented us from getting at least a point.

With his debut goal for us against West Ham, Andy Cole had demonstrated his finishing power and you could see he was still hungry for goals despite his massive tally of Premiership goals in his long career. I felt so blessed to be training and playing with all these fantastic footballers who I had watched for so long from afar on TV. Andy had a bit of a reputation at Fulham and elsewhere as being difficult to get on with but you can't judge anyone until you meet them, is a good personality and works well in training.

It gave me a real buzz, rather than being intimidated, in taking on the Chelsea strikers Drogba and Shevchenko at Stamford Bridge and we went there as a team riding high in the Premiership with real hopes of getting a result. It was exciting to be on the same pitch as Shevchenko, who was under a lot of pressure following some indifferent performances, but managed to score against us in a 2-1 win for Chelsea in which we really didn't do ourselves justice.

Despite presenting a sterner challenge than most strikers with his movement, aggression and direct runs into the channels, not to mention his hungry appetite for goals, I took a great deal of satisfaction that afternoon from being able to match an in-form Drogba physically, stop him scoring and cope on all the other fronts. In my first few games in the Premiership I had got by purely on adrenaline as I struggled to cope with not only the extraordinary pace and movement, but the demands on your mind, concentration and reactions. Every sprint is to the maximum and there's no respite and no standing still. Every week you come up against forwards who are sharper, quicker, and smarter than anyone you've ever known before. I was happy with my positioning from the word go, but anticipation is key to thinking ahead to see a pass in advance. At this level a very good first touch of the ball to bring it under control is also essential, otherwise that can give you a problem, as you often don't get a second chance.

When I am at right back I adopt the same simple maxim I use at centre half – whoever I am up against won't get past me. When opposing an out-and-out winger I will first try and intercept any passes to him, otherwise I will be looking to close him down as quickly as possible. As you know I am much happier at centre half and the above principles do largely still apply, where I am looking to rely on my positioning and timing to anticipate and intercept the pass before it has reached the forward or get tight enough to make it difficult for the forward to turn. If you let someone like Michael Owen get a run on you, or let him turn and face you one on one, then you are playing to his strengths. It can be fatal to let a top striker turn and make a run at you. Speed is the key to battling with the game's best forwards and I like to think that's often where I get the upper hand. Top forwards show great movement off the ball that demands alertness and the ability to read their runs in advance. A player like Michael Owen or Thierry Henry will drop back towards a midfielder of theirs with the ball and try and drag you with him. Then in a split second they will turn and run away from the ball so that it can be played over the top and behind you for them to run on to you. The art is to keep the forward in front of you rather than let him get in behind you where he can get a run in on goal.

We went to Newcastle in the Carling Cup on a horrible, wet night to play on a waterlogged pitch and I was given the captaincy for the first time at Pompey, in Dejan's absence and most of our first team regulars. I felt really proud on the night and tried to encourage people and lead by example, just as we had come to expect from Dejan our regular skipper. Not since my time at Barnet some years ago had I taken the captain's armband but I've never been offered it again! Whether that has anything to do with our 3-0 cup exit after a disappointing performance I don't know. Unfortunately many of our 'fringe' players had played very little first team football and their lack of match fitness showed on the night.

By now David James had proved what an amazing signing Harry had pulled off. Later in the season, in our goalless draw at Aston Villa, he broke the Premiership's clean sheet record of 141 held by David Seaman and I must admit I have been surprised how good he is. He makes saves that would be goals with 'keepers that had previously played behind me. Thinking about it a bit more, I estimate that 30% of the shots he saves would be goals with any other keepers – that's how highly I rate him. You just know that if a player gets past you and in on goal that Jamo will make a save. He is currently the best England keeper and I certainly feel he deserves to be in the England squad. Jamo's agility and reflexes are extraordinary for a big man, and so is his appetite for the game, particularly in training, where he works as hard as if he had just come into the game.

Jamo has been stuck with the nickname 'Calamity James' and for me that's quite wrong and utterly inappropriate. As a defender it's a worry to have a keeper behind you who makes wrong decisions and you feel the added responsibility of having to protect him. With a keeper like Jamo behind you there are no such worries and a defender can concentrate on his own tasks. In a position where decisions have to be made quickly, I reckon Jamo makes 99 good decisions to one bad. A big part of his game is that, as a powerful strong guy, he can take knocks without going down injured and I can tell you it's so reassuring for defenders to have a keeper who has no hesitation in coming out and dominating his area.

Jamo is a very intelligent guy and his interests go a lot deeper than those of a typical footballer. He's not scared of passing an opinion, even if it's unpopular, and, as well as his interest in art, the environment and sports psychology, Jamo has worked to raise Aids awareness in Malawi and has also set up his own Foundation to help farmers there to develop better farming practices. I understand that through his intervention a David James Foundation Scholarship was instigated at the University of Westminster from September 2007 to enable a student from Malawi to study there.

Sol missed our 3-0 defeat at Old Trafford through sickness and I joined him on the sidelines with a hamstring strain that had caused me to come off in the previous home game against Reading. My game was thriving in Sol's company and he was inspiring me to match his consistently high performance levels. I realised when the season was all over that I had never partnered anyone in the centre of defence for so long and that enabled me to get to know and read his game such that I instinctively knew what he was going to do in any situation. Sol reads the game well, uses his vast Premiership experience to good effect in most situations, tackles strong and hard and his timing is near to

265

perfection. During the course of the season I learnt from him how to do the basics well and not let your standards drop in training or in matches. Knowing that Sol very rarely made a mistake made my life easier and he never over-complicated anything. Very few strikers get the better of him and, rather than make it easy to beat him, he will force the player to do something special to get past him. He certainly won't go to ground to make a tackle unless it's absolutely necessary.

A great 'backs-to-the-wall' job at Liverpool in late November earned us another point in a goalless draw where Sol was under such pressure at one point that he split his boot and we had to play for a few minutes with ten men while he tried to make our bench understand his need for a replacement. It started a six-game run that yielded twelve points and put us comfortably in the top six and suddenly people were talking about a UEFA Cup place next season. At the start we had said that a good season would be a top ten place and I kept on saying that I really believed it was going to be our best season in the Premiership, but that was not with Europe in mind. In-house we were adamant that we needed to get to the 40-point safety mark as soon as possible, and anything else would be a bonus.

That good run up to Christmas included a 2-0 home win over Everton – a team who we always seemed to find difficult to beat at Fratton Park. By now it was clear to many clubs that our home crowd were very much our '12th man' and easing our path by making life uncomfortable and intimidating for our opponents. Everton tried to quieten our crowd by stopping us getting into any sort of tempo or 'head of steam' by slowing down the game through, for example, delaying the taking of goal kicks and throw ins. When we beat Sheffield United a couple of weeks later I could sense they were uneasy about playing at Fratton Park, intimidated by our home record and very wary of the noise from our fans. Against Everton however we started very quickly, got in their faces and were two up by the half-hour mark, and that was enough for a valuable three points.

Mattie Taylor scored the first against Everton with a volley from 35-40 yards – probably the best goal I've ever seen – and a goal worthy of the talented player he is. His career has been held up by injuries at times and by some switching between left back and left midfield, but now that he has settled into the latter position he is really making a name for himself. As the season progressed important goals from his left foot became a regular feature and justified his claim for England international recognition. I agree with those who think our players are overlooked by the international managers. It's probably down to the fact that we are not a club who have regularly figured in the top half of the table or in Europe. Certainly most of the England squad are playing in Europe week in and week out.

We employed the same defensive formation that had been so effective at Anfield and similarly packed our midfield for our first visit to Arsenal's Emirates Stadium. I found it an intimidating arena, like a bowl of red, but by far the best stadium in the Premier League. We took our two chances in the first half but Arsenal came back strongly to draw level, but, as underdogs, we didn't look at it as two points lost.

After Harry had given us a rare Christmas Day off we went to Upton Park on Boxing Day to meet a West Ham side, now under my old Charlton manager Alan Curbishley, who had shown me the door, who were in trouble in the relegation zone. From the kick off you could sense their nervousness and unease – giving the ball away easily, lack of communication between defenders and the keeper, making bad decisions on headers and tackles etc. We went for them from the off, taking advantage of the way they were playing, and to my amazement I managed to get myself on the score sheet twice with headers in the first half that brought our 2-0 win. It had been exactly two years to the day since I last scored, and I, not to mention my team mates, was simply amazed. After the second had gone in I was walking around the pitch saying out loud for anyone to hear: 'What IS going on?'

Both came from set pieces taken by Pedro from the left, the first a corner, and the second a free kick. In both instances the ball reached me at the back post and I was able to head high into the net. For the first I was able to shrug off Marlon Harewood's challenge, but for the second West Ham had changed my marker to a smaller guy in Hayden Mullins and I was able to lose him to get in a free header. I remember the thought going through my mind as I jumped to meet the second cross from Pedro: 'All I have to do is get this on target and it's a goal'. Such goals are a reward for all that work on the training ground to get in at the far post for set pieces but unfortunately, unlike that remarkable Boxing Day at West Ham, very much more often than not the ball doesn't reach you.

Before the game I had prayed over the phone with Mick, and he had said to me: 'Someone will bring glory to God today with their performance'. Afterwards I knew that my two goals would make me the centre of media attention and it would give me the opportunity to share my faith. With it being Christmas it couldn't have been timelier and I prayed that I would have the chance to get Jesus's name into my interviews. I needn't have worried as the first question from the assembled press corps immediately gave me an opening: 'Linvoy, you're a man of faith… it's Christmas so what do you put your two goals down to?' To which I replied: 'It's surely not a coincidence that I've scored at Christmas again… what a way to celebrate the birth of Jesus!'

The January transfer window signing of Lauren, a player we had all admired in a great Arsenal side, was yet another coup by the club, after he had been set to go to West Ham. He was another international with a host of domestic honours who had come as a right back as cover for Glen initially. Then Djimi

Traore arrived to cover the left back position and somebody pointed out that he was the fourth Champions League winner (to add to Kanu, Andy Cole, and Pedro) at the club. The calibre and experience of the players in the squad had been improved beyond all recognition to take the club forward. It was significant that, with so many experienced 'big-time' players in the team, they were not fazed by going to play at Arsenal, Liverpool, Manchester United, Newcastle and the like.

The quality of players at the club was all too evident in training where the tempo had increased, greater techniques were being displayed, better decision making was on show and there were only rare mistakes. All that was carried into the games of course and that rubbed off on lesser mortals like me. When you're surrounded by players on your side with a great touch, who have the close control and ability to beat players and be productive, you are more confident about passing the ball to them even if it's in a tight situation. In the past I would pass the ball to one of our players and he might well be unproductive with it or even lose it.

Every player harbours hopes of getting to Wembley in the FA Cup – I've never got further than the quarter final – and, with our form in the league, we fancied our chances. Unfortunately we drew Manchester United away in the fourth round and were edged out 2-1 thanks to an astonishing chip shot by Wayne Rooney for the winning goal, one of the best scored against us this season. I remember watching his chip sail into the air towards goal and thinking: 'Please let it be too high', but unfortunately it dipped under the bar beyond Jamo's reach. Any game in front of over 70,000 at Old Trafford is big enough but it was also live to millions on a Saturday evening on BBC TV and, very unusually for me now, I was surprised to find myself really nervous beforehand. So much so that I had to work hard to avoid the fear taking control of me and I prayed to God for help. I also try to address the fear by asserting that it has no authority over me – the affirmation I use to speak to it is 'no fear here'. Once the game started however the adrenaline and the focus kicked in and all the tension disappeared.

A couple of weeks later came the return with Manchester City at home, which I missed with a thigh strain, and there was talk in the media about 'revenge' following the assault on Pedro back in August. But we had no problem with City, who had done all they could by fining, suspending and then eventually selling Thatcher to Charlton. Unbelievably, after all he had been through earlier in the season, and after scoring with a typical volley, Pedro was the victim of another bad challenge that also went unpunished, when this time Joey Barton took him out by crunching down on his Achilles tendon and he was carried off. Fortunately the damage was not as bad as was at first thought, but it could have been a potentially long term, career-threatening injury. It was an isolated incident and players generally show a greater mutual respect for each other and their livelihoods these days than perhaps a decade or two ago.

Our problems with the facilities at our Eastleigh training ground were highlighted in February when the continuous rain left the pitches heavy and boggy. We would work at our usual high tempo but that level of activity on such pitches catches up with you eventually leaving you leg weary by the end of the week. In fact all our preparations were being hampered by the weather and the facilities. You should never use excuses for bad results but in our 3-0 defeat at Blackburn we were sluggish, slow out of the traps and guilty of some uncharacteristic mistakes. It was a real 'bad day at the office' and didn't reflect our recent performances. Blackburn took the characteristics of their manager Mark Hughes – gritty, determined, hard-working, highly motivated, and highly professional – and consequently were always difficult opponents.

After subsequently losing at home to Chelsea – with Drogba taking his only chance of the game to score with a magnificent volley – and two useful draws at Reading and Fulham, we took on top of the table Manchester United at Fratton Park on Easter Saturday knowing that we had beaten them twice at home during our short time in the Premiership. Three days earlier United had lost a tough Champions League tie with Roma and played for a long period with ten men so, despite being under strength with Sol and Pedro missing through injury, we sensed an opportunity to take another big scalp at home. We knew we had to start at a high tempo and to apply a pressure game on them, get at them and give them no time to settle.

I was looking forward to the game enormously and, despite having a healthy respect for what they were capable of, was not fazed in any way by coming up against big names like Rooney, Ronaldo, Giggs and company. We all know that these players can come up with something special and make things happen out of nothing. But, as I've said before, now I simply relish such challenges. Playing against Ronaldo is an enormous task and he's an absolute nightmare to mark. First you need the speed to keep up with him, and, if you do manage that, you then have to read his every little trick. When he's on his game there's no real way to handle him. You just have to hope against hope that you are at the top of your game and somehow cope, but it's a hit and miss business.

Our first half performance against United was exceptional and, not only were we ahead by a brilliantly-taken goal by Mattie, but we had kept the ball well and allowed United no time on the ball. In the latter stages of the second half Sir Alex Ferguson had five strikers on the pitch at one time but we held on to our lead until our win was sealed in the last minute by a second goal, when Rio Ferdinand nudged a back pass, under pressure from Benjie, past his own keeper Van De Saar. It felt quite amazing to have beaten United, who were virtually unbeatable in the league, and it was clearly the talk of the football world that weekend, opening up

271

the Premiership title race again. Looking back it was probably my best performance in a Pompey shirt.

I made two tackles in the game, both on Wayne Rooney in the penalty area; both of which attracted strong appeals from him for a penalty and were the subject of close analysis of the TV replays by the BBC Match of the Day pundits. There was no doubt that if either or both had been just fractionally mistimed it would have led to a penalty against us. The first challenge came after a headed clearance of ours had run loose and I slid in to clear the ball. A fraction of a second later, in attempting to reach the ball, Rooney fell over my foot and immediately leapt to his feet and ran to the referee to claim a penalty that was denied by Mark Clattenburg.

My second challenge in the second half, when we had only the single goal advantage, brought even stronger claims from both Rooney and his team mates. I have noticed that the bigger the club the more their players talk to the referee and work to put more pressure on him. It must have a bearing on the number of decisions in their favour. On this occasion the ball was played into Giggs just inside our half and he slid a perfect pass through the heart of our defence that put Rooney in with the ball with a clear run on goal. I went in pursuit of him and, as he reached the penalty area, thought: 'I've got to get in a challenge very quickly otherwise he'll score... but if I don't get it right it'll be a penalty and I'll be sent off'. It's amazing what messages from your brain you can absorb in a fraction of a second! I went down to make my tackle from behind, and had to overstretch to reach the ball. Fortunately I just managed to knock the ball away and in doing so brought Rooney down yet again. My heart was in my mouth as I got up and I would not have been surprised to have seen the penalty awarded. Later I recalled that after a very similar tackle by Dejan at Old Trafford earlier in the season the decision had gone against him.

I really don't have a problem with referees today. The pressure on them in the modern game is enormous and it's become more difficult for them as the pace of the games increases and more players dive and cheat in a deliberate attempt to get decisions. The situation has improved with the coming of professional referees but the more our referees are in the public eye and their decisions are highlighted extensively on TV the better they have to be. They have their bad days as we all do. New excellent technology is entering the game but we need something developed that can show whether or not the ball has crossed the goal-line.

On Easter Monday, two days after that Manchester United triumph, we were brought right back down to earth at Watford when fatigue, brought on by all the effort we had put into beating United, caught up with us. As a result, coupled with a complacent attitude, we took a 4-1 hiding from a team who were heading for relegation. Going into the game thinking we could win easily, we scored first but couldn't generate enough energy to combat Watford's direct strong-running football.

But that was all forgotten when we were back in the groove at home, and well in the reckoning for a UEFA Cup spot again, in beating first Newcastle 2-1 – a club that we hadn't beaten in the Premiership – and then adding another big scalp in a weakened Liverpool, who were concentrating on their Champions League encounter with Chelsea, by the same score a couple of weeks later.

Our comprehensive 3-0 defeat at Everton in our last away game was a blow to our chances of getting into Europe however and brought three issues into focus. Firstly we hadn't won away since my two goals at West Ham on Boxing Day, secondly we weren't scoring enough goals, and thirdly the lack of depth in our squad was being shown up with the spate of injuries to key players several of whom, like Gary and Benjie, had been carrying niggling injuries through games for some weeks. Our away form,

273

in particular, was a real source of disappointment and mystery to us and not something that we can put our finger on. We want to play well in every game and we don't set out to be more defensive away from home. Curiously, outside the big four clubs, few Premiership teams have good away records and it would be interesting to hear how they view the problem. I must admit that I don't know the answer. You can factor in the effect of the home support, a huge intimidating stadium, the travelling, the overnight stays etc but these don't go a long way towards explaining the situation.

We went into the final game of the season at home to Arsenal knowing that a win would enable us to slip into Europe if Bolton and Reading failed to win their games that afternoon. Given our record against the big clubs at home it was possibly to our advantage to play Arsenal, and we approached the game with the same high work rate we had employed so successfully against Manchester United. There was an end of season atmosphere in the ground as if the fans were waiting for something to happen here and elsewhere.

We played more direct football than normal but we didn't give them too much to shout about in the first half and the blustery windy conditions didn't help. I mistimed a tackle to concede a penalty but Jamo, who before kick off had been universally acknowledged by the players and the fans as a very popular Player of the Year, made a great save to turn away the spot kick from Baptista. At half-time Harry said to us: 'The results are in our favour at half-time so we have a huge opportunity here. We must up the tempo, win all our tackles and make it happen'.

In the second half we were getting lots of opportunities on the break and restricting Arsenal, and I was confident we would pinch a goal to clinch the win. When Niko Kranjcar scored from close in we ran off to celebrate with him and the goal was announced over the PA, but the Arsenal players were seen to be pointing to the linesman whose flag had not been raised. My thoughts were: 'Surely he can't not give it', but after speaking to his assistant referee Graham Poll disallowed the goal by indicating a free kick for offside. Whether the decision was right or wrong, we were shocked after thinking the goal would seal it for us, very disappointed at the way the decision was made and that it took so long for it to be reversed. To the referee's credit he was at pains afterwards to explain his decision fully to Gary O'Neil our skipper.

As it transpired, that 'goal' would have taken us into the UEFA Cup the next season but even to be still in contention for a place in Europe in the last game was a great way to end an amazing and exciting season. We took satisfaction from taking a point from a big club like Arsenal and, more than that, everybody at the club, including our supporters, was proud of what we had achieved in the season by finishing in the top half of the league and our highest league position for over 50 years. For next season we had set new expectations and built a foundation to continue to build on. Many of us had gained valuable experience, not least knowing as a team what we needed to do consistently in every game to achieve success.

Harry summed it all up afterwards in the dressing room: 'Everyone has done really well, and we've achieved something huge this season. We had an opportunity to put ourselves in the record books by taking this club into Europe, but unfortunately it was not to be. But well done everybody'.

I feel that the club needs to establish a good foundation in the Premiership before we can consider competing in Europe. We've not found our balance yet and moving from a club that had narrowly avoided relegation the previous season to one who is stepping out on to the European stage is a big step. We need to consistently finish in the top half of the league, feel comfortable there and come to recognise what it takes to perform at that level.

As we've seen elsewhere the demands and the high of playing in Europe can lead to flat performances when you come back to the league.

I had learnt so much from the season and as a defensive unit we had only conceded just over a goal a game and achieved the club's most clean sheets in a Premiership season. Great credit went to my team-mates at the back – Jamo, Sol, Dejan, Glen along with Noe, Lauren and Djimi – and on a personal level I gave all the glory to God. I'd been privileged to play against some of the best strikers in the world, and particularly relished my encounters with players like Henry, Drogba, Fowler, Anelka, Yakubu and Morientes. The foreign players have set us a great example by their good habits and lifestyles that are leading to more of our players being able to extend their careers as a consequence. The only downside is that our young players are finding it harder to break into the Premiership squads as clubs find that it's cheaper to bring in foreign players than to buy British.

My knee had been causing me problems towards the end of the season and two days after the final game I had surgery to repair some surface damage in the joint. Unfortunately, and most disappointingly, that prevented me joining a 16-strong Faith and Football group who were due to embark a few days later on an exhausting sponsored trek across the Egyptian desert for eight days culminating with a journey up Mount Sinai with the aim of raising £100,000 for our charity to help orphaned and needy children abroad.

Hours after coming out of hospital I had the good news that my agent John Mac had met with Pompey's Chief Executive Peter Storrie and had accepted his offer of improved terms for the last year of my present contract. It was a great way to end what had been my most successful season ever in terms of the number of games I had played and my consistently good form throughout.

In every game I played I felt as strong and as focused as I have ever done. During much of my career the pressure of maintaining that level of performance had been too much for me to take, but now I have the peace of knowing that God's power is driving me forward constantly. Without having to feel the pressure of success and with that power I still felt I had greater heights to reach. As a club we had the opportunity to build a successful future and to learn from past mistakes.

It gets harder as you get older but I felt really good about myself and had been playing with a new lease of life. Physically, apart from the niggles with my knee in the final couple of weeks, at the grand old age of 33 I felt fine. Harry hadn't yet told me I could take some training breaks if I needed to. He'd done that with one or two of the older players in the past but he must have been happy with me because so far I'd not had that tap on the shoulder. While I was at Portsmouth and playing well it gave me a chance to give a message about my life. Football changes so quickly however and when you finish playing you're forgotten. If you make football your life then when you finish you'll be disappointed but I believed that my life outside of football had already started. The overall picture in my life was more than just what was happening out on the pitch.

'To you alone, O Lord, to you alone and not to us, must glory be given because of your constant love and faithfulness'
Psalm 115.1

18

Whatever God Wants...

The surgery to repair and clear the surface damage in my knee at the end of the season meant that I spent the summer of 2007 on crutches. When I reported back to the physios in the first week of pre-season with the knee still showing substantial swelling it was soon clear that there would be no physical rehabilitation for some weeks for me. All our efforts would have to be directed towards reducing that swelling including the use of ice compression techniques and having the whole leg wrapped in the Flowtron inflatable boot.

The 2007/08 season was well under way by the time that swelling finally subsided but through the subsequent physical work there was always an element of discomfort and pain which I tended to treat as part of the process of recovery. I believed that I had to work through it and that eventually the pain would reduce. The leg and the knee were getting stronger and the surgeon was pleased with my progress so I was introduced to normal training. I had prayed, and so had others, for a quickening of the healing and I believed that it was happening.

After a month of full training it was felt I was ready to play in the reserve team and the plan was for me to have a gradual introduction starting with 45 minutes against the Chelsea reserves and then if that went well to try an hour in the next match. The first team had been strengthened in the close season and if anything looked like a team that could make a bid for the top six. I was excited at the possibility of having the chance to play with the likes of Sulley Muntari, Papa Bouba Diop and Lassana Diarra.

Twenty minutes into the first reserve game I had to make a quick turn and had a lot of pain in the knee but managed to continue with a clear feeling that something was not right although there was no swelling. That feeling was confirmed in the next 60-minute run-out in the reserve game against Arsenal and by now I was conscious that I wasn't running naturally but was being restricted in some way. Nevertheless I continued to feel at peace with the situation and even though I was not completely healed I knew that there was a purpose to what was happening to me.

I really began to lose confidence in the knee when, after one particularly intensive short run, I felt some really powerful pain in the area of the operation. Not only that the knee had begun to give way and lock when I put any weight on it. I was anxious not to speak negatively over it. I had learnt from the scriptures that to speak positively always leads to positive outcomes ('blessings') whereas equally speaking negatively only leads to negative outcomes ('curses'). After consulting the physios they were still of the opinion that I might have to be patient and work through such discomfort as part of the process.

Ten minutes into the next reserve game against Aston Villa the knee gave way. I really struggled with my performance for the remainder of the first half as a result and in the end had to come off. I was referred to a Harley Street specialist who, after taking a scan, felt that everything was OK and that more strengthening around the knee was necessary. No sooner had I started work on his programme however then the intense pain was back.

When my latest setback was reported to the manager's office

Harry suggested a referral to Dr Richard Steadman, a knee specialist surgeon based at Vail, Colorado in USA, who had pioneered a unique operative treatment for this type of injury. He had a huge world wide reputation in the field and had previously successfully treated the likes of Michael Owen and Alan Shearer. I was disappointed that a second operation was necessary but knew it offered hope and relief for the future.

As I flew to the States I was hoping against hope that I wouldn't leave for home carrying the news that my football career was over. On arrival at his clinic in the ski resort of Vail amongst all the snow and the mountains, I was met by Dr Steadman who was a tall imposing character who gave off an aura of authority and peace and immediately impressed me with his knowledge and explanations.

After a series of tests it didn't take him long to not only agree that something was very wrong but to fill me with confidence in his ability to fix the problem. The operation went well and afterwards Dr Steadman's reaction was: 'It was one of the most difficult I have ever done... two areas were damaged... I'm 70% sure it will all be OK'.

I stopped on for seven days for rehab at the Medical Centre and Trish and the children came over for a few days to keep me company. On my return I faced being on crutches again for two months and having treatment at home for eight hours a day lying on the floor or the bed whilst a hired machine slowly raised my knee up and down to cause the necessary movement without any weight bearing.

Back in England with jet lag, post-op blues and a massively swollen knee (three times the size of the other) I had two or three dark days when I began to believe that I wouldn't play football again. After some positive self-talk and, more importantly, scripture study which I found hugely comforting I was convinced that, even if my career was effectively ended, God still had a plan for my life. Not only that I realised only too well that there were people in far worse positions than me.

So that was it football-wise for me as far as the rest of the season was concerned. I had been told not to kick a ball for the foreseeable future and faced long hauls to not only recover from the operation but to work on first rehabilitation and then getting back to fitness. I faced the reality of my contract running out at the end of the season without having played any games and with no assurance of even being fit. That reality often came up in conversations and interviews and my standard response was to say: 'I'm more concerned about being able to play again rather than my contract situation'.

But it was hard not being involved with the squad in any way and not doing what I was supposed to be doing each day left a hole in my life. It was a great consolation however to be around the family every day, especially at weekends, a pleasure I hadn't experienced during all my years in football.

I couldn't get to any of the games or even into the seats in the stand – and that was at a time when the team was on a great F A Cup run which was to lead to our first Cup Final appearance since 1939. I watched the quarter final away to Manchester United on TV, like the fans, more in hope than expectation. But the longer the game went on, with the resilience we were showing, the more I had an inkling we could win it. When Sulley scored that vital penalty and then we were through to the semi final it was like a dream.

It was difficult to believe what I was hearing when, in post match interviews, Sir Alex Ferguson and his assistant Carlos Queiroz from United, were complaining at our over-physical approach to the game when that was simply not true.

Our Cup semi final at Wembley in late April 2008 against West Bromwich was my first away trip of the season and as a spectator rather than a player, seeing all our fans there, I was able to take in the atmosphere and the emotion of getting through to the Final after 'King' Kanu had scored the winner. There was no party afterwards but some real joy on the journey home. For the team there was still a lot of football to be played with the chance of qualifying for Europe before they could think about a final against Cardiff City. For me, thinking further ahead, months of rehabilitation were on the agenda into the summer.

Then, as if to answer our family prayers, and indeed those of our church, Peter Storrie, the Portsmouth Chairman, took me aside in the canteen at the training ground one lunchtime to talk about my contract and in just a few words allayed all my fears, simply saying: 'We'll keep you on for another season at Fratton Park, Linvoy'. I suppose I need not have worried because I had seen Harry quoted in the newspapers earlier in the season as saying words to the effect of 'Linvoy will be looked after' but it was still great to have it confirmed.

I was a non-playing member of the Cup Final squad who were fitted out with a suit and travelled to a Windsor hotel on the Thursday before the match before we went out for a meal locally. The restaurant laid on a karaoke and we were treated to a Bob Marley impression from John Utaka and an Elvis impression from Herman Hreidarsson that brought the house down.

On the day of the Wembley final itself I was one of the early risers at breakfast and it felt like a wedding day. I had watched the build-up to the Cup Final year after year on TV from a young age when it was televised through the morning of the game, and here I was in the middle of it all surrounded by the players and the staff, the journalists, the photographers, and the interviewers. Once we set off for Wembley on the coach with a police escort it was simply amazing to be on the road amongst a sea of blue and white with so many flags flying. I enjoyed seeing all the happy faces from both sets of fans and the sheer joy and expectation of seeing their teams at Wembley.

The traffic held us up and our arrival was delayed such that Cardiff were already on the pitch taking in the atmosphere. There didn't appear to be any more nerves than usual amongst the players but I detected an increased focus and a steely determination to do well. As I stepped down from the coach parked under the tunnel at Wembley it struck me momentarily – how good would it be to play and be involved – and a pang of regret came and went.

As I made my way along the running track at the pitch side to see where my family, parents and friends were sitting the Pompey fans behind the goal began chanting my name and it brought a lump to my throat. Back in the tunnel and the dressing room it was chaotic with what seemed like hundreds of staff and attendants buzzing around. The sounds of the musical build-up reached into the tunnel and, not being involved playing-wise, I could take in the build-up and sense the atmosphere building.

With the non-playing members of the squad added to the substitutes there were too many of us who wanted to sit on the bench, and it descended into 'musical chairs' as we jockeyed for places before the unlucky ones were left to stand and watch with the Wembley staff just inside the tunnel. Although we were favourites against Championship opposition we were anxious to score early on to settle the nerves. As it was Kanu scored eight minutes from half time and from then on it was just a question of hanging on to the lead.

Steve Claridge interviewed me at half time and said: 'You're in the driving seat because Pompey have never lost a game this season in which they have taken the lead'. It was difficult watching from the bench in the second half as we desperately hung on to that lead knowing that we couldn't afford to make a mistake. At no stage did I feel comfortable until the dying minutes when I felt we had done enough to win the game. We hadn't played well or dominated but that was true of every game in our Cup run. Happily the performance hadn't been reflected in the result yet again.

At the whistle I raced from the bench to try and get Trish and the children down to the pitch side to join in the celebrations, but a security guard wouldn't let them through so that plan was scuppered. Everybody in the squad went up to collect the trophy with those who played going first. It was a special moment when Sol Campbell lifted the Cup and our fans erupted and sang their anthem: 'When Sol went up to get the F A Cup I was there, I was there...'

It was a dream come true for me, just as it was for all those thousands upon thousands of Pompey fans in the stadium, back in Portsmouth and around the world. I had been taken on the old Wembley stadium tour as a 13-year old with my parents and had gone up the steps and lifted the trophy. Now 20 or so years later as I waited in line for my turn to lift the trophy for real I remembered that during that tour I said to my parents: 'When I grow up and become a footballer I am going to be doing this'. When I did get to lift it above my head the fans gave me one of the biggest cheers of the afternoon and people continue to remind me of that moment to this day.

I know that winning the Cup was something that the huge majority of our fans never expected to see in their lifetimes so there was an outpouring of joy coupled with disbelief. I have lost count of the number of stories of their experiences that day I have heard from fans since, almost all with tears of joy involved. What was great for me was to hear of how generations of families had been united in their joy and celebration whether it was in the stadium, back at home or the next day during our city-wide tour.

Harry was pretty calm but from the huge smile on his face there was no disguising the joy he felt. As successful as he had been as a Premiership manager in keeping teams in the top flight or into Europe it must have been one of the most satisfying moments of his career. You could see what it meant even to international players like Sol Campbell and David James and for the young players like Sulley Muntari, Lassana Diarra and Papa Bouba Diop it was clearly thrilling to win a major trophy in their first season at the club. Harry's dreams for the club, that had drawn players to come and play for him at Portsmouth, had been realised and many were surprised how quickly it had been achieved.

When we finally got back to the relative quiet of the dressing room, leaving all the noise in the stadium behind, there was a slight air of anti-climax as the players started to reflect and take it all in. But soon the cameras were flashing, the champagne was being sprayed around, and loud music poured out from the IPod as the room began to fill up as the press and a stream of visitors arrived.

Suddenly I was hit with a surge of self pity and disappointment that was to stay with me in my head for about an hour. I had been in dressing rooms as a player and celebrated winning promotions and avoiding relegations with all the joys and celebrations they brought. But this didn't feel like that and I was struck with a sense of having been denied one of the biggest moments in any player's career through not having played that day. Dozens of people were talking to me happily but inside the disappointment was gnawing away at me.

Was it a punishment from God or a lesson to be learned? Soon I felt God say to me that there was no question of Him punishing me, and I knew that He wasn't a God of punishment but a lover of good things. I had a choice – be sad or be happy. I chose the latter, pulled myself together and realised again how much it meant to me to see so many people so happy. After that I focused on enjoying the rest of the weekend, and consoled myself with the thought that I had been able to enjoy and appreciate the whole Wembley day from beginning to end better than the players through not having to be involved in the tension of playing.

Trish and the children were with all the staff, families and friends at the hotel, and after a meal the celebrations at the hotel went on until the early hours. The next day we were due to parade with the Cup in an open-top bus tour of the city before arriving at Southsea Common. Many of the squad, particularly the players from abroad, were unsure what to expect but when they saw the thousands upon thousands who turned out and the city streets go into complete gridlock you could literally see their jaws dropping. It took an hour to travel just one mile because of the pressure from the crowds. The reception at Southsea Common, where we took to a stage and were individually presented to the fans, was even more amazing with a crowd reported to have been 250,000 stretching around us as far as the eye could see.

With the comfort of knowing that I had another year on my contract in which to prove myself I was given a rehab programme to work to through the summer of 2008. When pre-season training came round again I was excited at the prospect of being part of the squad. I was like a new boy in the squad – after all I hadn't trained, played or travelled with any of them and they all knew me as 'Linvoy' but not as a player. On the pre-season tour of Nigeria I played for an hour against Manchester United and felt good although short of match fitness. I felt part of Harry's plans, despite having Sol Campbell, Sylvain Distin and Noe Pamarot ahead of me in the central defensive positions.

As I had missed out in the Cup Final, Harry had said that he would give me a run-out in the F A Community Shield match at Wembley against Manchester United. A week or so before that my agent John Mac had called me to say that Bristol City wanted to take me on loan for a year. I turned the offer down flat as I had set my heart on playing at Wembley. I was to be denied again however because three days before the game I picked up a groin strain and wasn't fit enough to play. It was one of my lowest points in football, after all the months of hard work I had put in to get over the operation, and the family and I were bitterly disappointed.

When I was fit again and after playing in a reserve game I found myself having another offer of a loan spell to consider. This time it was from one of my old managers Alan Pardew, now in charge at Charlton, who had been impressed with my form. I spoke to Harry who was keen on the idea on the basis that 'It would be good for you to get some games under your belt as there are not too many reserve games'. Unfortunately a misunderstanding arose over the length of the loan after Pompey and I thought that a three month loan to November 2008 had been agreed whereas Charlton announced it as season-long. Harry quickly insisted that only three months was involved as, as he put it: 'Linvoy is still part of my plans'.

For my part the whole purpose of the loan period at The Valley was to enable me to build my match fitness by playing games and I never considered the possibility of signing for Charlton. It was nice to go back to where it had all started for me but I knew that I could never feel at home anywhere else other than at Pompey and I couldn't bring myself to play for anyone else. Charlton were struggling and in desperate need of some good results and, in truth, I didn't do myself justice at all. I was soon missing Trish and the children through staying in a London hotel all week, playing at weekends and just getting back for a few hours on a Sunday. The time alone during the weekday evenings did give me a chance to gain some fellowship with the Lord through reading and learning scriptures and I build up a great relationship with the Charlton club chaplain Matt Baker. We even managed to set up prayers before Charlton's games with a number of players and staff attending.

I had a good relationship with Pards but it was disappointing when I began to be left out of the squad largely because of the number of loanees at Charlton and the need for them all to have a chance to play. It was frustrating for me and the family when I was away all week and at the weekend without actually being involved in the games. Charlton were in trouble at the foot of the table and soon Pards was sacked and replaced by Phil Parkinson. There was talk of the loan being extended but for me that was never an option and I was happy to return to Pompey in mid-December 2008. I reflected in hindsight that God moves us into situations for a purpose and that this loan might have been for the purpose of proving to me that my future lay with Portsmouth.

No sooner had I returned to Fratton Park than Harry left to manage Tottenham and Tony Adams had taken over. So I had experienced four managers in the space of about two weeks at both clubs – some sort of record. I felt good but knew how difficult it was going to be to break in the first team in defence and Tony greeted me by saying that he was 'happy to have me back' but added ominously 'you are going to have to work to get back in the team'.

Tony soon came under pressure with the results not matching the performances, with games that we should have won being lost or drawn. He was so close at times to getting big results but with no sign of improvement the players began to lose confidence in him. It was no surprise, as a reflection of the club's league position, when Tony was sacked.

I had not been named in any of Tony's squads and my situation became clearer when I was left to train with the younger players. That brought more personal frustration and with my contract due to expire it didn't bode well. Naturally I was anxious to hear what the club had in mind and Harry's words in the press some months earlier came back to me: 'Linvoy should be here in some capacity when he finishes playing'.

On meeting Peter Storrie I told him that I wanted to continue

289

to be involved with the club in some capacity and immediately he said: 'That's great, we would like you to take on a role helping out with the young players, as a player, a mentor and role model, as an assistant to Guy Whittingham the Development Squad coach. We will give you another year to enable you to make the transition from being a player while you move into your new role. Can you put down everything you feel you can do to help in that capacity? And we want to give you a testimonial'

I couldn't believe what I was hearing – that role was exactly what I was going to suggest to him. Storrie's thought processes matched mine precisely. Silently, under my breath, I exclaimed: 'Thank you Lord'.

I had become disenchanted and anxious about my direction and vision for my life. So it was a great relief to have God open this new door and give me a purpose. The extra year would enable me to complete ten years at the club player-wise and qualify for a testimonial match.

Paul Hart had come in as caretaker manager with a mission to take the club away from the relegation struggle and by now I was enjoying playing with the youngsters in the reserves. Paul steadied the ship and the team regularly picked up valuable points, only losing to Arsenal and Manchester United during that crucial run-in to the season. We were virtually safe by the time of the last two home games and, with injuries in the squad, I found myself on the substitute's bench each time. In the first of those against Arsenal the fans were continually chanting in the closing stages for me to be brought on but tactically it wasn't possible.

In the last home game of the season against Sunderland with a few minutes left we were 3-1 up and suddenly the fans throughout the stadium took up the chant for me to be brought on. When Paul Hart gave me the signal there were shivers down my spine and I was shaking as I checked that my boot laces were firmly tied so as to ensure that I didn't trip up as I went on. The team played their part by passing the ball to me at every opportunity and there were looks of disbelief from them as my every touch was cheered to the echo. I hadn't played in the first team for nearly two years and it crossed my mind that this could be my last – but what a way to finish.

I worked hard through the summer 2009 to ensure that there would be no problem with my knee through pre-season training and everything went well until I was involved in a friendly game against Havant & Waterlooville. The swelling in my knee afterwards came as a big surprise and led to yet another short hospital stay for a 'clean-up'. As I write this in September we are still waiting for the swelling to subside so that a further necessary operation can be undertaken, now not for the sole purpose of my playing again but the long term prognosis for mobility, stability and discomfort in my later life.

I am excited about my new role with Guy Whittingham and the development squad – working on a daily basis with a group of a dozen or so older teenagers who are away from home and about to grow from boys to men but are on the fringe of the reserve team but not yet strong enough to work with the older professionals. My role involves not only coaching football skills but imparting life skills and values to enable them to develop all-round not only as footballers but as people. It is recognised that there is a need for the youngsters to be mentored so they can develop mentally, physically and culturally and learn how to act in the right way as they learn to cope with the demands and pressure of the professional game. I've been through most of what they are going through on and off the pitch.

My additional ambassadorial role will mean that not only am I closely involved with the Pompey Study Centre, but also the club's media department and will provide the link between the club and the whole community so that we become aware of their needs and what we can do to help. I hope to bring my charity

Faith and Football and the other players' own charities – Kanu, John Utaka and David James for instance – closer to the club, and will help to promote other community initiatives in the fields of, for example, education, health, poverty, road safety etc.

Another useful role I intend to fulfil, alongside the existing Players Liaison Manager, is that of providing an introduction to new players as they arrive at the club – being the first to meet them, do the introductions and show them around the club and the city.

The level of intensity and energy that football demands at the highest level leaves players needing regular rest periods and I often struggled to find the energy and commitment to spend as much time with my children as I would have liked when they came home from school and at weekends. In my new role I will now look forward to being able to just go out and play with them, even for a precious 15-20 minutes, and for us to be together as a family more often. My aim for my children's futures is for them to be happy and secure in who they are, and prosperous in all things. They need to know the Word of God so that when they come to make their own decisions about their faith, although we know they may reject it, they will have enough evidence to know God is real and faithful. We have endeavoured to bring them up the right way and to give them the right tools, and I long for them to be great ambassadors for God wherever they go and whatever they do, grounded and strong in their faith and beliefs.

Our Faith and Football charity has grown year by year such that our activities have extended beyond Portsmouth to deprived areas of Birmingham and Plymouth under the control of newly appointed full time directors in the localities. At Plymouth our activities are under the patronage of Argyle football Rory Fallon and it was extraordinary how our connection with the football club down there came about. My good friend Lee Hodges was playing for Plymouth and he happened to mention to me over the telephone one day that a team-mate of his, Rory Fallon, had recently been baptised and had expressed a wish to meet me. God's hand must have been in what happened a week later when the draw for the F A Cup 4th round was made. Pompey were drawn at home to Plymouth so Rory would be coming to Fratton Park and very quickly arrangements were made for us all to meet before the match. By now the Plymouth club chaplain had been in touch with Mick Mellows about replicating our charity's inner-city Portsmouth activities in Plymouth, and following the meeting the plans were laid and executed.

The community football leagues that are our foundational activity now number sixteen over the three cities with up to 1500 youngsters being able to enjoy football free of charge, irrespective of their ability or background, thanks to the efforts of our dozens of trained volunteers. In addition to these leagues, for youngsters up to age 13 we are also launching programmes for older disaffected teenagers who are at risk of offending by the formation, organisation and coaching of football teams to play matches in the area which is supplemented by other evening activities through youth clubs. Through all this we are attempting to introduce them to healthy lifestyles, personal development and life skills through good male role models.

The Linvoy Primus Business Enterprise Challenge continues to provide an opportunity for secondary school pupils in both Portsmouth and Southampton to set up business teams and trade with the profits being donated to our charity, with the winning teams visiting the Goa orphanage to see the work that they have been supporting.

Our 'Extra Time' Literacy Scheme was launched a year ago in an endeavour to help under-achieving primary school children to improve their reading age. In partnership with the schools we offer one to one reading sessions after school to six and seven year olds with the permission of their parents using bible stories. This involves 35 mentors currently working with individual children each week and we have seen some amazing success stories arise from this activity which is due to expand considerably in all three cities.

Each year Faith & Football and the Portsmouth newspaper 'The News' work together to promote an annual 6-a-side tournament in July for local junior schools to celebrate the best in football bringing together teachers, players, parents and families for a great day of football and fun. The teams include many players, boys and girls, who do not normally have the opportunity to play elsewhere or represent their school in any other way. Organised by Faith & Football's team members the tournament usually attracts over 300 young players plus family members and friends; approaching 1,000 people, all enjoying football and friendship of the highest quality on a summer's day. It usually means I am involved in signing autographs non-stop for up to three hours – my own personal annual marathon!

Since the early days of our charity it has been the custom of the Christians at the club to meet with Mick Mellows every Thursday afternoon at his house for prayer and study. In addition for some years now, there's been an early evening meeting for an hour once a month at Fratton Park, that has become a regular event attended by Christian supporters of the club, along with some permanent and match day staff, when we pray for everybody associated with the club – management, directors, players, staff, supporters etc – and any issues involving the club. Players come to our Thursday meetings, sometimes with their wives, particularly if they are having difficult times in their lives and are in need of prayer. For us it signals an acceptance from them that who and what we believe in is real and important to us.

We had been praying at those Thursday meetings for more Christians to come into the club, and since then our prayers have been answered with a steady stream that started with the arrival of Jason Roberts in 2003. Jason made himself available to help out with our Faith and Football activities in the city before he was transferred to Wigan, and he was followed by Lomana LuaLua a few months later in 2004. Lua was surprised when, knowing of his already firm faith, I spoke to him about our charity on his arrival at the club. The football environment makes it difficult to find the time or the space to talk about such deep issues but, although he was initially shocked at my confidence in 'coming out' at the club in such a way, he was soon coming to our meetings and becoming a big part of our work in the city.

Before joining Pompey, our masseur Chris Neville had been thinking about life and its meaning for some time, following a life-saving operation on his baby boy, and we managed to have many personal conversations, during my massages, and in hotels during overnight stays, in which I told him how God had changed my life. Following an 'Alpha' dinner he attended at the football club, Chris felt called by God, and I am happy to say that he and his family have become Christians too and have joined a local church.

Andy Griffin was amongst the Pompey players who were seeking answers to several questions in his life, and once he had attended an 'Alpha' course at the club, along with Lua and Andy O'Brien, he too was converted after making the decision out of his own heart without any pressure on our part. Griff is now at Stoke City but I know that he has found an inner peace, love and security in his faith and through going on our mission to Mexico in 2006 that I had to miss, he had an encounter with God on meeting and working with street children.

Andy O'Brien moved to Fratton Park in 2005 and we knew that, with Shola Ameobi at his previous club Newcastle, he had been interested in the 'Christians in Sport' organisation. On his first training session after his transfer I spoke to Andy about my faith whilst we were jogging alongside each other, and that I thought God had brought him to Portsmouth for a reason. He gave me a quizzical look before he confessed that he had not yet made a decision about becoming a Christian. It wasn't long however, after Mick Mellows and I had answered some big questions from him, before, without prompting, he was ready to commit, saying: 'What do I need to do?'

Vincent Pericard, who subsequently moved to Stoke, came from a Christian background but, when he was having problems with his career at Pompey and more particularly his persistent injuries, he wanted answers from us. I went to his home to share my story and in doing so developed a close relationship with him that culminated in Vincent giving his life to God. His conversion was a great joy to his family and his father in particular who had been urging him to speak to me and become familiar with our work. Whenever I spoke to anybody with my testimony I always felt that it was not out of my own strength but with God's help.

Sean Davis, now with Bolton, is another player who had acknowledged that there was something missing in his life and had been seeking answers. Then one day Mick challenged him: 'Just give me an hour and I can tell you all about Jesus and how he gave his life for us'. It was the start of a journey for Sean and he has come to realise that he needs God in his life and his whole outlook has changed.

We have seen more people at the club who have proclaimed their faith and two more Christians, Kanu, Utaka and Benjani (now with Man City) moved to Fratton Park. Kanu has his own Foundation that helps young children with heart conditions in Africa and was already aware of our Faith and Football work through meeting Darren Moore during his time at West Brom. It was great when he told me on arrival that: 'I want to be a part of your charity work as well'.

Through all of this the club and the city have been blessed, and

I've been proud to be part of a group of players who were prepared to stand up for what they believed in, to give something back to the community, to put themselves forward as positive role models to youngsters, and above all to give the glory to God for what they have achieved. Our core of Christian players and staff grew to about 13 and our pre-match prayer group still meets.

The last two years have brought a real winding-down process in my football career and not being involved with the first team has allowed me to adjust to life outside that environment. A gentle voice has been telling me 'the time is closing'. A long road is about to end and I know I am being prepared and gradually led into an acceptance that I will not play again. I had already discounted playing for any other club professionally, even in non-league locally or elsewhere, and have no desire whatsoever to manage.

I had always had it in my heart to work with youngsters in need of help in whatever way God led me, whether it was in this country or overseas, in or out of football. With me the bottom line is what God wants – He brought me to Portsmouth and has guided my life and career every step of the way.

Index

Note: References to Portsmouth/Pompey have been omitted as they are too numerous to record from Chapter 7 onwards.

A Message from Linvoy

If you're a believer in Jesus Christ, I pray that this book will encourage you to keep on fighting the good fight. If you're not, then this may be the chance of a lifetime – your chance to call on Jesus as your Saviour, to get to a true Bible-believing church and find about a relationship with the true God of the universe. Trusting Jesus for life is the very first step to choosing life – abundant life. Jesus came to give us life, life to the fullest measure.

If you would like to have a relationship with God and you are ready to say these three things, then here is a very simple prayer which you can pray and which will be the start of that relationship:

Lord Jesus Christ,

I am sorry for the things I have done in my life. Please forgive me.
I now turn from everything which I know is wrong.

Thank you that you died on the cross for me so that I could be forgiven and set free.

Thank you that you offer me forgiveness and the gift of your Spirit.
I now receive that gift.

Please come into my life by your Holy Spirit to be with me forever.

Thank you, Lord Jesus,

Amen.